CHARACTER: ACTING AND BEING ON THE PRE-MODERN STAGE

Also by Edward Burns

*RESTORATION COMEDY: CRISES OF DESIRE AND
IDENTITY
THE CHESTER MYSTERY CYCLE: A MODERN STAGING TEXT

Also published by Macmillan

Character: Acting and Being on the Pre-Modern Stage

Edward Burns
Lecturer in English Language and Literature
University of Liverpool

MACMILLAN

First published 1990

Published by
THE MACMILLAN PRESS LTD
Houndmills, Basingstoke, Hampshire RG21 2XS
and London
Companies and representatives
throughout the world

Printed in the People's Republic of China

British Library Cataloguing in Publication Data
Burns, Edward, 1955–
Character: acting and being on the pre-
modern stage.
1. Theatre. Acting, to 1983
I. Title
792'.028'09
ISBN 0–333–44389–6

SB 1855 /35 . 11·90

To Carolyn Fleming

Contents

Preface

This book was begun during a term's sabbatical granted by Liverpool University English Department. Sections of the Introduction and of Chapter 1 were given as a paper to the Department's Renaissance discussion group in November 1985: thanks to those who took part – Philip Edwards, Kenneth Muir, David Mills, Nigel Bawcutt, Ann Thompson, Helen Wilcox, Nick Davis, Mike Watson and Mike Cladingbowl. A section of Chapter 5 formed part of a paper given at the Durham Seventeenth Century conference in July 1987.

Thanks are especially due to Nick Davis and Carolyn Fleming, for their interest, support and criticism, and to the members of the Early Theatre Group, who have bravely over the last five years endured a frankly experimental approach to performing a number of the plays written about in this volume – *Youth*, *Wit and Science*, *Measure for Measure*, the 'Antonio' plays and *Man equals Man* among them. The contribution of a uniquely (indeed bizarrely) loyal group has fed very rewardingly into this study. And of course it would not have reached its present form at all without the heroism of Tina Benson, Catherine Rees and Fiona Johnstone in negotiating between my typescript and the word-processor.

E.B.

Introduction

I   READING CHARACTER

'I see by this woman's features that she is capable of any wickedness'.[1] William Hogarth's observation on Sarah Malcolm, whom he visited in Newgate two days before her execution for murder, is the keynote of his subsequent portrait of her. She sits at a table in a plain cell which is painted in broadly behind her like a set of theatrical flats. Her head and upper body are lit brightly from an unseen source. Her arms are folded on the table-top, and she stares vacantly a little to the side, into the empty space that takes up nearly half the picture, ignoring both the spectator's gaze, and the rosary that lies on the table in front of her.

Hogarth's picture is a virtuoso demonstration of his powers as the great painter of 'character'. His virtuosity here is of a kind directly contrary to the flair with which his narrative prints invite exploration of a rich diversity of clues, a layered reading of events and relationships whose regression into almost infinite suggestibility is kept in due proportion by the artist's rigorous compositional skills. Narrative is eschewed here, the iconography of 'history painting' absent, the composition deliberately simple. We are to see by the woman's features, and by that alone, that she is capable of, not a specific crime, but of *any* wickedness. Hogarth's aim is to depict her character, in the sense of her nature, as directly as possible.

But if we did not know what she had done, would paint on canvas tell us that she was a murderess? What, in any case does it mean to see her *as a murderess*, as a being whose nature is that of a capacity for any evil, rather than as a woman who had, at the age of 22, killed three people, an old woman who employed her, and the woman's two servants. Hogarth's painting imprisons her more completely than Newgate did, in that it seeks to contain her essence; it condemns her more decisively, for it defines her acts as her identity, and invites the viewer to repeat the recognition the painter made on viewing her in her actual cell, that that identity is present in every physical accident of her being, written unmistakably upon her features. This of course says very little for the perspicacity of her employers. But the power of the painting is that it records, not a map of recognisable clues to wickedness, but a moment of moral perception. Her 'character' is this perception, it is Hogarth's moment of seeing. What he sees is

1

dramatised by a number of readable clues; she ignores the rosary, refusing repentance (Hogarth's Richard III has his back to a crucifix), she cuts herself off from the spectator's enquiring eye. (Let us assume that our visit to her cell is well-intentioned.) Her physiognomy would in itself say something to the educated eighteenth-century mind (to some it would say everything). But mostly we are disturbed by the absence of that social context of which her imprisonment deliberately deprives her. She sits as she might at her own kitchen table, but work and employers are absent (she saw to that). Her crime gives her an uneasy autonomy. She inhabits the picture space awkwardly, without theatrical flair, but she is not placed by her social superiors, either from outside the picture or from within. Hogarth's perception is the perception of his own unease.

Character is a two-way process. Sarah Malcolm is a powerful presence by virtue of her refusal to give anything away. Hogarth's perception of her is powerful in its rigorous definition. The resultant 'character study' records an unknowability, but this is its success, not its failure, in that it thus allows a double articulation of character, as a process of seeing, and a process of being seen, as a transaction between two human subjects.

Conceived of in this way, character is a creative perception, which constructs both observer and observed as its subjects—it identifies them, in other words, as somehow particular, and it does so through an essentially fictive method of selection, organisation and exposition. Writing (or painting or performance) which articulates this perception also extends it, because it 'constructs' other subjects—reader, viewer, audience. So character, as creative process, is open-ended and can be imagined as continuous. (This is the 'richness' of signification that the Hogarth picture produces.) What we call character in writing is essentially similar to what we call character in this everyday business of the recognition and formulation of other identities. A discourse of character, the developed visual and verbal language through which this process takes place has historically been central to Western culture, and it is that discourse with which this book is concerned.

If Hogarth's work stands close to the culmination of this developing language, then the Greek moralist and biographer Plutarch represents both an important source for later character-based writing and, with other classical biographers, an early instance of an attempt to define the individual human subject through such writing. His so-called *Parallel Lives* illustrate right and wrong choice by putting together in pairs the lives of Greek and Roman leaders whose careers seem to him to be in some way similar. Plutarch sets out his policy of constructing 'character' at the beginning of his life of Alexander.[2] He is writing lives, he says, not histories. The most spectacular actions may not provide clear instances of wickedness or virtue, but 'trivial things, sayings or childish jokes' often provide more of a revelation of human nature (*ethos*) than great military achievements. The Greek word *ethos* is of complex and precise philosophical usage; my translation of it as 'human nature' is only provisional, in that that term too has a history and a set of connotations all its own. But whatever we call it it is clear that Plutarch is referring here to something which he conceives of as separate from the actions of his subjects, something in which we can see good or evil quite apart from the value of particular acts. It is something which reader and writer derive from the narrative materials of the life under discussion, which they construct as an object of moral knowledge, and which can be seen to give the life a double coherence. This '*ethos*' is the centre from which the choices of good and evil which motivate action can be seen to come; its revelation is also the source of any value the 'life' as a piece of writing has for its readers.

Plutarch goes on to describe the process of constructing such a revelation of *ethos*, using an analogy which leads us back (or historically, of course, forward) to Hogarth and Sarah Malcolm. Portrait painters, he says, take likenesses from the face and from the appearance (*eidos*) around the eyes. These are the things in which *ethos* shows itself. They take little notice of other parts of the body, and in the same way, Plutarch claims, he should be allowed to concentrate on the 'signs of the soul' and to depict each life through those 'signs' rather than through the great conflicts in which his subjects may have been involved.

Ethos is presented, or made visible, by signs, signs which are like the *eidos*, the visible form, perceivable in the human face. The word Plutarch uses as a term for what he is doing is *eidopoiein*; the making of *eidos*, of that readable form. *Eidos* at its simplest means 'thing seen' but it is also used by the philosopher Aristotle for form, as opposed to matter.[3] In other words, it is the shape or structure which the different signs of 'soul' selected by Plutarch make up as a whole.

Plutarch's perception of Alexander, like Hogarth's of Sarah Malcolm, employs a creative selectivity to define and present his sense of that other human subject. Plutarch's description of the construction of his 'portraits' like Hogarth's brusquer remark on Malcolm, point to what character is, in the most inclusive sense of the term. Though we may call the visual and/or verbal end product of these processes a 'character' (as a category for certain kinds of texts) or use the term for the notional object those texts refer to (the character which Alexander or Sarah Malcolm somehow 'had' as particular beings), the term can be understood to unite these subsidiary meanings by standing for the whole process of which they are a part.

There is an important distinction to be made here between the semi-colloquial sense of character as moral nature, possessed by the individual and acting as the determining factor of their being, and character as a mode of perception and a discourse—a discourse in and by means of which such perceptions occur. Plutarch distinguishes *ethos* from the carefully described process of the construction and 'reading' of the form in which it manifests itself. English translations of Greek texts unfortunately tend to obfuscate this kind of distinction by simply translating *ethos* as 'character'. The sense of the English word to which *ethos* is closest is that of phrases like 'a man of good character', where the word is used to mean moral essence. Such usage records a shift from character as reputation, what one is known as, to character as essence, what one is. A servant is given a 'character' on leaving employment. Sarah Malcolm has, by her own act, irretrievably lost hers. Character comes to mean something like 'inherent quality' when this colloquial usage elides into another, when character is not a recorded perception with knowable social value but a moral quality in itself; someone has 'a lot of character', someone else 'lacks character'. Both these statements imply that 'character' is not even a quality, but a kind of intangible substance, an intrinsic structuring of the personality, which can be acted upon by 'character-building' activities, and thus developed or reformed. Its metaphorical overlap with 'back-bone' (as something a certain kind of person lacks) is graphically suggestive here. As the last few examples may indicate, the space in which classicism and authoritarian slang meet is the language of English education.

I shall return to both Plutarch and Hogarth later in the book. Their use at the moment is to help to define the notion of character as it exists in Western art. Like many critical terms character has its everyday colloquial currency. This perhaps is one of its advantages over the more carefully sanitised terminology of a more exclusive literary discourse. Those everyday meanings cannot be arbitrarily separated off, nor can one particular area of usage, like literary criticism, be privileged above another. All possible meanings of the word are continuous with one another, and definition is a matter of limiting the cultural context of a particular usage. But as the last example of the word's tendency to slither through related sets of moral connotations has, however sketchily, indicated, any consideration of a term so culturally central requires some preliminary mapping out of possible meanings.

'Character' has in fact a rather unusual history, in that its use in classical, mediaeval and renaissance writing is tied very closely to a sense of its derivation; the word is often written in its original Greek letters, and its meaning explained in terms of metaphor. In its original Greek, a character is a figure (letter or symbol) stamped onto a wax tablet. It can also be the object that stamps that figure. It thus comes to mean a readable sign in a very general sense—the mark by which something is known as what it is. It may extend to aspects of the human—marks of face and body, for example—but it always implies the reading of signs, whether those signs are purposive or not. The metaphor then tends to return us to the production and interpretation of signs in writing and reading, an emphasis which Latin writers reiterate by carefully maintaining a sense of the term's origins.

Within the study of rhetoric 'character' comes to refer to a particular use of language to be identified with a particular writer/speaker, or a particular group of writers or speakers. So a late Greek writer like Dionysius of Halicarnassus produces studies of the work of the established masters to demonstrate the 'character' of their writing (not their 'character' *in* their writing, as in post-Romantic literary criticism).[4] So also attempts are made to establish ways of speaking and writing proper to particular kinds of people, on whose behalf an orator may speak, or whose actions and words may have to be represented in speech and writing. The rhetorician must understand such signs and be able to reproduce them through an adaptation of his own style to a style fitting to broadly describable categories of person—old or young, male or female, vicious or virtuous, a flatterer, a boaster, or whatever. The 'stamp' of this other subject on the writer's own command of language is seen as an aspect of the need to fit style to matter.

The 'stamp' model of character can be applied to various aspects of this rhetorical communication of the nature of one subject through the medium of another language to yet another set of subjects, the readers and listeners. Discourse on rhetoric concerns itself with the arts of such communication as seen in the context of a writer or speaker working towards some goal, identified with the reaction of listener or reader. So knowledge and experience in the realm of character is essential to a rhetorician's success. The mark of character must be set on his own style, which nonetheless must be receptive and flexible enough to present the marks of other types and individuals, and finally he must know how to stamp those marks on the minds of his listeners, to move them to reception and appropriate reaction.

'Character' is thus a central concern of rhetorical study. But the term is tied very closely to its original meaning, as an example, metaphorically extended and elaborated, of one of the processes by which human beings recognise and are recognised as themselves. Throughout the post classical period, the middle ages and the Renaissance, rhetorical treatises and classroom texts developed exercises in character—what would it be proper for a particular person to say in particular situation? How would one give voice to an inanimate object? Such exercises often took as their basic roster of human types those parallels to the rhetorician's classification of typical figures which were to be found in classical comedy.[5] But the plays were seen not as objects of study in their own right but as useful tools in developing the art of 'character' thus understood, as a crucial aspect of rhetoric, of the study of language in its most sophisticated and culturally important form.

This protection of the term, its careful semantic definition, seems very much at odds with modern usage. If we return to the opposition I made earlier—between character as a process of knowing, and character as individual moral essence—we have a broad definition of a shift in usage. The first gives the term as the rhetoricians understood it, the second isolates that concept of human being to which the term now refers. The development of one out of the other is the central concern of the second half of this book. My own formulation seeks to place the second meaning in terms of the first—it aims to reinstate ideas of cognition, of reciprocal identification, of the mutual construction of identities, into a discourse of character, in order to open up to scrutiny the historical formation of that discourse.

II CHARACTER, ACTING AND RHETORIC

If one were to formulate the distinction between these two approaches to character in other than periodic terms—as 'modern' and 'pre-modern', for instance—one could speak of a 'substantive' and a 'transactional' concept of character. This would avoid the obviously over-simple assumption that the substantive moral mode had somehow swept the board and would also skirt the dangers of plotting the history of the term against a developmental model (and so seeing the later as a more 'mature' version of the earlier). Nonetheless, I offer a broad definition of an historical shift in order to avoid the more immediate hazard of a retrospective examination, a search for an understanding of 'character' taken in its modern meaning, in the writings of an ever-receding past. Shakespeare's use of the word character exists within the field of the 'writing' and 'sealing' metaphor, a field he does not significantly extend. Viola, in *Twelfth Night*, resolving to trust the sea captain who rescued her, says:

> I will believe thou hast a mind that suits
> With this thy fair and outward character[6]

Her metaphorical use of a term Shakespeare often uses simply to mean 'written language'[7] point to the ancient meaning of a word with whose provenance and history Shakespeare, like any educated man of his time, would be perfectly familiar. 'Character' begins to accumulate its modern associations when it ceases to be seen as the matter of readable signs, to which Viola is referring here, and instead takes on progressively more and more of the connotations of words from other, chiefly philosophical and psychological discourses—identity, personality, soul, self, or whatever. All these things are of immediate relevance to the ancient discourse of character, as the things to which (with different emphases at different times and in different cultures) it takes itself to refer. But the snowballing effect by which these terms have become assimilated to one another is historically recent, and it obscures the issue when taken as timelessly normal and so projected back onto the past. The moral judgement which Viola is making exists in the area which covers those later meanings of the word—she could be saying, 'I will believe thou hast the character which thy appearance suggests'. But instead the line spells out very carefully, very importantly for the play, that character is a reading of signs, with a complex and risky relation to a knowledge of the minds with which such signs may seem to suit.

Shakespeare is inevitably central to a discussion of character. The enthusiastic eighteenth-century recuperation of his texts for an emergent 'modern'—though somehow also 'timeless'—idea of character is a complex cultural phenomenon with an interest over and above the more inscrutable matter of Shakespeare's own dramatic practice. The festive climax of a process by which the eighteenth- century theatre had rendered the plays down into a series of discrete individual figures was David Garrick's great 'Shakespeare Jubilee' of 1769, in which a procession of Shakespeare's characters paraded through the streets of Stratford.[8] (Or would have done, had it not rained.) The new notion of character is a remaking both of 'Shakespeare' and of 'the actor'. Garrick's development of a new acting style, of a new mode of character-creation is often taken to mark the inception of a modern idea of the actor. As phenomenon and problematic, the 'modern' actor and the post-eighteenth-century 'Shakespeare', the Shakespeare whose 'genius' lies in his ability to produce, seemingly endlessly, perfectly individuated, perfectly coherent and perfectly 'real' representations of almost every kind of human being, crucially inform our received conception of character, and must therefore be examined if we wish to account for its history. The interdependence of the two provides us with a still lively field of preconceptions and ahistorical certainties, to be interrogated and worked through.

Shakespeare concordances give us only two references to 'character' in *Hamlet*, and both seem at first sight disappointingly literal for what is, after all, the most frequently cited play in controversies of character interpretation. 'These few precepts' Polonius says to Laertes as he is about to leave for Paris, 'in thy memory see thou character',[9] meaning, of course, 'inscribe' or 'write'. ''Tis Hamlet's character',[10] Claudius exclaims on receiving an enigmatic note from the prince, newly returned from England, but what he means is that he recognises the hand writing. But hand writing is individuated[11]—Claudius is trying to establish the authenticity of this message, so the metaphorical extension to less literal kinds of identification is pretty modest. Reading correctly and establishing the authenticity of an utterance are major preoccupations in this play, for the audience as well as for the *dramatis personae*. The 'precepts' which Polonius gives Laertes are preceded by advice from Laertes to Ophelia, tokens of his superior knowledge of the world, of Hamlet's position in it and his likely actions—they give a 'character' of Hamlet, in other words, and implicitly of Laertes too, which Ophelia is enjoined to impress on the wax-like surface of her own mind. Polonius continues the process, first on Laertes, then on Ophelia after Laertes has gone. It is the 'character' which she then bears, which her male relations have given her, which Hamlet in his turn 'reads' and re-inscribes, as the 'characters' of women, the rhetorical set-piece descriptions that define his reaction to her in the 'nunnery' scene, their next on-stage encounter.

This example points to the presence in the play of the two most obvious features of the 'rhetorical' mode of character; the metaphorical extension of the term's origin, and the classificatory taxonomy by which it delineates other human subjects. A concordance search cannot in itself fully uncover the presence of so complex a cluster of ideas. Polonius's use of the word follows Hamlet's physically enacted 'setting down' in his 'tables' of a more paradoxical precept for the reading of 'character': 'That one may smile, and smile, and be a villain'. This physical literalisation of the metaphor occurs at the end of the speech which begins with his stated desire to 'wipe' from 'the table of my memory' all but his father's 'commandment'.[12] Like Ophelia he receives the imprint of a character that then re-characters him; he has had written on him an apparently authoritative disclosure—of Claudius's evil—which then defines how he himself is read. The encounters, interpretations and questionings of *Hamlet* strain the 'identifying' figures of rhetoric to their limit. However busily the *dramatis personae* offer each other rhetorical characterisations—old man, madman, maiden, prince, villain, adulteress—in order to fix and define the action at least temporarily, the springs of the action and the authentic significance of utterances constantly elude both them and us. Hamlet can confidently attribute the authenticity of the 'picture' of his father that he produces for Gertrude to divine character imprints: 'Where every god did seem to set his seal/To give the world assurance of a man'.[13] In this play character is most clearly articulated in the context of memory, and its related images of recording and reading back. Only the players, secure in the types they play and confident of their rhetorical skill, can provide a space in which the language of character possesses an immediate power.

The play's exploration of the language of 'character' extends to a metatheatrical consideration of my other focus in this section, the actor, and what he is seen to be doing when he acts. Hamlet's advice to the players is periodically quarried for clues to Shakespeare's own notion of an appropriate acting style. Approached this way it can be interpreted endlessly, and claimed for almost any position.[14] But that is because we are looking in it for the traces of a non-existent object—Elizabethan acting theory. It is in fact the absence of this object that is historically interesting. One can speak of broadly two different kinds of performers (pre-dating, that is, the eighteenth-century 'actor'). The performance skills required of medieval and renaissance actors were almost unclassifiably miscellaneous, blurring considerably the boundary between those who worked in an established theatre or troupe (and are thus easily perceived as actors in our sense) and the many other kinds of participants in entertainment and performance, amateur and professional, which formed an important part of social and public life. In so far as there is an emerging sense of 'the actor'—that is, of a professional pursuing a dignified career—it would seem to come out of the assumption, by the leading players on the Elizabethan professional stage, of that body of rhetorical skills which had, since Aristotle, constituted the West's central discourse on the use and methods of writing and speaking. This kind of performer, then, is essentially a professional rhetorician, developing rhetorical skills—in particular the skills involved in 'character',—in order to present a theatrical performance. This defines him against the more humble kind of player or public entertainer.

Acting and rhetoric are never seen as distinct entities; the theory of acting is unnecessary, as are systematic manuals of its techniques, since the first is already present in the theory of rhetoric, and the second can be seen in one aspect as an aggregate of unclassifiable social and entertainment skills, and in another, in the special effects of master-rhetoricians like Alleyn and Burbage, as a development from within a long-established rhetorical tradition. The dramatic traditions of the universities, the Inns of Court and the choir schools had long explored acting and rhetoric as, essentially, the same. We must not make the mistake of taking rhetoric in its modern colloquial sense as something strained, unreal, nearly ridiculous. To talk of acting in terms of rhetoric is to consider it as a branch of the study of human communication, of the development of the skills of 'moving', 'delighting', 'persuading' and 'teaching' other human subjects, as classical mediaeval and renaissance culture conceived of it. This is how Hamlet talks of it to the players.

'It is a trivial grammar-school text, but yet worthy of a wise man's consideration', writes Francis Bacon in his essay *Of Boldness*. 'Question was asked of Demosthenes, *What was the Chief part of an orator?* He answered, *Action*. What next? *Action*. What next again? *Action'*.[15] 'Action' is the term for the physical expression the orator uses to amplify his verbal statements. Fitness to the matter conveyed is of course all important here. 'Suit the action to the word, the word to the action, with this special observance, that you o'erstep not the modesty of nature'.[16] Hamlet is not speaking simply of *gesture* here; 'action' (not 'acting') is the Elizabethan term for what actors do. Hamlet's remark encompasses, albeit very generally, a notion of the proper relation of acting to text. It is one that the 'First Player' has developed to the highest degree, 'his whole function [i.e. whole physical being] suiting/With forms to his conceit'.[17] And this too in a speech he has

had to start 'cold' at Hamlet's request. All he does then comes from
that text, from the set of heightened personalised images of revenge,
ruined majesty and extreme grief (the 'characters' offered of Pyrrhus,
Priam and Hecuba) and from the verbal devices that amplify their
emotional effect. He is not 'acting a character' in the modern sense. The
speech is Aeneas's in a way that sets a problematic contexting around
its effect. Aeneas moved Dido in another way than he intended.
Hamlet, and the compromised little court around him, stand in for
Dido, blurring the distinction between actors and audience in the
player's sample of rhetorical theatre. The player projects the 'characters' of revenge, ruin and grief provided by his vividly insistent text,
and does so with a mimetic skill whose confusing and implicatory
effect on Hamlet inspires the prince to try out some similar effects on
his uncle.

An extended examination of *Hamlet*, or indeed of Bacon's remark on
the player would reveal the issue to be more fraught, in ways that I
shall return to later in the book. But the questions – what is the player
at Elsinore doing? How does he achieve that effect, and why? – take us
to the consideration not only of Elizabethan acting, but of the modern
actor, to issues which both seem to raise. A famous, probably
apocryphal, story exists of how Polos, the great fourth-century
Athenian actor once achieved a memorable effect of emotional
authenticity. This is Lee Strasberg, the director of New York's
influential Actors Studio, and promulgator of 'the Method', re-telling
it to one of his actors:

> Using the affective memory, which the great actors used uncon-
> sciously, makes it possible for us to join the great tradition of acting.
> When Kean in Hamlet picked up the skull of Yorick, he cried,
> because he said he always thought of his uncle. The ancient Greek
> actor Polis [sic] brought on the ashes of his own recently deceased
> son when he delivered Electra's funeral oration.[18]

But are Kean, Polos, Strasberg and Hamlet's player all doing the same
thing? Affective memory (leaving its technical meaning aside for the
moment) is a good term for what Hamlet tries to do in imitation of the
player, and the result is fruitless and embarrassing to him, because it
has no purpose. (*Then* he decides to turn the actors' skills to use.) Had
the player recently lost a close relative? The whole point of the scene is
that he had not. Nonetheless, he is able to produce the emotion
mimetically and in doing so he fulfils the often quoted precept for
rhetoricians, formulated by Horace in his *Ars Poetica* as follows:

Just as human features break into laughter with those who laugh, so they weep at others weeping. If you want me to weep, there must first be some sorrow for you. Then, Telephus or Peleus, your misfortunes will trouble me. If you speak what has been allotted to you badly, I'll either laugh or fall asleep. Sad words fit a mournful face . . ..[19]

Polos provides an effectively extreme image (in itself a kind of character-mnemonic) of this commonplace.

The 'affective memory' to which Strasberg refers is a concept in acting technique evolved by the early twentieth-century Russian director, actor and theorist, Konstantin Stanislavsky. He derived it from the French psychologist Ribot, who believed that all previous experiences leave a trace on the nervous sytem, and can be re-experienced if the key to activating that trace is found.[20] Bertolt Brecht *is* talking about the same thing as Strasberg when he retells the Polos story in his *Dialektik auf dem Theater* (1953). The example is used to focus on the issue of empathy in acting. 'His own son has just died, and so he brought the urn with his ashes on to the stage and spoke the relevant verses "focusing them so painfully on himself that his own loss made him weep real tears. Nor could any of those present have refrained from weeping at that point?" [sic] I must say there is only one word for such an operation: barbaric.' Brecht's argument, of course, is not with Cicero, but with Stanislavsky and his followers. His rather maliciously witty choice of illustration makes a common device of twentieth-century acting seem strange, 'barbaric'. But his main objection is the lack of clarity, complexity and purpose in the effects it produces. 'His son may have been a scoundrel' says one of the participants in the *Dialektik*. 'That needn't stop them suffering, but why should I suffer too?' Brecht agrees, and proposes the example of a woman mourning her brother's departure to a war that is, the play argues, a just war—a situation whose contradictions would be nullified by a simple call on empathy, on an attempt to make character, actor and audience feel, or imagine that they are feeling, the same thing. 'Our actual emotion will come from recognising and feeling the incident's double aspect.'[21]

As we have seen, both 'character' and a mimetic form of empathy are central to rhetorical communication whether in a theatrical or a non-theatrical context. 'Action' is the medium of both. But what differs, and it defines character and the empathetic effect differently too, is the relation of action to text. By such an exact fit of word to action, by virtue of a 'function' trained to effect such a 'fit' with an almost disturbing ease, the player becomes the text's instrument. He is then himself discountable as a presence separate from that which he articulates. The Stanislavskian actor, on the other hand, creates a text for himself, out of materials he finds in/for himself, which he stabilises and organises as a character. This is the 'substantive' idea of character in its fullest translation into acting terms. The actor's character-text is different from the verbal text of the role. Their clash produces the 'sub-text': a layer of unspoken meaning on to which we project our illusion of the character's depth, coherence, reality. When Elizabethan commentators describe the effect of good acting being 'as if the Personator were the man Personated' (to use Heywood's phrase)[22] they mean that the perfected 'modesty' and 'cunning'[23] of player and text has produced a fusion of the two in fitting 'action'. No such clash is apparent.

This would suggest and seem to make possible a more fluid and open presentation of character than the 'Stanislavskian', one in which continuity and discontinuity, empathy and alienation, real and symbolic, are all equally available to both writer and player. The rhetorical language of character makes this possible. Stanislavsky's extraordinary achievement is to solve for the actor the problem raised by the substantive mode of character; the relation between this achieved construct of another being, and the actor's own self. His development of acting as a creative process allows the actor to negotiate that crucial 'duplexity', the doubleness of his being. The theoretical consideration of acting can be seen to date largely from the mid-eighteenth century, from the controversy surrounding Garrick's new style of character-creation. (Its most famous philosophical off-shoot is Diderot's exploration of the problematic of acting and character in the *Paradoxe sur le Comedien* (1773).) The defining line between the two aspects of the performer—which is character, which is actor?—is consequently the central concern of theories of performance, whether they are aimed at actors (Stanislavsky), theorists (the semioticians), both (Brecht) or neither (Artaud). Hamlet's player, coming from a different tradition, presents a problem of a different kind.

The issues surrounding character are complex and varied, in that the term's history encompasses so many aspects of the representation of the human subject. Drama, my chosen focus in this book, has the advantage of concentrating on itself, by virtue of its technical and intellectual eclecticism, a wider range of these issues than most other forms. Performance in itself creates a problematic of 'character', of the relation between acting and the self, which dramatic texts of all periods tend to reflect on, as a philosophical nexus, and as the source of disturbing or implicatory theatrical effect. Finally, in the case of the period I have decided to concentrate on—from the early sixteenth to the late eighteenth century—drama, particularly in the context of its changing representation of the human, is centrally implicated in the development of the culture as a whole.

The two final points need to be raised here. The first involves my use of the term 'the human subject', the second (though of course the two are interdependent) is a reflection on the method and structure of this book. The issue of the representation of the human subject in pre-modern writing has been the focus of provocative recent work, particularly in the field of seventeenth-century drama.[24] Contemporary debates form one context for such an issue, but so, it should be stressed, do the models of self-reflection and exegesis employed in pre-modern dramatic and rhetorical texts themselves. The mystique which post-romantic criticism tends to create around the representation of the human does not exist for earlier writers. However powerful and urgent their presentation of character may be, its origins can be accounted for and its aims evaluated. It is acknowledged as a language, as a purposeful construction of identifying signs. Behind this explicitness lies a describable set of assumptions as to the nature and value of what modern literature theory tends to refer to as 'the human subject'. Subject here is used in an extension of the grammatical sense of the term. Our subjecthood is our experience of ourselves as 'I' or 'we' (rather than as 'it', 'he/she' or 'you'). Literature or drama or any developed use of language creates what one can call 'subject positions'. For example, the process that we tend to call 'identifying with a character' (in the sense of a figure in a play or a story) involves our imaginatively occupying their subject position, our experiencing (locally and limitedly) what it is to *be* Lady Macbeth or Hamlet as subjects, that is, as we experience ourselves.

My examples here (and obviously it is not the only way of responding to those figures, though it is one it would be naïve to discount) illustrate a coincidence of character-effect and subject-position, but assume the essential separateness of the two things. In different texts, perhaps at particular points in those two roles, one works without the other. Thus the idea of 'the human subject', while admitting a specifically modern terminology into the discussion, does tend to clarify the precise use of the more ancient term.

On the second point, as may already have become obvious, my approach to character is largely diachronic. That is, I have chosen a series of texts which seem to me to provide interesting examples of a discourse of character, and have dealt with them in chronological sequence. Some of these texts declare a relation to each other which can be mapped in time. Scaliger's *Poeticae* for example is a critical conspectus of writing from a classical past. Aristotle's *Poetics* is thus instated as one of its sources, while itself citing the work of the Athenian dramatists as the basis of its own formulations. Other texts can be linked by shared ideas and devices, and when put in chronological relation to each other can be used to construct a tradition.

This kind of presentation tends to suggest other notions—'development', for example. There are neutral ways of using this term, but its usual sense of 'improvement' and so 'becoming more modern', I find unhelpful. Gombrich has pointed out that a 'developmental' model of the arts has passed into Western culture from the classics, via the renaissance art historian Vasari.[25] For the ancients, he says, it provides a model of progress, of the kind which is provided for us by an idea of technological progress. (For neither ancient society nor bourgeois culture could such a model be provided by society in itself, given an inherently conservative notion of society as a given set of natural relations.) Though questioned, this model still operates in Western discourse on art. Such assumptions become vividly apparent when we look at the usually unexamined—character, for instance. Though we do not believe we are cleverer than people in the past or write better, we do assume that character 'depiction' has developed/progressed, become richer, fuller, more subtle, taken on scientific 'discoveries', become modern, or at least modernish. This notion perhaps belongs with several others—the great author as mysterious genius, the peak of art as the 'depiction' of 'characters' with whom the audience 'can identify'—to form a constellation of definitions of art in which a post-eighteenth-century idea of character is centrally implicated. In these terms, progression or development is autonomous—harmlessly so, if we accept it *as a model*, but confusing if we try to work it through literally. It has a shape we associate with history, but in itself it negates history, as it suggests a contextless asocial process of 'discovery', of absolute betterment.

Furthermore, if a study of character is necessarily a study of the representation of the human subject, then it evokes that apparent impossibility, a history of the human subject.[26] The apparent impossibility lies in the paradoxical subjecthood that it would construct for the historian. If we claim that the subject has a history, that in the past it was somehow different, how then can we recover this from our present subjecthood? We know as subjects, so how can we know a different subjecthood?

I put this question not to imply the possession of an answer, but to introduce a note of caution into the uses of diachrony. The discourses of character I outline through my choice of texts interest me in their difference, and that difference is significant in that the literary culture of which a subsequent idea of character is a corner stone would seek to deny it. That being so, I could equally well present my material synchronically, in that always-there-together state in which presently existing texts *also* have their being.

The first chapter falls into two main sections. The first covers theories of character as encountered first in Aristotle's *Poetics*, the second the development of an idea of character in post-Aristotelian rhetoric, and in the literary forms of biography, '*persona*' and Theophrastean 'character'.

Notes

1. Quoted from *Hogarth* by Lawrence Gowing (London, 1971). Gowing reproduces the portrait now in the National Gallery of Scotland, Edinburgh (p. 35). I have taken the detail of Sarah Malcolm's crime from William Gaunt's account in *The World of William Hogarth* (London, 1978) p. 52.
2. *Alexander*: 2, 3 (my translation).
3. The same term is used by Plato, in the rather different sense of the ideal (that is, non-material, but real) form of a thing that can be said to pre-exist any material instance of that thing.
4. See, for example, his *On The Style of Demosthenes*.
5. For a useful introduction to renaissance 'character' writing, see Benjamin Boyce's *The Theophrastian Character in England to 1642* (Cambridge, Mass., 1947) pp. 36–52.
6. *Twelfth Night; or, What you Will*, ed. M. M. Mahood (Harmondsworth, 1968) I. ii. 51–2, p. 50.
7. *The Harvard Concordance to Shakespeare* (Martin Spevack, Hildesheim 1973) lists twenty uses of 'character' and twelve of 'characters'. The examples are spread fairly evenly along a range of literalness with 'written figure' at one end of the scale, and 'readable person' at the other.
8. For an account of this event see *David Garrick, A Critical Biography*, George Winchester Stone Jnr. and George M. Kahrl (Southern Illinois, 1979) pp. 577–85.

9. *The Tragedy of Hamlet Prince of Denmark*, edited by Harold Jenkins (London, 1981) I. iii. 58−9, p. 202.
10. *Ibid.*, IV. vii. 49, p. 366.
11. Hamlet draws on his ability to produce an official, non-individuated hand writing in forging the warrant for Rosencrantz and Guildenstern's execution. But on the whole he aims at a recognisable hand, as a mark of his superior status. See V. ii. 32−6.
12. *Ibid.*, I. v. 92−112, pp. 221−2.
13. *Ibid.*, III. iv. 61−2, p. 322.
14. For B. L. Joseph, in *Elizabethan Acting* (Oxford, 1951) it is an injunction to an almost Stanislavskian 'naturalness', a position more recently taken by Anne Pasternak Slater in *Shakespeare the Director* (Brighton, 1983). Lina Lose Marker on the other hand places the scene in the context of Elizabethan aesthetic terminology. 'Nature and Decorum in the Theory of Elizabethan Acting' in *The Elizabethan Theatre II*, ed. David Galloway (Ontario, 1970) pp. 87−101.
15. Francis Bacon, *The Essays*, ed. John Pitcher (London, 1985) pp. 94−5.
16. *Hamlet*, III. ii. 17−19, p. 288.
17. *Ibid.*, II. ii. 550−1, p. 270.
18. Strasberg is quoted in Foster Hirsch, *A Method to their Madness* (New York, 1984) p. 142. The story of Polos is told by the second-century (A.D.) Latin writer Aulus Gellius, in the collection of anecdotes and observations known as *The Attic Nights* (*Noctes Atticae*) VI. v. 7. For Gellius the point of the anecdote is that while it *seemed* that a story (*fabula*) was being enacted, the action presented was that of real grief.
19. *De Arte Poetica*, 101−5 (my translation). Telephus and Peleus are characters from tragedy.
20. Stanislavsky set out his theories in fictionalised form, as the narrative of a director's relation to his students. Affective memory, or emotion memory is dealt with in *An Actor Prepares* (London, 1980) Chapter IX, pp. 163−92.
21. From *Conversation about being Forced into Empathy* in *Brecht on Theatre*, edited and translated by John Willet (London, 1964) pp. 270−1.
22. Thomas Heywood, *An Apology for Actors*, London 1612 B4r.
23. *Hamlet*, II. ii. 436−7, pp. 262−3.
24. I am thinking in particular of three books that appeared during the course of my work on this—Francis Barker's *The Tremulous Private Body* (London, 1984), Jonathan Dollimore's *Radical Tragedy* (Brighton, 1984) and Catherine Belsey's *The Subject of Tragedy* (London, 1985). I will return to their work, and the issues it raises, in my final chapter.
25. E. H. Gombrich, *Art and Illusion* (London, 1960) pp. 9−10.
26. Belsey raises a similar point. *The Subject of Tragedy*, xi−x.

1

Ancient Theories of Character

I ARISTOTLE'S POETICS

Ethos, *Praxis* and *Pathos*

Aristotle tackles drama as one class of the human activity we call 'art'. For Aristotle all art is mimetic, and the objects of its mimesis are aspects of the human. Aristotle gives these aspects a triple classification at the beginning of the *Poetics*, as *ethos*, *pathos* and *praxis*. *Praxis* is what man does, *pathos* is what is done to him, and *ethos* is what man is. Drama differs from other kinds of mimesis in that it represents men '*prattontas . . . kai drontas*', acting and doing.[1]

For Aristotle things are defined by the end to which they develop, not by their beginnings (as in an historical mode of definition), or by their characteristic operations (as in structuralist or phenomenological accounts). The end of art is the representation or *mimesis* of the human. Drama is further defined by its medium — action — and tragedy is classified, as a form of drama, according to the objects it imitates. Certain kinds of persons and events are imitated in tragedy, other kinds in comedy.

Aristotle doesn't discuss the 'how' of imitation, and this leads to some ambiguities in his basic vocabulary. The 'doing' words — *prattein*, *poiein* and so on — by which he refers to action can be used either of the action imitated/represented, or of the action involved in representing — used either of Oedipus questioning Tiresias, or of the lead actor declaiming verses by Sophocles at the second actor. Furthermore the word *mimesis* retains a secondary meaning of 'performance'. So the protagonist could be said either to 'imitate' or to 'perform' Oedipus.

The language of the *Poetics* is in itself simple. Aristotle uses words familiar in both philosophical and everyday discourse. Such words acquire a vast and unstable set of meanings. A continuous history of commentary on the Aristotelian texts has developed and revised a range of possible interpretations, making up in itself the central discourse of pre-romantic literary theory. This renders the aim of an accurate one-for-one version of a text like the *Poetics* unrealisable.

Different readings of Aristotle are best mapped historically, as part of an account of a developing tradition of knowledge. Nonetheless, an attempt to pin down as clear and uninflected an account of his terms as possible remains a necessary preliminary step towards the discussion, not simply of 'Aristotelianism', but of that issue to which the *Poetics* are chiefly addressed—drama, specifically tragedy, as the mimesis of the human.

Such basic ambiguities suggest that, in fact, the distinctions implied are not important to Aristotle, which in turn warns us not to build too much on them. Aristotle has no real interest in questions of technique, of codes of communication. His refusal to account for the relation between the representation and the thing represented is implicit in the lack of a clear terminological distinction between the action on stage and the action to which that can be taken to refer. An English translation which respected this ambiguity would be unreadable, but attempts to clarify it invariably involve the introduction of an extra set of post-Aristotelian terms, whose connotations can incidentally obscure Aristotle's lucid argumentative moves.

Tragedy, in Aristotle's definition, is the *mimesis* of a *praxis*, the representation of an action in deeds rather than through narration. He then goes on to show that *praxis* (what we do) is more important to such a mimesis than *ethos* (what we are). One of his reasons for giving *praxis* the priority is technical; it is possible to present plays *without ethos*, and many recent and some of the older playwrights have done so. It is equally possible (indeed easy) to write detached speeches demonstrating *ethos* (*theses ethikas*) but it is impossible to present a play without *praxis*.[2] Aristotle provides no examples of plays without *ethos*, and though his later definition of *ethos* may bring one closer to conceiving of them, the hint seems too vague to impose illustrations or analogies on it at this point. But given the overlap of *praxis* onto Aristotle's other 'doing' words, it seems unquestionable that action of some kind is required, as by definition. It is in this form then that the human is *primarily* represented in drama—its representation as *ethos*, as the qualities of its being, is secondary, approached through *praxis* or, sometimes, not at all.

Another reason for the priority of *praxis* and of *mythos*, or plot, the structural principle of stage action, depends on Aristotle's teleological mode of definition and thus intermeshes with his consideration of the proper priorities of human life elsewhere in his works. Tragedy is a representation of life, and the end of life is either *eudaimonia* or *kakodaimonia*. These are often translated as happiness and unhappiness, respectively, but they are broader in implication, referring to materially good or bad conditions or 'fortunes', for example. They are rather states of being than feelings in the modern sense and so are neither subjective nor fleeting. This idea is developed in the *Nichomachean Ethics* (ethics means 'about *ethos*' and is thus the study of human being), as is Aristotle's contention that *eudaimonia*, properly understood, is a kind of action. Thus life is defined by its end, which is achieved through action, and which is in itself a kind of action, an active state of being. For Aristotle, contemplation is the best of such states. *Ethos*, what we simply are, cannot in itself achieve this end; so again it must be secondary to *praxis* in the representation of life, of which such achievement is, for good or ill, the defining end.[3]

Ethos is required in representations of life in the presentation of conscious choice—or *proairesis*. Again this concept is discussed more fully in the *Ethics*. This kind of choice is the choice of an action, made by a mature person in full control of his or her mental faculties. Where the choice is not an obvious one (a straightforward case of self-preservation for example) it reveals a particular *ethos*. So these moments of significant choice are the 'showing' of *ethos*.[4] Presumably then a play without *ethos* is a play structured around something other than choices made by the participants, though in the surviving canon of Greek plays this could only apply to a few minor figures—Hermione in the Euripides *Orestes*, for example.

So, if we translate *ethos* as 'character', we must remember that the Greek word overlaps in function with only a limited number of the connotations of the modern term. *Ethos*, *pathos* and *praxis* are three categories for aspects of human existence which modern writing would present differently, and in a different relation to each other. One could use Aristotle's terms to describe this modern idea of character as *pathos* and *praxis* subsumed into *ethos*, in that acting and being acted on can be seen to be organised by some essentially static notion of individual being, and that it is in this that they find any ultimate meaning. If we project this view back on to Aristotle, he can be seen to wilfully downgrade something 'we all know' to be centrally important, to reverse the priorities of a liberal humanist literary education, by which we are taught to downgrade action, and its organising principle, plot, in favour of this more developed, more 'human' literary concept. Characters that exist 'for the sake of the action' are crude, we are told, but action that illustrates character is properly sophisticated. Nonetheless, Aristotle's triple categorisation, however understood, has informed Western dramatic theory as its historical base, as has its underlying assumption, that representation of the human is drama's defining end.

Greek Tragedy and the 'Showing' of *Ethos*

Aristotle is concerned with the methods of tragedy, and applies his conclusions critically, to distinguish the proper and improper use of those methods. He derives his theory of dramatic representation from the work of the Athenian dramatists, taking his examples from their theatre practice.

At one point Aristotle describes how a writer constructs a tragedy. He starts from a plot, a *mythos*. Then he adds names to it, usually taking them from one of the great legendary families in which such an incident may have occurred. Then he builds in incidents and episodes which fit the basic scheme. Aristotle gives us here, not an eye-witness account of the tragedian at his desk, but a narrative version of the priorities of poetic creation as earlier defined by him in opposition to those of 'history'. History deals in the particular, in named individuals and known facts, where poetry deals in universals — *katholos* — valid as possibilities and thus of wider application, more useful philosophically as tending to broadly valid human truths. In comedy this is clearer, he says, as the characters' names are fictional, but in tragedies the use of familiar names merely heightens the credibility of the events, it is not essential, as it is, limitingly so, to history. The preliminary stage in his account of composition is, similarly, described as *katholos*; the universal is conceived of first, then named and placed in the context of a known family.[5]

This balance of the general and the particular is worked out in detail in his specifications for the representation of *ethos*. Speeches may present either *ethos* or generalised thought (*dianoia*) or narrative. Some characters, messengers for example, present only thought and narrative — *ethos* is not apparent, as they make no choices.[6] This brings one to a distinction between kinds of persons represented — *faulos* or *chrestos*. In neo-classical (seventeenth- and eighteenth-century) uses these come to mean 'low' and 'high' respectively, low appertaining to comedy and high to tragedy, the distinction tending to replicate class distinction. This last is undoubtedly the case for Aristotle too, whose political system assumes a natural and unchanging hierarchy of abilities in which a ruling class of citizens is alone capable of governing — of exercising proairetic choice and pursuing *praxis* in the most developed form of human life. Slaves and artisans are not *unjustly* deprived of this because they are so constituted that it would have no meaning for them anyway. To translate *chrestos* simply as good would therefore be to shift the distinction he makes. It can also mean useful, good of its kind. Here it means good in the best kind, good in a given system, a given categorisation of the human. When Aristotle says, in the first of his specifications for *ethos*, that women or slaves can be good in this sense, he is pointing to exceptional cases of two classes generally to be considered inferior.[7] The nature of tragic action is such that women and slaves are called on to display qualities of *ethos* which are generally irrelevant.

A choice of speech or action which is good/useful/good-of-its-kind demonstrates a good *ethos*. Important characters would have to be *chrestos*, in that choices made by characters in the *faulos* category would have no meaning, and thus could not instigate a meaningful action; they would simply scramble the plot as the plots of farces are scrambled. This then is perhaps the most crucial of the four specifications, as the relation of *ethos* to *praxis*, in *proairesis*, can be seen to depend on it. Just as *chrestos* cannot simply be translated as good/virtuous in Christian terms, so one cannot take this formula to mean that good choices are evidence of good qualities. The choices do not exist to dramatise a goodness of heart which is our real object of knowledge. They are the points at which the necessary interrelation of *ethos* and *praxis* becomes visible, and thus the structural nodes of the plays' 'making visible' of life in action.

The second specification, that representations of *ethos* should be *harmottos*, is clarified by examples and is close enough to other terms with the same root to present few problems. It is not *harmottos* that a woman should be manly or too clever, or, in the case of a named pseudo-historical character, it is not suitable for Odysseus to perform a lament. *Harmottos* means fitting, in other words, proper to the class of character (woman, old man, slave, warrior) or proper as a representation of a particular figure, and so proper to the class 'representation of Odysseus', for example.[8] Horace expands influentially on this point in his *Ars Poetica*,[9] and from this it was developed further by European dramatic theorists as a principle of 'decorum', assimilated to the aim of verisimilitude, of a fitting representation of the real. That, in reality, people often transgress their generic category is, of course, neither here nor there.

The third specification, *homoios*, is much more problematic. No examples are given for this, and all the clarification offered is that it is not the same as either of the previous terms.[10]

Homoios means, simply, like—but 'like' what? Any term we add seems to beg a host of questions. T. S. Dorsch's translation, for example, translates it as 'life-like', whose connotations of realist *mimesis* assume far more than Aristotle wants to say.[11] This is the tendency of several commentaries. Seymour Chatman wants it to mean 'like an individual' but this again implies a different kind of discussion, an attempt to import a modern sense of 'realistic character' back into the *Poetics*.[12] Another possible interpretation is 'like itself', not in the sense of consistent, but like other representations of the same identified *ethos*, like Odysseus, or whoever. This is possible, but it seems too close to *harmottos*, as applied to the Odysseus example, to require Aristotle's definite qualification that this is a different specification. I think *homoios* may differ from the first two terms in not referring to the person's fitness to or value in his or her category, nor (to anticipate) to the likeness to self of the fourth specification. Rather, *homoios* means like things outside the represented *ethos*, outside the representation itself.

This is suggested by other uses of the term in the *Poetics*. In talking of pity and fear, the states of mind which tragedy evokes in the spectator, Aristotle remarks that we fear the situations of those like (*homoios*) ourselves.[13] Pity, by extension, is what we feel for others. For fear to be evoked by a character's situation we must be able to classify ourselves with them; a kind of annulment of difference takes place, powerful perhaps because paradoxical and temporary, an annulment prepared for by the universality (*katholos*) of the basic *mythos* and allowed by an *ethos* which is sufficiently 'like' for us to class ourselves with it.

Modern ideas of empathy and lifelikeness are not wholly irrelevant, however. What Aristotle actually says could be a precondition for both these concepts, and thus allows them a place in a post-Aristotelian tradition. But empathy implies a very un-Aristotelian psychology—we do not 'feel with' the ethos revealed; we recognise it as like us, but the effect, the *pathos*, the thing done to the audience, is done by the *mythos*, the structure of the action, at its high points of recognition and reaction, and its effect is an 'invocation', a 'summoning up' even a 'conjuring' of a particular state of being—all these terms are possible translations of Aristotle's deliberately recherché choice of word, *psychogogia*.

Ethos has to be recognisable—though this word again implies the wrong model of perception. It has to be 'like', and perhaps can be seen to operate by analogy with the mediaeval English idea of 'kind'. It is in any case the precondition of a cancelling of difference on which the effect of Aristotelian drama depends. Characters who are not 'like'—frogs, birds, allegories, eccentrics and the more foreign kind of foreigner—belong in comedy, but the tragic action can reveal likeness in a temporary cancelling of the difference between a male audience of citizens, and the characters of women, 'good' slaves, or dignified barbarians (like Aeschylus's *Persai*).

The fourth specification turns on the term *homalos*.[14] This seems to mean 'consistent', like self. Aristotle concedes the possibility of an *ethos* which is inconsistent in itself, so he seems to mean that the representation must be consistent—an inconsistent ethos should be consistently represented as inconsistent. Aristotle's example, Iphigeneia in Euripides's *Iphigeneia in Aulis*, clarifies what he means but raises further problems fo r a modern reader. Iphigeneia responds to tragic crisis in a discontinuous set of proairetic displays—of girlish fear, of daughterly duty, and of mature resignation—all perfectly *harmottos*, *chrestos* and *homoios* in themselves, but adding up for Aristotle to something distinctly not *homalos*. For the modern reader this may suggest 'character development' (one of the few Greek roles to offer the possibility of such a reading) but for Aristotle Euripides is violating probability to achieve a set of shock effects. It seems a more purely aesthetic criterion than the other three, a formalist demand for an orderly surface to the representation, undisturbed by jagged effects of discontinuity.

Action, Choice and Recognition; Tragedy in Practice

For Aristotle a tragic *mythos* can be abstracted from a play, paraphrased, and still retain its effect; this is almost a test of true tragedy.[15] There is no analogous structural principle in the representation of *ethos* of a kind that would allow it to be thus detached and transposed. If there was it could be called character; character in modern criticism can be seen to stand to *ethos* as *mythos* does to *praxis*, as a way of structuring an account of a particular being. It follows then that Aristotle does not envisage the discussion, even the conception of, say, Sophocles' Oedipus, as detached from the *praxis* that constitutes his *Oedipus*. The various revelations of *ethos* which the play contains are organised by the action and are inseparable from it. To recap on Aristotle's description of these 'showings' of 'what men are' in drama, and to lead up to a reconsideration of the place of the human subject in the structure of an Aristotelian theatrical *praxis*, I intend to follow him in taking examples from two of his favourite plays—Euripides's *Iphigeneia in Tauris*, and Aeschylus's *Choephori* (*Libation Bearers*). The *Poetics* are not a manual of practical criticism, but an application of some of Aristotle's formulations should illuminate both them and the body of plays from which they were derived.

In the Tauris play Iphigeneia introduces herself in a sixty-five line speech, largely concerned with telling the story up to that point. She identifies herself first by describing her genealogy, then by naming herself, then by telling 'her' story, the story of the Aulis play.[16] This first section of the speech cannot be acted 'in character' in the modern sense. It is not *ethikos*; it deals in narration and *dianoia* (impersonal thought or observation). She puts her name to a situation first defined for us by other means—genealogy and narrated *mythos*. Her situation is presented not as individual experience, but in an objective narration, which thus renders it *katholos*.

The *praxis* of the Tauris play can be said to begin after Iphigeneia has identified its location, and moved her narration into the present. She exercises *proairesis*, and so demonstrates *ethos*, in speech and in ritual action, often the only kind of *praxis* available to a female character at this point in a play. In response to her dream of the destruction of her father's house—the *pathos* which instigates the action—she chooses to perform a funeral for her brother, Orestes, whom she supposes to be dead. But she chooses also to question the goddess Artemis's purpose in rescuing her from Aulis and the rightness of the human sacrifices at which she is now called upon to assist.[17] This proairetic speech-act (*logos*) is typically Euripidean in its potentially blasphemous daring. Together with Iphigeneia's response to the dream it displays an *ethos* which combines family piety with a rebellious if impotent tendency to question the apparently oppressive decrees of the gods. It is an *ethos* entirely *chrestos* (good of its kind), *harmottos* (fitting in all possible categories—princess, exile, woman, member of the house of Atreus), *homoios* (the situation presented in a way that opens up its potential relevance to ourselves) and *homalos* (consistent with itself, and with what we have learnt from the opening narrative).

The disguised Orestes and his friend Pylades fulfil the same criteria. On their first appearance Pylades states his decision to steal the image of Artemis, as the oracle has instructed. This forthright *ethos* is contrasted to the demoralised Orestes, who wants to leave it there.[18] Again, all the conditions can be applied to show that this is the correct *ethos* in each case. The progress of the action involves the characters in further sets of choices which amplify and complicate our sense of them. Iphigeneia in particular negotiates the situation in which she and her brother find themselves, showing bravery and cleverness of a kind unsuspected in her initial helplessness. The idea of *proairesis* and its place in Aristotle's scheme may incidentally help us to explain the apparent paradox that a society which imposed strict limitations on women nonetheless produced uniquely powerful representations of women in its tragic drama. Precisely because the range of choice is so limited for women, the trap (no choice, no action, no being) in which Medea, Electra or Iphigeneia find themselves, and the choice of action and consequent revelation of being that they find as a way out of it, are more sharply defined than for the male characters, who only in carefully constructed circumstances can make such vertiginous transitions through the proairetic moves they make.

It also becomes apparent that in Euripides in particular a notion of being of the kind that Aristotle outlines is problematised by the play itself. In other words the actions of Iphigeneia, Orestes and Pylades raise the questions: What is good? What is fitting? What categories are relevant? or even, what kind of behaviour is consistent; should we accept these people as like or alien? In the Tauris play this is resolved, though by a device Aristotle dislikes, the god in the machine. In Euripides's *Orestes*, a play which Aristotle thinks is faulty, there is no such resolution; nobody seems clearly *chrestos*, *harmottos* or *homalos*, to the extent that the play has been taken to be non-tragic. The characters are irredeemably *not homoios*.[19] Euripides continually tests at the limits of the tragic mode. Those values which Aristotle formulates as rules are themselves laid open to question, even destruction, in the tragic crises the plays enact.

Though Aristotelian criticism does not possess a discourse of character it does nonetheless place the issues with which that discourse concerns itself at the centre of dramatic representation. In modern terms, identity is seen to reside in the unique individuality of each separate consciousness — for the Greek dramatists and for Aristotle it is defined socially, by family and state. Orestes's madness and Iphigeneia's dreams are for us aspects of their consciousness — for the Greeks they are *pathos*, things done to them (by the gods). Though we each possess a particular *ethos*, that is not for the Greeks the source of our defining reality, it is not 'ourself'. We are defined by the end to which our life tends, and that is achieved through our actions. This absence of a discourse of character, of the presentation of unified individuated selves, aligns Greek drama with Brecht and the modernists. But Aristotelian poetics are opposed to Brecht in placing a notion of the human at the centre of drama, a notion based on sameness rather than on difference, in seeing as the end of drama an identification of the spectator as subject with the subjects established in the action, a recognition of common (*katholos*) and implicitly unchanging humanity. But the vehicle of this recognition is not that organising principle of *ethos* which we call character, but *mythos*, the structure of action. This is one more reason why *ethos*, according to Aristotle, need not be represented in tragedy. It is *mythos* that produces those moments of reversal and recognition which invoke tragedy's greatest effects.

At one point Aristotle calls *mythos* the *psyche* of dramatic praxis.[20] *Psyche* can be translated as soul, life or breath; it is the 'form' of a human being, in that it organises and gives purpose to other faculties. This perhaps startling metaphor is picked up again in *psychogogia*, that quasi-magical term used by Aristotle for the effect of 'conjuring up' or 'summoning' that reversal and recognition scenes have on the audience.[21] This terminology should remind us that though Aristotle makes *ethos* secondary to *praxis*, he does not, as a modernist might, do so in order to downgrade those values which *ethos* involves, and which have become part of our sense of 'character'. These values, that centrality of the human subject, is affirmed *through praxis*; the plot is fittingly called the soul of the play, for it is through the plot that the audience participates in that larger recognition scene that the whole play can be seen to be.

An idea like *psychogogia* is literally relevant to the climactic reversal/recognition of Aeschylus's *Choephori*. The first half of the play consists of Electra's recognition of Orestes, their prayer to their father's ghost and finally the decision to revenge, which has followed on from a long ritual establishment of the identities transgressed and denied by Clytemnestra's crime. It climaxes first with the recounting of the murder to the victim's grave, and then at the chorus's account of Clytemnestra's dream, with the prophesy that identifies Orestes as revenger and restates his filial identity in relation to her – in her dream she gives birth to him as a snake that kills her.[22] Recognition affirms identity – all its signs are re-established by the *mythos* and then fulfilled in action.

This may be for good (Iphigeneia) or for bad (Oedipus) but these two favourite examples of Aristotle's emphasise the importance of 'recognition' as tragedy's proper climax, the establishment of an identity otherwise nullified or disastrously transgressed, an identity in which relations to family and state inhere, but to which *ethos* is relevant only instrumentally. The best recognition scenes are produced by the necessity of the plot (*Oedipus*), the worst by signs alone (whether physical marks or self-declarations) in that these last bear none of the significance of the accumulated action with them.[23] Aristotle's account of the *mythos* of *Iphigeneia in Tauris* ends with the recognition scene. The manner of their escape is incidental, he says.[24] The 'likeness' of Iphigeneia and Orestes, of Orestes and Elektra, is the climactic revelation which 'summons up' in the audience a state of being which attests to our likeness to the characters on stage. Whatever the specific qualities of Greek plays, the theoretical construct which Aristotle derives from them has as its aim an affirmation, on stage and in the auditorium, of a human subject taken to be universally 'like' men, not as they always are, but as the height of their development would show them to be. Such a construct, as 'Aristotelian drama', gave the West its most persistently influential model for accounts of the nature and purpose of dramatic representation.

II   CHARACTER AND RHETORIC IN POST-CLASSICAL TRADITION

Characters and *Personae*

An idea of the human is at the centre of Aristotle's uniquely wide-ranging and massively influential intellectual project. He and his school produced studies in all branches of human knowledge and enquiry. For Aristotle the most important of these is politics, the science of the most developed human condition, man as member of a state. The set of definitions which Aristotle presents in the *Poetics* is less valuable as an account of the literary and theatrical practice of the Athenian dramatists of a century or so earlier than as the ground work of a study of literature as a branch of the science of the human, sharing terms and methods with philosophical, political and even medical enquiry. It is its implication in this system of knowledge which ensured the currency of the terminology it developed, a currency continuous in Western writing up till at least the late eighteenth century.

It is clear that one of the problems facing renaissance commentators is that of fitting a newly acquired knowledge of Aristotle's actual text to terms and ideas ultimately derived from it, as from other Aristotelian treatises, but adapted and modified by their passage through classical and post-classical Greek and Roman writers on rhetoric. That this tradition continues to take precedence over Aristotle's *Poetics* can be at least partly accounted for by the kinds of assumptions that rhetorical discourse on literature makes as to the function and nature of writing. One basic kind of argument, crucial to mediaeval and renaissance discussion of literature and drama is notably absent from Aristotle's *Poetics* – argument about the *purpose* of art. *Mimesis* is for Aristotle a natural, almost instinctive human activity.[25] Furthermore, he takes for granted the existence of developed mimetic forms, like drama, as part of the life of the state. He does not then have to define their purpose, let alone use an idea of their purpose as the basis for study. Most renaissance accounts of literature, on the other hand, are cast, explicitly or implicitly, in the form of the 'apology', a defence of art against attacks, assumed or real. The study of rhetoric, the terms it sets for the consideration of the techniques, effects and uses of a developed language, is more immediately relevant to arguments concerning the use and purpose of literature as a moral and political instrument within the state.

This may help to explain the initially puzzling pre-eminence for later writers of Horace's *Ars Poetica*, the verse epistle to the Pisos, over the more complex formulations of the *Poetics*. Though Horace's ideas are simple, even bland, compared with Aristotle's, he locates poetry in a knowable social praxis. Where Aristotle's text remains puzzling, in its denseness of formulation, and in the cultural strangeness of its premises, Horace both describes and enacts an accessible function for poetry. It is in this light that we should see his vastly influential prescription for 'character'. Aristotle's prescription, that a depicted *ethos* should always be *harmottos*, that is, 'fitting' to its particular category or combination of categories (young/old, male/female, free/slave, and so on), becomes the keynote of Horace's account, taking the place of all more complex considerations. But such 'fitness' for Horace comes from, and is evidence of, the poet's knowledge of the world, of human natures and human manners (the Latin word *mores* implies both).[26] His use of the categories which determine 'fitness' and his ability to produce fit styles and ideas place him as, if not more, precisely as they place the people he describes. This position of knowledge and right judgement is the basis of the poet's role, in his own writing, and in the state of which he is a part. Horace's mode of address to his aristocratic patrons in itself enacts this controlled fiction, this knowing construction of a poet's role. Like Hamlet's address to the players, his poem places its demands for a fitness of style to matter in the frame of 'advice' offered across class difference. In Horace's case this placing, the demonstration of the poet's power to construct a role for himself in the world, is more important, more crucial to the poem's influence, than any detachable 'theoretical' precept. Language, for Horace, is deciduous: 'As, over the years, the trees change their leaves . . . so the old generation of words dies and the new-born flourish and grow strong . . .'[27] His comparison of linguistic change to natural decay and, implicitly, to human ageing, opens up a still wider perspective on the notions of clarity, simplicity and fitness of style which his poem promotes. The act of writing is seen to take place within an unending condition of change – social, natural, even linguistic. Within this the poet creates a limited stasis, a carefully stabilised relation between himself, his writing and his world.

For classical and post-classical writers, *ethos*, *praxis* and *pathos* continue to provide basic categorisations of the human. The distinctions they imply still operate, as does the teleology they work from – the end, that is, that they set for representations of the human, that of moving hearer or reader, by a kind of participatory recognition, towards human happiness and human wisdom. They still define the subjectivities constructed by the rhetorical text, the reader/listener, and writer/voice that it implies. Character, on the other hand, is the initially metaphoric designation of a species of device by which things and people outside the text – outside its writer-reader relationship – impinge upon it, leave their stamp on its supply receptive language.

In rhetorical writing the term character is, as I pointed out in my introduction, always used with a sense of its origin as metaphor. As a mark stamped on one thing by another (or, as the thing that stamps that mark) the term requires a sense of 'fitness', of a fit between particular kinds of language and particular persons, a correspondence between particular 'signs' and certain categories of human being. Cicero uses the term 'character', in its original Greek form, for the 'ideal type' of orator whom, rather on the model of Plato's ideal republic, he presents in *The Orator*. The platonic concept of the *idea*, or ideal form of a thing, is an unhelpful cross-current here, but his usage seems enough in the context of the Greek rhetoricians' use of 'character' to denote the typical features of a particular writer's style.[28] Character is in this sense a style by which a particular person or particular category of person can be recognised. Elsewhere, in the *Topica*, Cicero uses character as the term for those categories of person which provide the orator with subject matter. Out of a knowledge of these types he can, like Horace's poet, generate descriptions by following the rules of 'fitness'. The kind of knowledge of human nature which Cicero demands of the orator is basically opportunistic.[29] His account of rhetoric is closely tied in to the example of his own success as a political and judicial orator. Cicero wrote in the last days of the republic, and Horace is the poet of the new imperial age. It is not difficult to see in their work a shift of emphasis, between Cicero's, on the influence which a discourse of character gives to those who can use it, to, in Horace, the quieter but safer position of power which rests on the knowledge which that discourse implies.

So, 'character' in classical writing on rhetoric is one of two related things. It is that use of language by which an individual or a group can be recognised. Or it is a recognised category of person, which provides the writer or speaker with a knowable quantity of material (or *res*), knowable because the definition and associations of that category are agreed on socially and re-articulated in the contract between writer and reader.

This last conception of character is one that can seem repugnant to modern readers. There is certainly a distinct difference of emphasis between the place and value given to the depiction of other human subjects in this account of literary practice, and that accorded it in the 'modern' (that is, post-eighteenth-century) discourse of character which has replaced it. If we recognise this difference, we ought to be able to avoid the trap involved in seeing the rhetorical idea of character as a primitive version of the other, as generalised sketch or crude stereotype. The difference lies in a different conception of the literary text. Rhetoric takes the text to be essentially intersubjective – that is, it is seen as a use of language directed by one human subject to another. Its aims and methods are to be examined in that light. The emphasis is thus always on the relationship between the 'voice' of the text and the authority that is assumed to lie behind it, and the mind of the reader and the reactions consequent on his or her reception of the text. 'Character' is the mode by which other human subjects impinge on the text, from outside this intersubjective relationship. They may leave their mark on it by means of a *'mimesis'* – the 'performance' or 'imitation' of their voices, of their 'characteristic' use of language – or by means of the 'placing' and 'identifying' moves that the concept of decorum and the multiplication of the categories of *personae* allow. But the relation of writer to reader is of primary importance, and character functions to articulate and extend this, to construct those textually primary identities more fully. 'Character', as a literary device, does not, to use a modern terminology, 'create' 'independent' 'fully-rounded' 'human beings' – it does not, in other words, present other human subjects as if they were the autonomous sources of the languages that make up the text. This kind of (again largely post-eighteenth-century) literary practice seeks to circumvent the direct writer-reader relationship of rhetorical texts which when it re-appears seems embarrassing – it is often referred to, in a tellingly paradoxical phrase, as the 'intrusive authorial voice' (intrusive into what? Into its own statements). The devices that come under the heading of 'character' in rhetorical writings are not crude early attempts at this. They have a different task to perform, in a conception of writing which explores the complexities of human communication by elaborating and reflecting on its own premises – on, that is, the intersubjectivity of the text.

Modern concepts – like 'the stereotype' (normally used per-joratively, as tending to misrepresentation of what it is taken to refer to) or E. M. Forster's 'flat character's[30] – are thus of limited relevance to a discussion of the *personae*, as these general classifications of the human were called. Both modern terms presuppose the existence of substantive (real, rounded, individual) 'character' to which 'flat' or 'stereotyped' presentation is inadequate. The ancient technique of the *persona*, on the other hand, derives from its schematisation of the social codes of 'character' – dress codes, typical behaviour, common physical types, and so on – a flexible basis for the articulation of character as social interaction, as implicated in the knowledge of a particular world, a world whose codes can be elaborated, confirmed and subverted in that contract between writer and reader which the text represents. A stereotype is more simply predicative. 'Golden-hearted whore' differs from 'courtesan' in that the first closes off possibilities of further reading or development; its most sophisticated use is as a kind of short-hand, in the service of narrative compression. But 'courtesan' – or 'nurse' or 'braggart' or whatever – exists as the basis for elaboration. The skilled writer offers persuasive realisations of the *personae*, complicating, shifting or strengthening the reader's sense of the world the text articulates.

Exercises in developing *personae* form an important part of rhetorical training. The urban comedies of the Roman writers Plautus and Terence, and their stylistic source, the Greek 'new' comedy, the form established by Menander – were often performed in schools, the aim being not so much to appreciate their specifically dramatic qualities as to explore the character categorisation that they offered.[31]

An often cited and, in the seventeenth century at least, highly influential example of a similar exercise is the collection of 'characters' written by the Greek teacher and rhetorician Theophrastus. Theophrastus was a pupil of Aristotle's, and like many other such, continued the Aristotelian project with studies in various fields. Most of his work is lost, but it is significant in this context that later writers on rhetoric credit him with the invention, or at least the formulation, of the doctrine of 'fitness', that congruity of style to matter to be developed by Horace.[32]

The 'characters' of Theophrastus are a collection of short sketches of kinds of social behaviour, tending to begin with the definition of a particular deformation of right behaviour – miserliness, flattery, or whatever – then illustrating it by a series of speeches and actions ascribed to one human example – the miserly man, the flatterer. The deviations from the social ideal presented here are, significantly, often examples of the wrong use of language – boorishness, boasting, for example. Other categories like meanness and drunkenness, are, like misuses of language, essentially deformations of social interaction, things that obstruct the proper conduct of those day-to-day relations which provide Theophrastus with the context of his illustrations. The 'characters' are thus exercises in 'fitness', in the development of a rhetorical device. Though Theophrastus locates each example in the acts of an imagined individual, that individual is not psychologically or morally accounted for, his acts are not described in order to point to some identifiable self; rather, the fiction of a self is used to organise a set of recognisable instances of a particular mode of undesirable social praxis. A particular reader, or someone known to that reader may well participate in several of the 'characters' – they are not exclusively individuated, as their reputation as distant ancestors of modern character 'creation' may suggest. They codify distinct kinds of misused language and bad behaviour, demonstrating the skill of the rhetorician in rendering the 'character' of each of them, and his wisdom in knowing them and judging them correctly.

The character metaphor then describes one way in which aspects of human life can be seen to be dealt with by a literary text; not, that is, as generalised precepts or philosophical wisdom, but as some real identified thing, which exists outside the text and has made its mark on it – the mark which identifies it. The writer's skill with language makes this mark possible. He becomes flexible enough to imitate, or at least to know, the identifying languages of others, and his worldly wisdom regulates his use of such knowledge, as it is also a knowledge of himself and of his place in his world. This process has an obvious professional relevance to the political and judicial practice of the great early rhetoricians — the law and day-to-day politics are essentially concerned with the identification and representation of others. Outside the Roman republic and the Greek democracies, where the arts of rhetoric were initially formulated, devices like character, while still recognised as a social and political language, come to acquire a more literary function, as tending to place, after Horace's example, the poet in relation to his world. Later still, for mediaeval writers like Geoffrey of Vinsauf, the conception of character as categorisable subject matter, from which *copia*, or setpiece descriptions, can be generated, takes precedence over mimetic character, character as rendered voice.[33] The development of different skills at different times and places bears witness to the changing role and status of rhetorical practice in different societies. But all such uses stay within the carefully conserved sense of the original metaphor. All present character as the reading and writing of an identifying language. All see that language as the 'imprint' that human subjects conceived of as outside the text, outside its writer-reader relationship, stamp onto it, as their identifying mark.

Ethos, Biography and the Purpose of Writing

Diogenes Laertius labelled the Theophrastian 'characters' *ethikoi characteres*, that is, characters dealing with *ethos*.[34] This may be taken to be a way of distinguishing them from other uses of the rhetorical devices of character, those not focused on the presentation of a single being. Theophrastus's presentation of the signs of different social languages, of different ways of placing the self and others within the discourses which make up social interaction as he sees it, depends on the fiction of an encounter with an individual subject who brings some of those signs together, and is thus potentially readable as possessing some particular *ethos*. Diogenes's bringing together of 'character' and the business of 'the showing of *ethos*' points to one reason why the Theophrastian characters seem to offer an ancient prefiguration of modern 'character drawing'. That 'showing' is the task we expect 'character' to perform. But it also indicates that for ancient writers the two terms were essentially discrete. If they were not, Diogenes's phrase, a phrase with the force almost of paradox, would be simply tautological.

'Character' and *'ethos'* can be shown to retain distinct meanings, developed in post-Aristotelian, pre-renaissance writing along quite different routes. 'Character' is absent from the *Poetics*, however much modern translations may wish to put it there. Aristotle, as I pointed out earlier, has no word analogous to *'mythos'* (plot) to fulfil the same function for *ethos* as *mythos* does for *praxis* — that is, to make it self-coherent, detachable and transferable, as we expect 'characters' to be. Nor is there any term to carry out character's role in rhetoric, as the set of linked signs which stamp the impression of a distinct being on the poet's language, and through that, on the reader's mind. The 'showing of *ethos*' occurs by different means — at moments of choice, in the articulation of action.

In classical biography *praxis* and *ethos* are two separate categories, under which the matter of the 'life' is presented. They are related to each other differently in the work of different writers, but always in their conjunction forming the nub at which right and wrong action become open to judgement.[35] The basic structural pattern followed by biography is a bi-partite presentation, first of 'deeds' and then of 'qualities'. The earliest example is Xenophon's eulogy of Agesilaus, which proceeds from an account of 'what was achieved in his reign' to an assertion of 'the virtue of his soul'. But the point of the piece is that we see the link between these two. Such achievements make his nature (*tropos*) visible, and it is through such virtue that great actions become possible. Most importantly of all, we are led to recognise his correct operation of moral choice, for the great (*kalos*) above the base. Unlike history, this requires no proof — just mention his deeds and they are immediately credited, Xenophon says — we assent to its *philosophical* rightness, convinced by Xenophon's rhetorical skill.[36] Biography developed into a genre of writing quite distinct from history, and its practitioners tended to combine antiquarian interests — in ancient or foreign customs, for example — with a background in ethical enquiry. Differing from history, as Plutarch points out, in its selectivity, it differs also in the basis of that selectivity — it tends more to the *katholos*, as Aristotle saw it in poetry, than it does to the specificity of history, in that it aims to present instances of good and bad choices of action in a broadly valid and thus more 'philosophical' way.[37] Selectivity may of course shade unashamedly into fiction; such things as physical appearance, as described by Suetonius, are predicated by the pseudo-Aristotelian science of physiognomy, which classifies physical features as expressions of character, and this, in its accordance with the overall ethical scheme of biography, is more valid than actual physical evidence.[38]

Suetonius's *Twelve Caesars* uses the *praxis/ethos* pattern to present a series of contrasted portraits of good and bad emperors, starting with the near perfect balance of the two elements in Julius and Augustus, and proceeding to figures like Caligula and Nero, where the pattern is itself obscured or even burlesqued in a seemingly random catalogue of grotesque anecdote. Evidence of the personality of a good ruler – his physical appearance, customary behaviour, dress and basic nature, as Suetonius lists them in the biography of Julius Caesar ('*formam et habitum et cultum et mores*') – is seldom necessary to account for his actions, which, in their copiousness and self-explanatory rightness, point clearly to virtue.[39] The biography of Julius, in dealing with a man only potentially emperor, holds these elements in a complex and open-ended relationship. The idealised Augustus however is a ruler almost without personal quirks. The *ethos* section focuses attention on private and domestic life ('*interiorem ac familiarem eius vitam*') and it is in this that we see his *mores* and the fortune of his home life.[40] Such exemplary and orderly divisions of interest are nowhere to be seen in the lives of the wicked emperors – the *ethos* section has to bear the weight of explanation for their failure to come up with any satisfactory *praxis*, and the disjointed anecdotes and descriptive details which convey the evidence of bad *mores* overload the writing to derange the balanced form of ideal biography (like the *Agesilaus*) creating a disorderliness in the 'Life' to match the ethical deformation of its subject.

For Plutarch the *ethos* of his subjects provides a primary focus. As he points out in the life of Alexander, he does not have the historian's duty to record every great event in so full a career; small incidents may tell one more about a man's nature, just as in portraiture we read character from the eyes, and do not need a full length depiction of the whole body.[41] If biography is a kind of portraiture, it aims, not at 'a likeness' in the modern sense, but at a representation of an underlying *ethos* or, to use the Latin term for basic unchanging character, the *mores* out of which are made those ethical choices to which the reader's more serious attention is directed.

As the example of biography shows, the model of an *ethos/praxis* distinction set up by Aristotelian dramatic theory undergoes a change of emphasis in those later writings which observe a similar distinction. Where Aristotle sees action as the primary focus of attention, with choice (*proairesis*) as its crux, later classical writers see action as the clue to character (*mores*) which in turn provides writer and audience with models of correct and incorrect ways of making choices. As the *Poetics* share terms and values with Aristotle's ethical and political writing, the change is easily described in political and philosophical terms. Aristotle's notion of *proairesis* predicates an audience of male citizens, the governing group in a democracy. Action and choice are thus more immediate to them than to an audience in imperial Rome, for whom effective *praxis* is the prerogative of a separate class of being. *Mores* becomes the more valid topic, not only because, as Suetonius shows, the fate of the empire depends on the *mores* of a few unpredictable figures, but because the sphere in which choice operates for others has become more exclusively personal and domestic. This in turn allows for a wider application of the vocabulary and concerns of an ethical notion of human life, in that groups excluded from proairetic choice in the Aristotelian sense, as not of the governing class, are seen to be presented with the more private choices of vice or virtue implied in a Roman concept of personal *mores*. Later forms of writing weight the relationship between *praxis* and *ethos* differently. *Ethos* becomes more clearly instated as writing's origin (in the writer) and end (in the reader). Finally, it defines the purpose of writing – however its effect may issue in *praxis*, the reader's *ethos* is the text's field of play.[42]

Notes

1. Aristotle, *Poetics* 1.47a 3.48a.
2. Ibid., 6.50a.
3. Ibid., 6.50a; *Nicomachean Ethics*, I. iv. 1–3.
4. Aristotle, *Poetics*, 6.50b; *Nicomachean Ethics*, III. ii. 1–2.
5. Aristotle, *Poetics*, 9.51b 17, 55a–55b.
6. Ibid., 6.50b.
7. Ibid., 15.54a.
8. Ibid., 15.54a.
9. See this chapter, pp. 00.
10. *Poetics*, 15.54a.
11. Aristotle *et al.*, *Classical Literary Criticism*, translated with an Introduction by T. S. Dorsch (Harmondsworth, 1965) p. 51.
12. Seymour Chatman, *Story and Discourse* (Princeton, 1978) p. 110.
13. Aristotle, *Poetics*, 13.53a.
14. Ibid., 16, 54b, 55a.
15. Ibid., 14, 53b.
16. Euripides, *Iphigeneia in Tauris*, 1–66.
17. Ibid., 34–41.
18. Ibid., 77–115.
19. Aristotle, *Poetics*, 15.54a.

20. Ibid., 6.50a.
21. Ibid., 6.50a.
22. Aeschylus's *Choephori*, 523–50.
23. Aristotle, *Poetics*, 16.54b.
24. Ibid., 17.55b.
25. Ibid., 4.48b.
26. Horace, *Ars Poetica*, 114–8.
27. Ibid., 60–2 (my translation).
28. Cicero, *Orator*, iii. 10, xi. 36. See Introduction, p. 5–6.
29. Cicero, *Topica*, LXXXIII. 22.
30. E. M. Forster, *Aspects of the Novel* (London, 1927) pp. 65–75.
31. See Benjamin Boyce, *The Theophrastan Character in England to 1642* (Cambridge, Mass., 1947) pp. 38–9. Menander, according to Diogenes Laertius, was a pupil of Theophrastus, *Lives and Opinions of The Eminent Philosophers*, V. 37.
32. See Boyce, *The Theophrastan Characters*, p. 17.
33. For Geoffrey of Vinsauf, for example, the description of persons, as generated by rules of fitness, is dealt with under *descriptio*. *Prosopopeia* is the rhetorical term for giving a 'voice' to an object animate or inanimate, and, as in later rhetorical writings, the two are the essential separate devices from which 'character' effects may be created. See *Nova Poetica*.
34. Diogenes Laertius, *Lives* V. 48.
35. See Patricia Cox, *Biography in Late Antiquity* (Berkeley, 1983) pp. 8–9.
36. Xenophon, *Agesilaus*, III. 2.
37. Aristotle, *Poetics*, 9.51b.
38. Cox, *Biography in Late Antiquity*, pp. 13–15.
39. Suetonius, *Lives of the Caesars*, I. 'The Divine Julius', XLIV. 8.
40. Ibid., II. 'The Divine Augustus', LXI. 1.
41. See Introduction, p. 3.
42. Both *ethos* and *mores* can simply mean habitual behaviour, so make no distinction (as a modern term like 'human nature' does) between inherent and acquired characteristics, or between observable 'manner' and the 'real' self. The ethical significance of this can be traced back to the Aristotelian notion of virtue. In the *Nicomachean Ethics*, Aristotle sets out to establish what virtue is, in relation to an idea of the soul. There are three things existing in the soul, *pathos*, the effects of outside forces, and hence, roughly, feelings, *dunamis*, powers or faculties, and *hexis*. This last translates as 'possession', that is, something simply 'had'. Virtue comes under this aspect, for while neither feeling or faculties are in themselves open to moral judgement, Aristotle's argument posits the existence of something 'had' which determines 'whether we are in good or bad relation to our feelings' [*pathe*, things that happen to us] – something which, in other words, governs their direction and extent. This, as *ethos*, is both being and habit, in that it is through the consistent exercise of conscious proairetic choice of the good that we are good as beings. *Ethos* and *praxis* exist here on a kind of loop, which *proairesis* activates, and that loop is one's moral life. Aristotle, *Nicomachean Ethics*, II. i. 1–3, II. v. 1–2.

2

Rhetorical Character: History and Allegory

If, as I suggested in the last chapter, the rhetorical text is essentially intersubjective, then the subjectivities that it seeks to construct are represented from within that tripartite division of the human which Aristotle reasserts at the beginning of the *Poetics* as *pathos, ethos* and *praxis*. Mediaeval and renaissance accounts of literature – or of any other form of developed linguistic use, any other rhetoric – are formed at base by Aristotle's terminology, by the definition and evaluation of the human that it implies. The pre-modern notion of character can be seen to depend on a particular definition of the human subject, a particular notion of the role of writing and theatre in relation to that subject. These terms, in other words, give rhetoric a basic framework for understanding not only those subjectivities that can be taken to be depicted within the text (as 'character', in whatever mode) but for the operation of the text itself, as the meeting of the subjectivities of writer/voice and reader/listener. *Pathos, praxis* and *ethos* provide rhetorical theory with a continuously open problematic, existing in division to provoke the attempt to re-unite.

An outline of that Latin post-Aristotelian terminology, by which rhetoric sought to account for its own effects and purposes can be completed by a consideration of the term *affectus*. This is, in derivation, a close parallel to Aristotle's *pathos*, as meaning a thing done to the mind, rather than something done by it, or something in its own possession (*ethos/mores*). Its usage in Ciceronian texts, taken up by later writers, is as a term for feelings caused by some outside object, and so of a more changeable and transitory nature than the underlying traits designated by *mores*. It is on the *affectus* that the writer-rhetorician has his effect. By working up the *affectus* (*pathos*/feeling) of his statements, he shifts and educates, for good or evil, the *affectus* of his audience. The two terms, *affectus* and *mores*, constitute a model of the human subject, which in itself implies a model for the methods and aims of verbal art. Cicero in *The Orator*, uses the Greek distinction between *pathos* and *ethos* for two different kinds of rhetoric, the first

39

tending to operate on the listener's emotions, the second as a presentation of the speaker's own *mores*, tending to convince and calm.[1] The skilled rhetorician has both styles at his beck. The power to effect and thus potentially to change the listener/reader, to participate in the educative process which forms his *ethos*, his *praxis*, and thus the end of his whole being, is assumed as the aim of rhetorical art at its highest development.

In this chapter I want to explore a sequence of renaissance and late classical texts in terms of the basic rhetorical model. Two literary categories provide the focus: history and allegory. Pre-modern definitions of the two genres are not necessarily identical with our own. This may become especially clear when one considers their relation to each other. Both offer culturally dominant modes of representing the human, modes in which the issues involved in that representation can be explicitly worked out. The foundation of both is a development of rhetorical character devices, in a context where the construction and purpose of 'character' is itself at issue. The classical terminology diagrammatically summarised above can be thus both illuminated and problematised from within readings of these texts. Equally, the sense of a developing rhetorical tradition should justify linking the otherwise heterogenous. A trajectory from Prudentius's *Psychomachia* to the theatre of the Elizabethan history play links conventionally discrete areas of inquiry. But the concerns on which the texts themselves reflect can be seen to be continuous, even across so long a span of time.

I   CHARACTER AND ALLEGORY: SCALIGER'S *POETICAE*

The sixteenth-century Paris-based scholar Julius Caesar Scaliger makes a carefully revisionary attempt in his *Poeticae* (1561) to sort *persona*, *idea*, *character* and *mores* out from one another. The *personae* are the roster of basic types derived from classical writing, and dealt with under tragedy and comedy. A *persona* is 'an animated object in an invented scene, an imitator of the real'. He calls it 'a thing', he goes on to say, because we accept as *personae* anything to which reason and language is attributed – the frogs, clouds and wasps of Aristophanes, the ghosts of Greek tragedy.[2] Nonetheless, the terms in which he defines his *personae* are human and social. *Personae* in comedy are distinguished from each other in their condition of fortune, their occupation, their official status, their age and their sex. Tragedy is similar but more dignified; here *'gravitas'* is proper to all participants.[3] Out of these categories, Scaliger generates further sets of sub-categories. There are, for example, in comedy fourteen types of women. (He says there are *many* kinds of young men but can come up with only three – studious, athletic and pleasure loving.[4]) Each *persona* has its fit set of signs – in dress, behaviour, physiognomy and so on.

Scaliger is particularly careful to sort out *character* from *idea*, perhaps because of the confusion caused by Cicero's use of the words in the *Orator to Brutus*. There Cicero is writing about the 'idea', or form, of the perfect orator. He also talks of the *character* (that is, identifying style) of this orator, and says that the two words mean the same thing.[5] For Scaliger however there is an important difference. 'Form' and 'idea' are terms for the intellectual reality of a thing, a reality which determines the nature of that thing and which can be said to exist independent of any material instance of it. For Plato, who formulates this doctrine, the form (the idea of 'table') is more real than the object (a table). This reality exists apart from the 'figures' or 'signs' which make up 'character'. Character is then the set of signs which denote and identify an object. Scaliger wants to distinguish this from the actual 'form', the discrete reality of that object.[6] He also wants to explore his definition of character (essentially a summary and sifting of all the available classical definitions) on as wide a scope as possible. 'Character' is a quality particular writing has, the mark of a distinct style. But on its broadest definition it need not imply the depiction of individual being, of particular *ethos*; it can operate in terms of generalities, in terms of the non-human as well as of the human. According to Scaliger, 'character is a diction equivalent to the matter, whose sign consists in substance, size and kind. Fame is in its substance, *a marvel*. In its size, it is *huge*. Of its kind, it is *awe-inspiring*. The diction is similar to the matter. For in this "voice" [my inverted commas] *the marvellous* consists in harshness, *the huge* in greatness, *the awe-inspiring* in holy terror'. He then goes on to give the familiar metaphorical derivation of the term. Character can thus be used of an abstraction without even personifying it (without using the rhetorical device called *prosopopeia*).[7]

This in itself distinguishes *'character'* from *'persona'*. If one made 'fame' into a *persona*, by giving it language and reason, 'animating' it and inventing a 'scene' for it, and then developed its 'character' along the lines described here, one would have, by bringing the two devices together, created a figure of that genre of pre-modern writing we call 'personification allegory'. I shall return to the issue of allegory in my next section. Here this admittedly extreme example shows the extent to which *ethos* and character (that absent term of the *Poetics*) had developed in rhetoric along distinctly separate routes.

Nonetheless, *ethos* is a crucial concept in rhetoric's attempt to account for its own means and purpose. Scaliger comes towards the end of his magisterial conspectus of rhetorical study on the question that lies behind the whole project – what does the poet teach?[8] In doing so he comes closest to disagreement with Aristotle's *Poetics*. Aristotle's setting of *ethos* below *praxis* seems to subvert the rhetorical concept of how and to what end literature and oratory work. Scaliger's *Poeticae* grafts commentary on Aristotle onto a digest of the Roman authorities on rhetoric, seeing him in the light of works by Horace, Cicero and Quintillian. Scaliger sets himself the task of pulling together into a still more coherent and purposeful form the definitions of ends and means provided by ancient theory. Primary here is the issue of 'teaching' understood not simply in terms of providing information and example, but in terms of working on the '*affectus*', the receptive feelings of reader/listener, and so remaking the reader's subjectivity through the depiction of analogous human subjects by rhetorical means. A large portion of the *Poeticae* is taken up with a close reading of significant moments from Virgil's *Aeneid*, significant for Scaliger in that they show how Virgil's rhetorical skills operate to present moments of choice in the narrative in a way that affects the reader both with the immediacy of those choices and with a sense of the rightness or wrongness of the way the figures in the story make them. He thus restructures Virgil's epic as a field of play of rhetorical modes. Scaliger's 'new' text aims to reconstruct the reader as subject by means of the power those modes possess. A slightly later example of a text which explicitly proceeds from similar assumptions and so, unlike Virgil's, need not be recast to accommodate them is Spenser's *Faerie Queen*. Spenser's declared aim 'to fashion a gentleman or noble person in vertuous and gentle discipline'[9] is achieved by the elaboration of his discourse by all available character-devices, all of which feed back into the constant restructuring of the reader as subject. But Aristotle's account of the priority of *praxis* over *ethos* seems to threaten this version of the practice of writing and reading. How can a play without *ethos/mores* have any meaning or purpose? Everything in it would happen contingently, merely.

Scaliger has started this section of his argument off by asking – what does the poet teach? – and it is on this assumption of the purpose and methods of writing that his account of character depends. Does the poet teach actions, which come from the passions, (*affectus*) or does he teach 'the way . . . from which the faculty of acting well originates'? Either of these would be ruled out by the *ethos*-less play, which must then be seen to be a pointless exercise. Scaliger reformulates Aristotle's point in line with the distinction made in later rhetorical writing between feelings caused by outside forces (*affectus*) and unchanging 'nature' (*mores*). Orestes, in killing his mother, acted against his (basically virtuous) *mores*, but in accordance with his *affectus*. So, though *mores* and action are essentially separate, may even contradict each other, *affectus* must be seen to lie behind action. The *affectus* of the reader/audience are worked on by the poet, through his depiction of the *affectus* of the *dramatis personae*; figures like Orestes make such states of mind present to us and move us to our own choice of good or ill.[10]

In saving Aristotle for his more purposive account of writing, Scaliger recasts the *Oresteia* as a completely different kind of play, belonging to a completely different tradition, the tradition to which *The Faerie Queen*, Scaliger's reading of the *Aeneid* and the English renaissance history play all belong. The difference between this tradition and the Athenian drama (as Aristotle describes it) lies in the centrality of the missing term of the *Poetics*, character. Instead of Aristotle's representation of the human in *praxis*, the rhetorical tradition works through character devices, devices which play on the reader/audience's subjectivity, and seek to remake it. Such devices operate in a freer way than those employed in later 'substantive' character presentation, in that the only stable subject positions offered by such a text are those of speaker/writer and reader/listener. Subjectivity and character are conceived of and accounted for separately. Scaliger's version of the *Oresteia* is one that Pickering, working within the assumptions to which Scaliger gives academic formulation, puts into dramatic form.

II PRUDENTIUS'S *PSYCHOMACHIA*: ALLEGORY AND SUBJECTIVITY

'Character', in Scaliger's summary of rhetorical practice, creates a fluent boundary around what we normally think of as 'allegorical' writing. Where the modern reader tends to separate off 'allegorical' from 'real' character, the rhetorical tradition would tend to make no such distinction. Allegory is in its simplest definition a way in which one thing is represented by another; chastity is a woman, love is an arrow, a woman is a rose. The equivalence between things represented and the thing representing it may be immediately accessible to us, because the convention by which it works has a continuous cultural history, however anachronistic its terms (love/arrow). Or it may depend on a metaphor which seems commonsensically apposite, and so is not necessarily perceived as 'conventional' at all (love/heart). Or it may depend on a system of ideas with which we are no longer familiar – the pelican represents a particular kind of love, as it was thought that it fed its young by piercing its own breast, and this in turn referred to Christ's self-sacrifice.

One basic resource of allegory is to use familiar human realities to present what one may think of as abstract ideas. Such ideas may be represented as individuated human figures, and an action developed between them which acts out a statement of general moral or philosophical truth. Personification allegory, as this is called, involves the use of the same character devices as a presentation of Alexander, the ideal orator or a courtesan. That is, the signs which identify it are given in a way which attributes their genesis and articulation to an individual agency. The resultant 'character' of Chastity is no more or less real than the 'character' of Alexander, in that the meaning of chastity, or for that matter of Alexander, is not located in an assumption of their existence as individual defined beings in historical time and mappable space. Allegorical reading locates the meaning of Alexander or Chastity in the relation that the set of signs which identify them have to ourselves as readers – to our experience and our history.

Allegory also provides a way of setting up the audience's relation to the text, that of its accepting/rejecting/working – through analogues and identifications for itself. The issue of the 'subject' constructed by these texts takes one back to the rhetorical tradition and the definitions of text and subject that it assumes; again, these assumptions do not in themselves differ from allegorical to other kinds of writing, and so do not mark allegory off as a special genre. Allegory is, essentially, a reading process, one continuous with rhetorical assumptions as to the purpose and methods of writing, speaking and reading. The late Latin Christian poem, *Psychomachia*, is often claimed as the first developed allegorical poem. Whether or not this is the case, it offers a useful basis for a discussion of allegory and character, and an explicit and sophisticated source of illustration of its workings.

Prudentius's poem presents two narratives. It retells the biblical story of the patriarch Abraham, as a preface. The main narrative of the poem, which then follows, is of a battle between virtues and their opposites. After the virtues' victory, Concord (*concordia*) reigns. The virtues are now seen as *'sensus pacificos'* — peace-making feelings — and their military unity and orderliness is celebrated.[11] They go on to build a city. The poem ends by accounting for its own existence. It was Christ's will that we should recognise the 'hidden perils' concealed within the 'closed body'.[12] The military metaphor which the poem has used to effect such a recognition is validated by an appeal to the Christian reader. At the beginning of the 'battle' section Christ is invoked in terms of this metaphor — 'say, our King, what military force arms the mind, that it can expel sins from within our breast'. And at the end, we are invited to recognise 'how often' have we felt just such conflict and release.[13]

The two narratives represent two basic kinds of Christian allegory. The story of Abraham is to be read as 'typological' allegory. If we read a story this way we read incidents and figures in it as having the significance of a model or 'type' of something outside that story. The 'type' is normally fixed in the historical past, the person or event of which the 'type' is a model is in the present, or in an epoch seen as continuous with the present. The Abraham story is, for Prudentius, a 'picture, noted down in the past (*praenotata*) to be a model (*figura*) which our life remakes (*resculpa*) in correct proportion (*recto pede*).'[14] He goes on to reinterpret the story, finding its meaning in the way particular incidents can be seen as figures or models of moments in the life of a Christian, a life which, as events in themselves, they historically pre-exist. So, the battles which Abraham won on behalf of the faithful are models of those battles which the Christian must win for himself. Then, just as Abraham's aged wife became pregnant, so the barren soul will be made fertile by the embrace of the spirit. The pattern followed by both these readings of the story is the same, but the participants are identified differently in each. Both sameness and difference derive their significance from Christian history, the basis of typological allegory. The sameness reveals a pattern whose source is ultimately the will of God, the difference is the difference between the old pre-Christian order, and the new. The incarnation, when God, as Christ, became both human *and* divine, establishes a new meaning to human events, in the light of which pre-Christian history is re-read.

The poem returns to this issue in a speech of Chastity's uttered during the battle. How is it that Lust, her enemy, is still on the loose, when Judith destroyed it in the person of Holofernes (whom she famously beheaded)? Ah, that's because Judith, existing as she did *before* the incarnation, is only a model (*figurat*) for 'our times'. Now, in the Christian epoch, power/virtue (*virtus*) has passed into earthly bodies in a *real* form (*vera*).[15] Chastity is of course an entirely apt spokesperson for the incarnation, for a new notion of the body consequent on it, and for her own role in defending the body from attempts to win it back to a pre-Christian state. That this extends to an explanation of allegory may seem surprising, but it is typical of the poem's explicitness about its own procedures. It is explicit in order to justify itself, to claim divine sanction for its origins and purpose. As an historical event which creates a new meaning for the human, particularly the human body, the incarnation demands new modes of reading and writing, of which the poem is itself an example. So Judith's action is not to be understood as an historical or epic event, in which she achieved a once-and-for-all-end. Its meaning lies not in the identification of her and Holofernes as historically distinct people, but in the pattern of their encounter. Ultimately its meaning is to be located on the atemporal plane of Christian reality, on which the virtues (themselves of course examples of such *vera virtus*) are taken to exist.

This may seem to give the other mode of allegory, personification allegory, a more important role. What Charity says seems to suggest that she and the other virtues are instances of such '*vera virtus*'. Their narrative takes place in the Christian present, and so *they* determine the meaning, assign the identity, of the historical past. It is however the Abraham story which makes the battle narrative possible – events are taken from it and expanded into metaphors of the Christian experience of conflict and resolution. Both kinds of allegory are thus in a necessary creative relation to each other. The epic style narrative thus created is justified by its relation to Abraham, seen as an example as well as type, of interest in himself as an example of a man who lived out similar conflicts to a successful end, as well as for his part in the pattern.

The virtues and their opponents are identified by visual details and actions generated by means of the rule of fitness. They are to this extent Theophrastean '*ethikoi characteres*'. These details implicate them in a knowable social world, and are ordered by Prudentius's narrative development of the war/peace metaphor. *Luxuria* has perfumed hair and wandering eyes. She comes to battle drunk, getting up from her couch to step on pools of spilt wine. She fights with flowers, not with the sword.[16] Virtues and vices are assigned speeches expressive of their natures – Pride, Wrath, Soberness, Concord all use their rhetorical powers in fit style and to fit end. These character devices identify 'feelings' (*sensus*) assumed to be present in the reader. The aim is not simply to effect the 'recognition' that Christ's will requires of us (as the end of the poem states). The poem sets out to actively strengthen the good *sensus*, and weaken the bad, by giving 'faces' to one and unmasking the other. In Prudentius's initial statement of self-justification, he has attributed to God the 'arming' of the virtuous party to our internal struggle. The poem itself is one such weapon; 'The method [*ratio*] of conquest is present [that is, to us, as readers] if we are enabled to note at close quarters the features [*facies*] of the virtues, and the opposing monsters [*portenta*] with their deadly strength'.[17] It is the poem, in its divinely required project, which offers us such a 'method', and it is the character language of classical rhetoric which enables it to do so.

Questions about the subject constructed by the poem, or about the kind of reference made by its allegory, can be answered via the answer to a much simpler question – where does the battle take place? Prudentius repeatedly refers to the forces that fight as *sensus* and locates them internally – in the body, in the breast, in the heart, and finally even in the bones.[18] The body then is the site of the battle. And the city that the virtues build at the end of the poem is the new Jerusalem, as shown to John in *Revelations*,[19] but it is also the body remade, a set of constructed interiorities, with Wisdom enthroned at the centre. Prudentius appeals to the body as the seat of our experience as individuals, an experience he wants to rename, in effect to remake, as specifically Christian experience.

There are two further things to say about this. Firstly, that the body is a kind of metaphor here. Body, heart, breast, are not bits of real anatomy, but emblems of self-hood, as we experience it from within individual bodies. (The body, in this theological context is not conceived of as part of that self, so it is not metonymy, though admittedly the complex of religious and early medical ideas relevant here make such an apparently simple matter of stylistic definition very much more difficult than it seems.) Secondly, this interiority is of a kind that works without an idea of an exterior. We cannot read Prudentius's virtues as simply an elaborate way of presenting *as if* outside us what we are to take as really *inside* us – 'inside' as the feelings and thoughts of a James or Flaubert character are 'inside' them, closed within an 'inner life' itself closed off from an outside world.

The notion that allegories either present or simply imply a unified human subject, of whom all the other figures are simply personified aspects is a misrecognition of the form that can lead to a severe curtailment of our reading of it. Such a reading sets up a model of inner and outer – either the personified forces are inside an assumed subject, like fishes in a bowl, or they find their meaning by reflecting things inside him/her and thus, by virtue of that interiority, more real than they are. This is to transpose back onto allegory a 'modern' post-Romantic notion of the 'inner life'. Metaphors of 'innerness' are often, even insistently, used in allegory but in such a way that does not imply a corresponding outer, a line which defines the individual subject. Such a line does not exist for allegory, the point of which is precisely that it can represent forces and ideas working within the field of the human *as a whole* – in societies, institutions, bodies, souls, spheres of thought, conceived of as continuous with each other, represented by metaphorical structures which apply to the human in all conceivable aspects.

I stress this point in order to counter a common misrecognition of allegory. 'Psychomachia' has become a generic term for allegorical presentations of psychic struggle, but its application often depends on a mistranslation of the term, a misreading of the poem.[20] The battle does not take place 'in' the soul, in this sense. The battle metaphor destroys the distinction between inner and outer. The forces that fight here are public as well as private, common and individual, material and abstract. Concord, for example, is a peace we feel within, but it is also the peace of the well-ordered state – of the Church, of a Christian empire. Just as Chastity gives voice to the doctrine of the incarnation, the dogmatic formulation of her principle of being, so Concord makes a point close to Prudentius's own social praxis, as a colonial administrator. 'Public peace consists in private fellowship in the country and in the market place. Domestic dissension disturbs the state.'[21] It is in the nature of allegory that all these contexts for the idea of concord are equally significant. To present Concord or Chastity as individual subjects is to allow us to see the activity of such 'forces' across the whole field of the human. Conversely, it allows us to see the human as a continuous field of praxis, in which public/private, self/world distinctions do not operate. Our sense of our bodies, that primary marker of selfhood, is invoked by Prudentius as a bridge device, a primary empathy or 'recognition' which renders the whole scope of the poem open to us.

The *sensus* the poem identifies are located in the reader, acted on and reconstructed by the poem. It thus operates within a rhetorical notion of its design on its reader. The text describes, and by describing seeks to effect, a remaking of the reader-as-subject, the Christian reader, to whom the poem offers a powerful self-definition. The basic components of allegorical narratives – of its metaphorical action – present the human subject in and as conflict, resolution, building. The audience/reader participates in this; the process of recognition required to read the allegory through is itself a process of rebuilding, of the structuring of a subject. 'Participates' is of course a doubly apt word. The subject thus 'built' is simultaneously part and whole – part of a wider notion of the human, whole in its achieved self-hood, aware of itself as an unstable assemblage, aware of a 'truth' which grants an ultimate integration with the divine whole.

When the virtues have won the battle, their peaceful military order is celebrated. 'No part of the mind hides inactive, closed off in some fold of the body . . . all the tents are exposed to view, tent flaps open, canvas drawn back . . .'.[22] The metaphors work both ways – the perfect institution should be as one mind, the mind should function like the perfect institution. Peace for the Christian is the active peace of established military strength, and its battles are won for each individual as well as for the Church as a whole. The basis of the metaphor is the perfect unity of parts given mystical expression in the Trinity (the three-fold nature of the one God) and it recurs throughout the poem. 'Non simplex natura hominius'[23] as Prudentius says at the end of the poem; the human is split *and* one. The two Christian doctrines which Prudentius persistently returns to – that of the Trinity and of the incarnation – are the justification of his allegorical procedures. Christ too provides a mystical principle of unity, as both human and divine. His will is presented as the ultimate source of the poem, and it is his intervention which effects the shift in metaphor for the body/self, no longer now the field of dissension, but the new-built temple of Wisdom. As the word made flesh, Christ is sanction and origin of the procedures of Prudentius's allegory, the division of the human subject and its eventual reintegration in different form, by means of the divinely authorised metaphors of the biblical text.

III   ALLEGORICAL DRAMA: THE TUDOR INTERLUDE

The kind of allegory developed by Prudentius translates readily into dramatic form. The action of the poem is in itself a kind of 'theatre', watched and reacted to by God and the saints, enacted by figures who declare their identity in visual symbols and combative rhetoric.[24] In that the action implies spectators, the space in which it happens is the space of the arena as well as of the battlefield; it thus extends the metaphoric connotations of that action, to use theatre as well as combat as an analogy for the human.

Allegorical theatre tends to make the same metaphorical use of the conditions of performance. Stage space, the presence and actions of the performer, the fact of spectatorship and the use of disguise and transformation can all be reflected on in the performance and used as metaphors for the set of relations – a man/God, world/self, body/soul, and so on – which offer a definition of the human. That 'definition', actualised as the event and circumstance of a play, offers the site for a theatrical psychomachia, an agon of identities.

European theatre has notoriously retained this tendency to reflect on itself, to mirror its own processes, to produce meaning and structure out of this. (A term often used for this phenomenon is 'metatheatre'.) Theatrical action is of course especially open to analogical reading, in that it is itself constructed out of analogies, of things or people that we are invited to take as something other than what we 'know' them to be. But when theatrical self-reflexivity is part of an allegorical mode, the theatre analogy, rather than existing as a static 'frame' for debate, or as a circular paradox of 'form', is the basic pre-condition of a play of identities that in itself constitutes allegory's presentation of the human.

The action of an allegorical play is thus more than simply the translation into a particular mode of a statement that could be made in another perhaps simpler way. To summarise the narrative of a play like the Tudor 'interlude' *Youth* is to make a statement to the effect that 'Youth is inclined to Riot, which brings on Pride. Pride leads to Lechery. Such vices seem to be his servants, but in fact take control of him. Charity can save him, but, without Humility, Charity is powerless. Youth must reject Pride and Riot, and accept Humility and Charity'. Those 'abstractions' are of course the *dramatis personae*, and the logic of their relation to each other is the action of the play. But the dramatic life of such a story lies in the conflict of self-definition which these characters present. Allegorical *personae* are literally self-justifying. Their most complete utterance is the presentation of the grounds of their own being. Charity opens the play *Youth*, by presenting first the typological basis for his meaning/identity in the image of Christ on the cross, one to which he will return later, both in his use of the doctrine of redemption to persuade Youth, and (in a coincidence of comically and doctrinally motivated action typical of the interlude form) in the scene where the 'vice' figures place Charity in the stocks and mock him. Charity uses his entrance to naturalise this derivation as a spatial actualisation of what is also a genealogical claim to divinely sanctioned identity – 'I am come from God above'. And he goes on to give a series of textual sources for his being, sources which, being in themselves metaphorical, establish for us a divine origin for the allegorical mode – 'I am the gate, I tell the,/ of heaven, the joyful citye . . . . I was planted in his hart./We two might not departe.'[25] In contrast, the unregenerate Youth introduces himself in terms of his physical being – 'I am goodle of persone,' – and goes on to itemise his bodily well-being in a way that seems to leave Charity puzzled and/or scandalised – 'Why do you so praise your body?'[26]

By the same token, the most aggressive act of an allegorical persona is to challenge/destroy the uttered being of a rival. In John Redford's secular allegory, *Wit and Science*, Wit's progress towards winning the hand of Science (learning) is interrupted by a competition for his attentions between Idleness and Honest Recreacion.

[HONEST RECREACION.] Wyll ye leave me, Honest Recreacion,
    For that common strumpet, Idellnes,
    The verye roote of all vyciousnes?
WYT. She sayth she is as honest as ye.
    Declare your-selves both now as ye be.
HONEST RECREACION. What woolde ye more for my declaracion
    Then evyn my name, Honest Recreacion?
    And what wold ye more her to expres
    Then evyn her name, to, Idlenes,
    Dystruccion of all that wyth her tarye?
    Wherfore cum away, Wyt: she wyll mar ye.
IDELNES. Wyll I mar hym, drabb, thow calat, thow,
    When thow hast mard hym all redye now?
    Cawlyst thow thy sealfe Honest Recreacion,
    Ordrying a poore man after thys facion,
    To lame hym thus, and make is lymmes fayle
    Evyn wyth the swyngyng there of thy tayle?[27]

Idleness wins, at least for the moment, but by doing so calls into question the play itself, designed as it is by Redford as honest recreation for the boys of St Paul's, training their wit in music, rhetoric and dance, diverting them from the idleness on offer in their immediate environment.[28]

Mark her dawnsyng, her maskyng and mummyng.
Where more concupyscence then ther cummyng?
Her cardyng, her dycyng, dayly and nyghtlye —
Where fynd ye more falcehod then there? Not lyghtly . . .
Serche the tavernes and ye shall here cleere
Such bawdry as bestes wold spue to heere.
And yet thys is kald Honest Recreacion,
And I, poore Idlenes, abhomynacion.
But whych is wurst of us twayne, now iud[ge] Wy[t].[29]

The climax of allegorical drama is thus a combat of definition, whose weapons are the character-languages at the *personae*'s disposal. As readers or audience of allegory we are offered identifications of our response to given figures and given situations, often coercively, by those very figures. It is the nature of allegory that such identifications are conflicting and unstable, in ways that are developed in the action of the play. We do not, in other words, find a single figure or group of figures, with whom we 'can identify' — that is, use as a stable position from which we can 'identify' everything else. Rather, the action unfolds by virtue of its withholding from us that goal. Its structure is a structure of transition, the shifts in the basis of meaning effected by the course of these contests. When we reach a position from which all the participants in the action can be put into a settled relation to each other and to us, the play ends. It has constructed a model of the human, of the presence of 'abstractly' named but insistently actual forces in the human, and of the playing out of those forces, as a process of conflict, resolution, and reconstruction. In *Youth*, as in all religious allegory, the grounds of that reconstruction is the exposition of the relation of the human to the divine as borne witness to by the biblical text. In 'plot' terms, it is this that persuades Youth to take on the virtues rather than vices, but, more crucially, the set of identifications provided by the biblical text is the base out of which the whole of the allegory is generated.[30] The biblical text serves as the final, authoritative definition of the subject, no longer open-ended as when it was still 'in play', but expansive within its own terms. The prize is the right to redefine — to redefine the *dramatis personae*, the audience, and the playing-space itself.

The genre to which *Youth* belongs is often referred to as the 'Tudor interlude' — a name for shortish allegorical pieces written in England in the late fifteenth and early sixteenth centuries, and dealing in religious and political ideas. Such plays represent one of the most developed and flexible forms of allegorical drama. The interludes are written to be performed by small professional troupes, normally numbering six.[31] The props are simple and to some extent standardised. One of the most salient features of acting practice – the complex doubling necessary – is hardly ever reflected on in the plays. Doubling never works thematically – the convention of playing assumes that each character when established is taken as a separate entity, however many of them a particular player may have to present. We discount the individual player, and so there would be no linking factor 'in play'. This has several easily observable effects. One is that, if character effects are not to be identified with the individual presence of a player, then characters can be arrived at by a wide variety of means – personifications, historical individuals, supernatural forces all bear equal weight, as the means of presenting them (the rhetorical means of word and 'action') are all equally accessible; the audience is not, as in most later theatre, drawn to attribute more 'reality' to characters most 'like' the individuated human beings the actors are in 'real life'. They are also infinitely producable, the only limits to the number of characters in a play being its length (though of course there always has to be at least one person off-stage changing role, in order to keep up continuity). The arrival and departure of characters is thus not predicated by any assumptions about real time and space. They can define the space they arrive in however they like, and so planes of historical time, contemporary audience time and timelessness are equally representable, a necessary precondition of the more complex allegories (allegory in itself being the precondition of such a playing convention). The action of the play can be moved on by shifting its modes of representation, thus contracted or expanded by means outside realist assumptions of theatrical language. Most importantly to this discussion, it creates a fluidity in the definition of character which focuses the audience's attention not on distinct 'embodied' representations, but on risky negotiable identities, established through conflict and/or treaty and thus played out, not within an assumed or represented consciousness, but as relationship rhetorically constructed and controlled. One particular class of interlude player has an intensified power of transformation and impersonation at his beck – the 'Vice'. The term itself seems to be derived from 'vyse' or mask.[32] It defines, in other words, a kind of meta-role, a role defined by its ability to transgress definition, its identity lying in its operating in only provisional identities. It can thus be seen as an intensification of a tendency conventionalised in the rules of interlude playing – doubling of roles, open definition of space, and so on.

The plays are 'interludes' in that they are part of a social event – a banquet, a royal visit, a dynastic celebration – which they do not in themselves define. This makes possible their close and fluid relationship to the audience, who are not the 'invisible' generalised audience of the public theatre, called into being, in the most literal sense, by the event of the performance, but a group already visibly involved in some social praxis other than theatre-going. A dialectic is thus possible, between the audience's awareness of a set of identities allowed for or even confirmed by the overall context of the performance – identities constructed for them by the ideologies ritualised as religious observance, membership of a professional body, attendance at court or the life of a great feudal family – and the identities offered it by the performers. By setting a particular rhetorical relation to the audience – of mocking familiarity, of preacherly persuasion, of dignified command – a particular player makes the space theirs. Defined on one side by the player's self-presentation, and on the other by the audience's reception of it, the playing space becomes continuous with the identity of each; we are implicated in the play by the identities the player offers us – his tavern-mates, his subjects, his fellow-Christians, his flock – and the players compete to 'fix' that identification on us. In the case of individuals, the identities offered may be directly typological, offering to currently powerful figures analogues from biblical or secular history. But the audience as a group is invited to recognise and assess the performance as an analogue of itself, of its position within a religious or (in the case of the secular allegories performed at the Inns of Court, the Choir schools and the Universities) a political or intellectual ideology and praxis. The process of conflict, resolution and rebuilding which structures the psychomachia (both Prudentius's poem and the genre derived from it) operates as the action of the play, and as the experience of the audience. This is the way it constructs its audience as subject, a 'construction' the ends of the plays explicitly celebrate.

Both Bale's *King Johan* and Pickering's *Horestes* develop a detailed 'play' of the identifying devices of allegory in the service of a debate about power. Not an open-ended debate, but a debate whose 'end' is the affirmation of power – Tudor power – as that 'something else' beyond play. In doing so they problematise aspects of allegorical drama in a way that incidentally allows us a more open access to them. The two plays are often seen as 'transitional' in literary-historical terms. It may be more accurate to see them as pieces which build that structure of transitions, of which allegorical drama consists, on the largest and most original scale.

The opening speech of *King Johan*, in which the king introduces himself, establishes his authenticity by demonstrating a harmonious working of all the identifying systems open to allegory. He names himself – 'To show what I am I thynke yt convenyent' – after eight lines outlining the scriptural basis of kingly power. Then he demonstrates his right to that name by geneaology, by the sacrament of coronation, and by his just praxis as ruler and reformer.[33] He establishes also his power over the stage space, which becomes a kind of audience chamber in which he hears the complaint of widow England and the counterclaims of characters who represent aspects of government, of ecclesiastical and civil politics.

That England has become a widow – a poor but dignified widow, claiming protection from the king – delays Johan's initial recognition of her. She is a widow, she explains, because God, her spouse, has been exiled by the corruption of the Church.[34] This misfit between her *persona*-like identification as widow and the allegorical identification she is forced to declare is an effect developed by Bale to dramatise the shocks of recognition, and the perils of misrecognition, which govern the taking of correct political action. Systems of social categorisation like the *personae* are developed in the middle ages into the depiction of the various 'estates' of society, figures defined by occupation and social status, rhetorically elaborated into detailed presentations of the identifying features and, often, the characteristic faults, of a particular 'estate'. (Chaucer's *Canterbury Tales* offer a large scale development of 'estates' characterisation, as Jill Mann has shown.[35]) In *King Johan* allegorical 'naming' and 'estate' identification play off against each other in order to articulate the crisis that faces Johan; a crisis of power which is also a crisis of identity. Nobility asks Johan why he is talking to 'Sedycyon' and tells him to beware his trickery. So far so good. But in *persona* Sedycyon is a monk, and Nobility, assessing him in his light, ends up giving sedition his support.[36]

Sedycyon offers scurrilous identifications of events and characters in this first section of the play, but Johan's overall control places these as minor disruptions. When Johan leaves, Sedycyon is free to redefine the stage as the playing space of the interlude – 'I loke for felowys that here shuld make sum sporte'.[37] In the central section of the first part of the play the ecclesiastical characters play with the counters of allegorical identity. They explain their allegorical genealogies, act out undignified physical emblems of their relation to one another, and confess to secret identities. Usurpid Power reveals that he is the Pope, and when challenged as to his lack of 'your thre crounys, yowr crosse keys and yowr cope' replies that 'Thou knowest I must have sum dalyance and playe/For I am a man lyke as an other ys.'[38] To that extent the identities given by the 'sporte' of the interlude are primary. The actor's basic playing-roles — as good 'felowys' — allow the other identities (all the categorisations and ludicrous subcategorisations of the estates of the clergy, relished by Bale in virtuosic comic listings, and the allegorical names that mark their relation to Johan) to seem provisional identities claimed and exploited by the anarchic 'fantasye' of vice-like figures. While this provides the most entertaining section of the play ('sporte' for the 'felowys' that the audience themselves become in this context) it serves also to expose the sinister chaos which appears to Bale to be the consequence of that multiplication of identities to which dramatic allegory tends.

King Johan makes considered and intricate reference to allegory and acting, in ways that seem marked by a considered philosophical distrust of both. The abuses of which the play accuses the Catholic clergy include 'popetly plays',[39] a term which can be extended from actual theatre to religious ceremony and ritual. All this amounts to 'fantasye' of one sort or another in that it operates without proper reference to scripture, scripture being for Bale, and his exemplary monarch Johan, the only basis of true knowledge. When Usurpid Power comes back in his 'estate' role, as the Pope, he instigates an excommunication ceremony. In following the 'felowys'' rowdy song, the ritual seems to be simply the translation into a different mode of the dangerously flexible symbolic language which for Bale makes players and priests equivalent. To be a priest is to be a player, a player with a wide choice of both social (estate/*persona*) identifications, and of the self-assigned moral identifications of a dangerously duplicitous system of values. In a sense then the 'player' identity is more valid for these figures than the dizzying lists of orders and hierarchies which, in their baseless 'fantasye' they invent for themselves.

The excommunication presents symbolic language as if it worked as a kind of sympathetic magic, in which actions performed on inanimate objects would be reproduced as an effect on human beings. Here, blasphemously, the Pope acts as if this language enabled him to control God:

> Lyke as this same roode turneth now from me his face,
> So God I requyre to seqyester hym of his grace;
> As this boke doth speare by my worke maanuall,
> I will God to close uppe from hym benyfyttes all;

He then goes on to assign historical identities to Private Wealth, Sedycyon and Dissymulacyon in turn;

> To coloure this thyng, thow shalte be callyd Pandolphus
> Thow, Stevyn Langton; thy name shall be Raymundus.[40]

The audience then is to trace a progressive intensifying of deception in the layering of roles that the players take on, and to recognise in this progression (from personified quality, to 'estate' to 'historical individual') a revelation of the real identity of evil working in the world. The Pope's 'I will' gives him a position, identified as evil intent, anterior to any of these three modes of naming. It is in fact the identity of all these figures as players which creates a sense of diabolic agencies 'in play'. The interpreter's speech at the end of the first half of this two-part play puts down opposition to Johan to 'Satan the Devyll, which that tyme was at large',[41] an agent whom the play need not (perhaps dare not) dramatise, given the diabolic overtones of the vices' 'play'.

King Johan works itself out as a clash between identifying systems. As a rhetorical *agon*, it pits one way of constructing and assigning identities against another. As we have seen in *Youth* and *Wit and Science* this is to some extent true of all the 'flytings', the verbal conflicts of personification allegory. The complexity of Bale's play depends on a conflict between two different interpretations of allegory itself, of the modes of reading and writing/speaking, and thus of the knowledge of truth which it presents in its opposition of an anachronistically protestant ·Johan to a player-Pope.

When Johan returns in the second half the playing space is now the space of this contest. Johan seeks to reassert himself by using scriptural authority. He attempts to cut through the deceits of the Church's identity games in unmaskings which threaten to destroy the conventions of allegory and of interlude playing. 'Me thyṅkes this bysshope resembleth moch Sedycyon', draws attention to the play's 'doubling' of roles.[42] This, as I have said, is normally a discounted 'invisible' device in the interlude, and is so here in some cases (England doubles Clergy, for example). But Johan wants to draw attention to the players as players, to use *this* identification to discredit their self-proclaimed roles, just as Usurpid Power has drawn attention to it as the source of his false authority, and its compelling if short-lived effect on others (fittingly so, of course, given his name). Johan tries to act as the agent of the making 'playne' which the interpreter promises the audience in the second half. The allegorical device of representing 'Commonalte' as blind is carefully explained by England:

> His outward blyndness ys but a sygnyficacyon
> Of blyndness in sowle for lacke of informacyon[43]

The making plain of this not particularly abstruse point is a marker of how far the play has moved towards a distrust of allegorical device.

The interlude player's relation to his role is reflected on in the plays presentation of Johan's death, interpreted by Protestant historians as assassination by the Church. Dissimulacyon swaps identities, from Bishop Raymundus to Simon of Swinsett. Sedycyon persuades him to poison the King even though this will mean he must, as Simon, poison himself as well. As Dissimulacyon, he will however survive, since the relics and prayers that commemorate 'Simon' effect the survival of dissimulation as an aspect of Catholic ritual.[44] So, like the interlude player, Dissimulacyon can endlessly construct identities for itself, within an infinite variety of modes, and, like an allegorical personification, it can survive an earthly embodiment, *must* so survive, if conceived of on the eternal scale of religious allegory.

The defeat of the player-priests is eventually effected by the intervention of Veritas (truth). Truth in effect establishes a new basis for the reading of action and character, through its mutually validating relation to the figure who leads the play to its denouement, Imperial Power.

We have been told before in the play that chronicles 'will', or in the audience's time *do*, misrepresent Johan;[45] they are thus an extension of the Church's vice-like multiplication of baseless identities. But Veritas, in one of those speeches in which personifications expose the conceptual basis of their own being (thus the attribution of individual agency to such concepts allows them to be presented as literally self-justifying), outlines to the audience, whom he/she addresses as 'fryndes', what the true basis of a knowledge of Johan's actions was – 'excellent writers' and the proper understanding of his relation to scriptural authority, as given in precept, and example.[46] Imperial Power has his base in 'Veritas', in the proper interpretation of scripture. But Veritas, after making the situation 'playne' to Nobylyte, Clergye and Civile Order, is seen to have been acting on Imperial Power's Orders – 'Have ye done all thynges as we commanded yow?'[47] he asks on his entrance. As in Pickering's *Horestes*, Truth is a social as well as an ideal value – perhaps it is more crucially so. Truth enacts and so represents a social relation, to Imperial Power, which it validates as 'true'. So Truth is knowledge of the 'real' but it is also 'obedience', for these are one and the same thing.

Personification allegory explores abstractions as aspects of the human in interaction with each other, and so allows an explicit identification of that interaction as a social praxis, as the action of power. This is the point to which both *King Johan* and *Horestes* come. Imperial Power and Truth, in league with each other, establish a new basis for reality against which both allegory and playing, so dubious in the player-priests' hands, can be plainly read. Allegory and acting are thus themselves 'remade'. Bale's use of the 'vice' figures points to where modern misrecognition of the term – 'vice' as opposed to virtue – has some validity. When Bale reflects on the processes of doubling, it is to inflect them as an aspect of evil, of the untrustworthiness of his Catholic player priests. In doing so he marks a terminus in the interlude tradition. But the 'vices' have never been seen to be ultimately trustworthy. The ends of the plays involve their expulsion, in the name of a true source of identity as established elsewhere. When they leave, the play ends and we are pointed to something else, beyond the play, where meaning lies. Imperial Power disposes of Sedycyon by having him quartered – where the vice in *Horestes* is banished, and those of the religious interludes tend to slip ambiguously away, defeated but surviving, Imperial Power can literally dismember Sedycyon's identity, thus marking that particular Tudor spectacle as an emblem of Imperial Power's rights over the basic site of human identity, the body.[48] Imperial Power has thus established control over the assigning of 'true' identities, just as truth has become the servant of power. History, based in scripture, replaces the 'fantasyes' of the Church as the site of meaning and identity.

King Johan has often been seen as a transitional piece in the development towards the secular history play, in putting an historically defined character into an allegory. The play does not however make a generic distinction as between two discrete modes of characterisation; as I have suggested earlier, there is no essential difference between the depiction and interpretation of historical figures and personifications within a rhetorical mode. (To assume so is to assume that because there was a real Johan, to assign his identity to a character in a play must be to invest that figure with the values we now ascribe to 'real' individuality. He is to be read in the play however by the same process as the reading of England, Sedycyon or Clergy, distinct from each other as kinds of concept, but not as kinds of 'character'.) The play itself enacts a transition; its action is that of a shift, a remaking of meaning and identity, describable as a shift from allegorical reading to history, from disguised meaning to making plain, from Catholic trickery to

Protestant Truth. When Elizabeth is invoked at the end of the play by Nobylyte as 'that Angell, as Saynt Johan doth hym call/That with the Lordes seal doth marke out his true servauntes/Pryntynge in their hartes Hys holy wourdes and convenauntes',[49] he means that she *is* the angel, is herself foreseen in Revelations, not that she can be seen as it, if read allegorically. She is that angel historically; historically, the identifying stamp, the divinely ordained marking of character, is hers. The play describes power, using the freedom given by the allegorical mode to trace the operation of power across the whole field of the human, and to present it as a process, a developing praxis of identification.

Pickering's *Horestes* also places an 'historically' defined figure in an interlude structure. Horestes, like Johan, is to be read allegorically, as facing historically recurrent problems of political praxis, applicable generally and to a particular situation, here the conflicting claims of kinship and of correct political action as represented to Elizabeth in the threat posed by her cousin, Mary of Scotland.[50]

The conflict between a narrative/historical identification of *Horestes* and that provided by the interlude structure is worked through in the play to a conclusion which to some extent coincides with that of *King Johan*. Epic rather than drama provides the identifications which link the characters in the play to an 'already known' 'historical' narrative. Though Pickering's working out of the issues involved in Horestes's crime shows some interesting parallels to Scaliger's consideration of the same act, he seems not to have arrived at it, as Scaliger has, from a meditation on a tradition of drama now almost incomprehensibly remote. *Horestes* is adapted, not from Aeschylus's or any other dramatic treatment of the story, but from the account given by Lydgate in his *Troy Book*, itself based on early mediaeval tellings of the Troy tale in Latin and French, rather than on classical sources.[51] Horestes is not then some throw-back to a classical form of drama, not an attempt to re-establish such a tradition. It is an exercise in historical allegory, whose sources merely happen to be classical. Its central *agon* is articulated as a problematisation of those identifying practices which in the rhetorical tradition are both character and a political praxis in themselves.

Horestes, when he appears, presents his situation to us as a conflict between the way his feelings 'provoke' him to revenge his father by killing his mother, and what 'Dame Nature teles': that he should forgive her. He calls on the 'godes of war' to resolve this conflict. Instead, the 'vyce' turns up. We have already seen him, in the short

comic action which begins the play, stirring up a fight between two
rustics, calling himself 'Master Pacience'. Here he claims 'Amonge the
godes celestiall I Courrage called am', and as such resolves Horestes's
dilemma.

> My thinkes I fele all feare to fley, all sorrow, griefe and payne.
> My thinkes I fele corrage provokes my wil for ward againe
> For to revenge my fathers death and infamcy so great.
> Oh how my hart doth boyle in dede, with firey perching heate.
> Corrage, now welcom by the godes; I find thou art in dede
> A messenger of heavenly gostes.[52]

Horestes is then able to embark on the narrative strand in the play
which defines his 'historic' identity. 'Courrage' is experienced by him
as a 'feeling' which provokes his will, and thus in turn allows him to
instigate the narrative of historical praxis. The 'heate' Horestes now
feels validates the /vice's self-identification, at least for Horestes, and
instates him as the messenger of the gods, thus giving Horestes a claim
to divine sanction, which he can use later in the play to impress
potential allies.

Horestes is 'hero' and instigator of an historical narrative. His will
provides the motivating force of the story, and we are invited at
various points to see him arrive at decisions. He therefore provides a
clear focus of identification for the audience, as a figure whose
subjecthood is 'open' to us, and which we share as we share the subject
position of the 'hero' in simple narratives, in following the story
through. This, at least, is the tendency of this strand of the action. By
enmeshing the story of which Horestes is subject/hero in an interlude
structure, with its much more complex and open-ended construction
of subject positions, and its fluent character-language, Pickering
deflects the audience's identification with Horestes that this simplifying
coincidence of function (hero) and subjecthood ('I') might seem to
offer.[53] We have after all seen that Horestes could only take up this
position after the vice, by (mis)identifying himself, had given Horestes
a way of accounting for and resolving the split in his subjecthood, the
split between feeling and nature.

The terms of this split are exactly those of Scaliger's (roughly
contemporary) problematisation of Orestes's crime, and his
modification through that of Aristotle's account of tragedy. Orestes,
Scaliger said, acted against his *mores*, but according to his *affectus*;
against nature, in Pickering's terms, and according to the feelings

Horestes seeks both to internalise ('my harte doth boyle') and to validate externally ('Corrage now welcom by the godes').[54] The vice and Dame Nature, who enters later to attempt to dissuade Horestes, act out the terms of this model of the subject. Horestes acts with the vice Patience/Courage/Revenge, who rhetorically reorders his initially confused 'wyll', but must in the end be rejected; Pickering represents the separateness and yet interdependence of the vice and Horestes as a master/servant relationship, in which the vice seeks to transfer his services to Menelaus after the murder, but must be driven out to beg when the 'amity' in which the play ends makes him redundant.[55]

By aligning the rhetorical skills of the vice with the *affectus* (feelings produced in the mind by external forces) of the rhetorical model of the subject, Pickering presents the Orestes story as an allegorical contest, not simply in the psychomachia operating on and through Horestes, but in the contest for the audience's attention and assent and for the playing space defined by it. The play becomes the kind of drama which, for Scaliger, Aristotle's account of the *Oresteia* so plainly was not, the drama which finds its purpose in working through the depicted *affectus* of its *dramatis personae* and on the *affectus* of its audience. The contest in this case is the wresting of the play away from the vice figure to the 'amity', the social and personal concord, established at the end by Duty and Truth. Truth proclaims to the spectators the educative value of the play then coming to its end. All the forces that have been 'in play' end in a proper relation to each other, with the audience recognising the validity of the values Truth represents to it, and accepting the model of themselves that they have been offered.

The interlude form, and the vice as an intensification of interlude tendencies within a certain role, make available a fluidity of identity, which overrides the epic structure. The short-range effect of this, as Marie Axton has pointed out, is to neutralise the problems evoked by Horestes/Orestes's actions in the name of that political expediency which first requires and then expels the vice-figure Patience/Courage/ Revenge as a force within the state.[56] But the play has a larger political project, paralleling that of *King Johan*, of a redefinition of the determining source of identity. In *King Johan* this was a Protestant project, a move from Catholic 'playing' to the mutually validating interdependence of Imperial Power and Veritas. Here the process of the play is guided by Councell to Fame and then to Truth. Councell, as repository of advice derived from historical *exampla*, represents the authority at the base of this process. Fame is its operation in the world, and Truth its establishment through power. To Idumanaeus, fame has initially represented fatality, but in Councell's interpretation it becomes a constructive projection of individual identity, and thus the solution to the fragmentation of Horestes's subjecthood as faced by him at the beginning of the play and explored in his relation to the vice.

Fame, in European humanist tradition, is the process by which history is made, the process by which the individuals of whose stories history is made up join the 'already known'. It is also the process by which they are defined *as* individuals. They become an epitome of their deeds, a kind of schema of the virtues/vices that those deeds represent, a schema organised by the relevance of those deeds to us – that is, their relevance in an allegorical mode of reading. Fame – writing, reading, speaking – defines 'characters' whose function and constitution can be accounted for in terms of a rhetorical tradition of character. They are thus continuous with the mode of character-drawing practised by Plutarch, and represent a kind of writing revived in the Renaissance as part of the formation of a secular scripture, a master-text of history – the text that fame produces. As such a text, 'history' is still subject to what are essentially allegorical modes of reading. A form of typology still operates. To return to the Abraham story as Prudentius uses it, Abraham is both an *exemplum* (someone in the past who acted in a way we can learn from) and a 'type' (incidents in his life can be read figuratively, as the pattern of later events). Renaissance historiography is perhaps closer to the first than to the second (outside the theological/historical framework of the Christian story, the relation between the two becomes less stable) but a typological reading habit still applies. That is, history is to be read back in typological patterns – *x* is like *y* is like *z* – but these have to be accounted for in some other way than by reference to Christian theology. Rhetoric itself in constructing 'fame' is the key to the process as we shall see.

The process of fame, in constructing typologies, is conventionally opposed in humanist writing to genealogy.[57] Is identity passed on by the aristocratic family, or does the individual achieve it by actions which link him or her into the process of fame? In *Horestes* this debate lies behind the discussion Idumanaeus and Councell hold about the hero. For Idumanaeus he is Agamemnon's son. This identification would seem to fit him into a tragic pattern, a mediaeval *de casibus* view of tragedy, outlined by Idumanaeus in his first speech. But Councell identifies him differently – he is like Achilles.[58] In other words, his own deeds and qualities align him through a fame network to one not kin to him, while the kinship pattern would link him into a repetitive tragic scheme. This is perhaps another example of the way in which 'nature' is overridden in the play's pursuit of political praxis. It also diverts the play generically from the rather dour circularity on which Idumanaeus seems initially to set it. (As the interlude form does not obey classical generic rules anyway, this flexibility is readily available to it.) Typological reading of this kind is essential to the operation of the history play. If Horestes is Achilles, so is he also the successful Tudor monarch – Elizabeth I, the ultimate audience of the play. *Horestes* increasingly marks out for itself an 'historical' space – this seems to be the function of military spectacle in the play, hard though that is to imagine given Pickering's small cast. Horestes's interiority – emble-matised in stationary poses – finds its place on the historical stage, though uneasy in its original interlude context.[59] Interlude practice is itself displaced, expelled. The vice's attempt to disrupt Fame, by drawing attention to her tacky theatricality is a game one, but it fails.

> Who! berladye, Nan, thou art trym and gaye!
> Woundes of me, she hath winges also!
> Who, whother with a myschefe doust thou thinke for to go?[60]

This is the only moment in the play where two allegorical figures interact with each other. Mostly such figures exist in an emblematic relation to the historical figures, but this interaction is, aptly enough, in the form of allegory's most crucial *agon*, the conflict of identifying systems.

IV   ACTING, FAME AND THE HISTORICAL INDIVIDUAL

Bale's Veritas, Pickering's Councell and Fame all point to the enduring textuality of history. Rhetorical practices define, record and reproduce the 'characters', the schematised representations, of the virtuous dead, and thus ensure for them a kind of survival. It is in this light that I want to look at the two most celebrated descriptions of the experience of Elizabethan acting, the only two (though possibly interrelated) particularly elaborate contemporary accounts of an Elizabethan play on stage. The public theatre plays of the later Elizabethan period show a particular concern with the presentation of historically defined individuals. If, as I suggested in my introduction, Elizabethan acting takes onto itself the techniques and terminology of classical rhetoric, and thus accords itself a more dignified status, then acting becomes part of the mechanism of fame, and the representation (in the strict sense of 'making present again') of the historical figure is its highest aim. The theatre building itself – the newly permanently pseudo-classical amphitheatres of Burbage's Southwark[61] – is redefined by this newly apparent purpose, or rather, this focusing on one aspect of the historical allegory developed in the interludes and the Inns of Court plays.

'To turne to our domesticke hystories', Thomas Heywood writes in *An Apology for Actors*:

> what English blood seeing the person of any bold English man presented and doth not hugge his fame, and hunnye at his valor, pursuing him in his enterprise with his best wishes, and as beeing wrapt in contemplation, offers to him in his hart all prosperous performance as if the Personator were the man Personated, so bewitching a thing is lively and well spirited action, that it hath the power to new mold the harts of the spectators and fashion them to the shape of any noble and notable attempt. What coward to see his countryman valiant would not bee ashamed of his owne cowardise? What English Prince should hee behold the true portrature of that amorous King Edward the third, foraging France, taking so great a King captive in his owne country, quartering the English Lyons with the French Flower-delyce, and would not bee suddenly Inflam'd with so royall a spectacle, being made apt and fit for the like atchieuement. So of *Henry* the fift . . . .[62]

In a parallel passage from Nashe's *Pierce Penniless*, which may be a source for the Heywood, Nashe sets out to prove 'playes to be no extreame, but a rare exercise of vertue . . . .'

> First, for the subiect of them (for the most part) it is borrowed out of our English Chronicles, wherein our forefathers valiant acts (that haue line long buried in rustie brasse and worme-eaten bookes) are reuiued, and they themselues raised from the Graue of Obliuion, and brought to pleade their aged Honours in open presence: than which, what can be a sharper reproofe to these degenerated effeminate dayes of ours?
> How would it haue ioyed braue Talbot (the terror of the French)

to thinke that after he had lyne two hundred yeares in his Tombe, hee should triumphe againse on the Stage, and haue his bones newe embalmed with the teares of ten thousand spectators at least (at seuerall times), who, in the Tragedian that represents his person, imagine they behold him fresh bleeding.[63]

The context of both pieces is a defence of theatre, a defence resting on a description of its function. The *Apology for Actors* (printed in 1612, but most probably written some years earlier) is the most substantial piece of commentary to come out of the Elizabethan theatre. Heywood says he speaks as one of many (with conventional modesty, as the least of many, 'the youngest and weakest of the Nest wherein I was hatcht').[64] The 'three briefe Treatises' of which it consists counter detraction by asserting the theatre's 'Antiquity and ancient Dignity', and by defining 'the true use of our quality'.[65] It presents itself as a summary of the theatre's knowledge of itself and of its history. Nashe's piece is part of a disquisition on the seven deadly sins – playgoing is cited as one of 'the Means to Avoid Sloth'.[66] Theatre, for Nashe, leads to virtuous action through its uniquely powerful deployment of rhetorical effect.

To a modern reader, the *Apology* is best known as a quarry of information on Elizabethan acting technique. As I suggested of Hamlet's advice to the players in my introduction, any evidence is equivocal, largely because it is cited as traces of a non-existent object, Elizabethan acting 'theory'. The controversy in this field between the 'naturalists' and the 'formalists', between those who read passages such as this as evidence of Stanislavskian technique and illusionist effect, and those who prefer to argue for a formalised (and thus in a more colloquial sense 'rhetorical') presentation of feeling.[67] If one uses the *Apology* in this way one can find evidence for both sides. Heywood says of the boy actors, for example,

to see our youthes attired in the habit of women, who knowes not what their intents be? Who cannot distinguish them by their names, assuredly knowing, they are but to represent such a Lady, at such a time appoynted?[68]

The problem lies not so much in a misreading of Heywood as in selective quotation (and selective reading within that quotation) from a writer who provides as wide a variety as he can of approaches to the matter of what acting is and what it is for. It lies also in a misrecognition of the text, whose larger claims for theatre show this passage in a different light. The *Apology* is as inclusive an attempt as possible to establish the role of a newly institutionalised public theatre in the city, here specifically the city of London. Rhetoric and history provide the main lines of defence.

Historical works, according to North's preface to his Plutarch (1579), 'teache the living, revive the dead'.[69] The dead are revived by virtue of their fame. They become the epitome of their deeds, their history, and history itself is a collection of such epitomes. It exists *outside* time and is opposed to mortality. But it is not static, it recruits into itself through 'emulation'. Knowledge of an individual's history produces the desire to equal it. Fame therefore has its own genealogies.

In the first of the *Olimpiads*, amongst many other active exercises in which *Hercules* ever trimph'd [sic] as victor, there was in his nonage presented unto him by his Tutor in the fashion of a History, acted by the choyse of the nobility of Greece, the worthy and memorable acts of his father *Iupiter*, which being personated with lively and well-spirited action, wrought such impression in his noble thoughts, that in meere emulation of his fathers valor (not at the behest of his Stepdame *Iuno*) he perform'd his twelve labours: Him valiant *Theseus* followed, and *Achilles*, *Theseus*. Which bred in them such hawty and magnanimous attempts, that every succeeding age hath recorded their worths, unto fresh admiration. *Aristotle* that Prince of Philosophers . . . having the tuition of young *Alexander*, caused the destruction of Troy to be acted before his pupill, in which the valor of *Achilles* was so naturally exprest, that it imprest the hart of *Alexander* in so much that all his succeeding actions were merely shaped after the patterne, and it may be imagined had *Achilles* never lived, *Alexander* had never conquered the whole world. The like assertion may be made of that ever-renowned Roman *Iulius Caesar*. Who after the like representation of *Alexander* in the Temple of *Hercules* standing in Gades was never in any peace of thoughts, till by his memorable exploits, hee had purchas'd to himselfe the name of *Alexander*: as Alexander til hee thought himselfe of desert to be called *Achilles*: *Achilles Theseus*, *Theseus* till he had sufficiently Imitated the acts of *Hercules*, and *Hercules* till hee held himselfe worthy to bee called the sone of Iupiter.[70]

Heywood's elaboration of a popular example demonstrates the crucial role in the process of art, here any art that can be likened to the presentation of plays. Fame cannot exist without monuments, without writing, rhetoric, representation. It seems unhelpful here to employ a distinction between written history and the history that writing represents. History, for the Renaissance, is a collectively produced text. Representations of individual acts of persons become part of this text, but as they do they become something else, they acquire a new meaning. History is a representation, not of what has happened ('the past') but of a timeless idea.

Nashe's and Heywood's claim for the history play – in both their accounts the most significant kind of play – could be described as follows. The theatre is a crucial part of the moral and social life of the city (any city) because actors and playwrights have skills which give history (thus understood) material form. They present the individuals of the past and their deeds in a way that erases present time and place in the spectator's mind, creating instead a moment of that which transcends time and place – a moment of history. And because such presentations evoke the desire to emulate, the spectator himself may be recruited into history, thus continually renewing that text, and continually attesting to the existence of 'virtue', to which it can be taken to refer. For North, narrative history creates a mental theatre:

> what can be thought more pleasaunt or profitable ... than sytting as it were in the Theatre or Stage of mans life (the whiche an Historye hath most exquisitely furnished in all points . . .) to be made ware and wyse at the perilles of other men, without any daunger on his owne behalfe?[71]

For Heywood and Nashe the public theatres are spaces in the real world which fulfil the same function as that mental space, but more adequately, by virtue of their ability to embody, to 'revive the deade' by more concrete means. It is within this structure of ideas, rather than in anachronistically imported terms of naturalism, that we should understand the praises of actors who present historical characters 'to the life'. But what of the second part of the process – emulation? Again, modern terms are unhelpful. The spectator is not, I think, 'influenced', as children are said to be by violence on television. It is not, in other words, to be understood in quasi-psychological terms, as a half-willed encroachment on the interior life. Rather he or she recognises 'a pattern' as Alexander did in Achilles. The well 'expressed' 'impresses' through resemblance, through what Sidney calls 'a conveniency to ourselves'.[72] The individual spectator/reader sees a blank in the text of history, in the shape into which he or she can fit. This is Sidney's 'delight' and the 'secret pleasure' of Spenser's Arthur when he reaches the hiatus in the history of Britain given him by Eumnestes, or 'good memory' in the castle of Temperance.[73] The play does not change the spectator (as modern censors fear): it offers him/her a sign, a depiction of an aspect of themselves and invites him/her, for good or ill, to acknowledge it.

In the context of popular, or at least 'public', theatre this nexus of ideas may seem problematic. If an ideology of fame owes its earliest formulations to the rulers of the Italian city states, and is transplanted to Tudor England as an attractive way of accounting for individual power above and beyond, sometimes even in opposition to, the demands of feudal genealogy, then what relevance has it to an account of an apparently 'popular' form, like the public theatre play? Do 'fame' and 'emulation', the interrelated processes which drive Renaissance historiography, have any application to a heterogenous commercial audience?

Heywood's own plays provide an answer here. His history plays are largely concerned with the City, with the formation of its historic identity and the growth of its institutions. City opposition to the theatre came not just from purely religious interests, but from civic authorities inclined to see such assemblies as unruly, or even potentially seditious.[74] In the *Apology* and in the plays preceding it, Heywood works out a contrary assessment of his art and its role in the life of the City. His transplantation of initially humanist or aristocratic modes of historiography is ambitiously explicit and full, possibly influential, and certainly very popular. The plays themselves present arguments for the value of history, a value as dependent on the City's independent political identity. The process can be seen at its most diagrammatic in the second of his two plays, *If you know not me You know nobody*, on the life of the young Elizabeth. It is subtitled 'with the building of the Royall Exchange'. The growing prosperity of the City under Elizabeth is seen to culminate in the establishment of one of its most famous monuments. Gresham's triumph is placed by an earlier scene in which Heywood makes one of his clearest statements of purpose. Dr Nowell takes Gresham and other City notables to see his gallery of famous citizens. Nowell, as his name suggests,[75] acts as the City version of Spenser's Eumnestes, giving the history of each worthy, correcting the legend of Dick Whittington, pointing out the surviving legacies of custom and institution, the monuments by which each is still remembered, thus moving his audience to recognition –

'We that are citizens are rich as they were/Behold their charity in every street . . . / And yet we live like beasts, spend time and dye/Leuing no good to be remembered by' — and so to virtuous emulation:

> Why should not I liue so, that being dead,
> My name might have a register with theirs,
>
> Why should not all of vs, being wealthy men,
> And by Gods blessing onely raised, but
> Cast in our minds how we might then exceed
> In godly workes, helping of them that need.[76]

Elizabeth turns up puzzlingly late in what had promised to be a chronicle play about her, and then it is through the medium of pursueant who interrupts the mercantile intrigue of the first section of the play to borrow a hundred pounds on her behalf.[77] When the Queen opens the Exchange later in the play she is greeted familiarly by the wealthy merchant who lent her the money — 'Knowest thou not me Queene? Then thou knowest nobody'. The title of the play is teasingly turned away from the queen to the City institutions on which she is financially dependent. 'Bones-a-me woman, send to borrow money/ Of one you doe not know.'[78] The economic relation between City and monarch is exposed and affirmed at the climax of the play. Citizen history is corporate history — not the individualist history of intellectual humanism, nor the dynastic history of the feudal aristoc-racy, but the history of institutions.

The presentation of the historical individual is only one of many still lively modes of rhetorical 'character'. Allegorical and social personae offer Heywood, in an account derived largely from Scaliger, the means of claiming a purposive role for theatrical imitation, an articulation of social and moral identity in dramatic action. To put the *Apology's* argument in the context of mainstream rhetorical theory is to resolve some of its apparent inconsistencies. The audience's response to 'lively and well-spirited action' and its awareness of an artifice, a set of conventional signs, in, for example the depiction of women by boys, only contradict each other if we import the modern terms of a debate of 'alienation' versus 'empathy'. Rhetoric allows one both to respond to the power 'action' possesses to 'new mold the harts of the spectators' and to remain aware of its origin and methods. It also allows, as we have seen, of a wide variety of modes of character definition. In the more socially inclusive of the Elizabethan history plays, like Heywood's *Edward IV* or Shakespeare's *Henry IV*, these different languages may be used, as we shall see, not only in one play, but in one single figure. But an emerging ideology of fame takes a particular pre-eminence in this group of plays, as the most powerful construction of the audience-as-subject, as the determining character-language within the plays.

In *Henry VI* Shakespeare problematises the idea of fame, using Henry V as its absent and Talbot as its present object. Nashe bears witness to the exciting and implicatory effect of this, though as the cycle progresses we are more likely to be aware of the nihilistic processes of civil war, seen almost as a kind of anti-history. In the first play of the cycle, Talbot is the central figure. The play consists of two actions: the war in France, and the beginning of civil war in England. Talbot and his French opponent Joan seem set to take their place in an heroic historiography, conventional in its assumptions and worked out on a large scale. Talbot is presented explicitly in terms of those issues which concerned Nashe in his citation of the role in *Pierce Pennilesse* – fame, glory, emulation, survival, a chosen and shaped historical identity. The scene of his death, fighting side by side with his son, hammers out in ballad-like rhymes a mnemonic of survival in fame, to be opposed to the destruction of Talbot and his line, as a monument which exists outside temporal narrations of events. But this moment is qualified by two scenes, one before and one after. In the first, Shakespeare invents a gloss on the idea of heroic identity. The Countess of Auvergne invites Talbot to her castle in order to betray him to the French. She is disappointed in his presence;

> It cannot be this weak and writhled shrimp
> Should strike such terror to his enemies.

'No, no', Talbot replies, 'I am but shadow of myself/You are deceiv'd my substance is not here.' He blows his horn and his soldiers enter. 'These are his substance, sinews, arms and strength.'[79] Defeat of Countess. And after Talbot's death Lucy asks for his body, listing his titles and honours in a twelve-line speech. 'Here is a silly stately style indeed', the peasant Joan replies,

> Him that thou manifi'st with all these titles
> Stinking and fly-blown lies here at our feet.[80]

Again, the contradictory effect of the gloss cracks Talbot's heroic identity open, to present it in shattered forms. This mode of presentation is not anti-heroic. It can act as a strategy of engagement.

We assert and fix his identity ('embalme' him, in Nashe's words) in an imaginative response (our 'teares') which conquers the destroying effect of time. Furthermore, the Auvergne fable tells the audience that they can all participate in the heroic identity by seeing themselves as his followers, by assenting to his 'triumphe'.

In his first history cycle, Shakespeare presents history as a set of interrelated tragic careers, a series of presentations of *individual* power, worked out across the three plays with a careful, even oppressive, consistency. This marks a break between Shakespeare's plays and the socially and generically inclusive chronicle plays of his contemporaries. By seeing their stories – their histories – as tragedies ('What scene of death has Roscius now to act?' Henry asks his assassin, Richard of Gloucester),[81] the characters in the final section of the tetralogy are complicit in that erasure from history of which Richard is the ultimate agent. Shakespeare's next trilogy, the *Henry IV/V* cycle – returns to conservative formal models, to make its own considered adjustment to the ideas of fame, rhetoric and history on which they are based.

V   CHARACTER AND POWER: SHAKESPEARE'S SECOND HISTORY CYCLE

In the first part of Heywood's *Edward the Fourth* Edward is seen from the perspective of different class positions, as represented by the tanner Hobs, whom he meets when disguised, and by the City merchants. Edward has no desire to rationalise his role, in personal terms. It is Heywood's definition of the social relations defining that role which creates suspense around the king's wooing of the merchant's wife, Jane Shore. Edward is presented in part one as a figure of romantic comedy in his own estimation, but in the estimation of others he is an agent of absolute power in a carefully articulated class society. The point at which the two converge – when he issues his summons to Jane, a summons whose refusal none of Heywood's socially conformist characters could even imagine – is unseen by the audience, and Edward next appears in France, in a chronicle-defined action of political negotiation. The second half thus shifts away from explicit social argument and redefines its protagonists in different modes. Once the King is cordonned off into a linear narrative of events in France, Jane becomes an emblematic figure of true repentance, a monotonous but compelling icon of all the virtues but one. No intersection between 'royal' history and the play's middle-class characters is permitted until Gloucester appears, rendered by Heywood as a sketchy, summarised version of Shakespeare's Richard. Heywood's monarchs are primarily defined by their function; their identity is fractured or marginalised by the demands of a corporate history of London, a history of institutions in which the monarchy is primarily an institution defined by its relation to other institutions. Heywood's presentation of a liaison across social class, which is also a conflict of social class, multiplies versions of Jane's identity, just as it must render opaque that of her lover and king.

Across the two plays, that to which Jane-as-characterisation *refers* (those things which Jane can be used to characterise) has to shift; in part one, she is the representative of a social class; in part two, she is the instigator and chief participant in scenes emblematic of a Christian morality, albeit in a middle-class context. As the *Apology* argues throughout, theatre, the City's monument, not only presents the City's history, but teaches how to live in the City. Characters like Jane, and incidents involving them, become part of a moral mode that works through memorably emblematic moments of stasis and silent action – 'Here they put the body of young *Aire* into a coffin', one stage-direction specifies of the impoverished Jane and her husband, 'and then he sits down on the one side of it and she on the other.'[82]

Such shifts in mode seem not so purposefully articulated as those of the allegorical histories that precede the plays, or those of the Shakespeare trilogy of a year or so later. They are equally the product of a Tudor awareness of the implication of power in a praxis of identification, but Heywood seems less interested than the Shakespeare of the *Henry IV* plays in exploring this for its own sake. Like Jane, Falstaff is both the victim and the representation of his monarch's pleasure, and his 'fall', even more clearly than hers, focuses the presentation of a complex analysis of identity and power.

The ahistorical space around the chronicled events of the *Henry IV* plays is presented by Shakespeare as a comic underworld in which the prince encounters not, as in Heywood, the social realities which define his role, but an array of socially unrepresentative vice-like characters. Only the carriers (in part one) come from a world outside the self-defining theatrical spaces of the tavern and the court, and Hal never meets them. The tavern is an interlude-like space for the free play of identities. Hal's and Falstaff's banter consists largely of naming games, of grotesque elaborations of each other's physical characteristics, of disguise and imitation. The climax of this is of course the 'play extemporary' in part one, where each in turn play Hal and his father. Their evolution of the play has gone through several stages. It is initially proposed by Hal (to Poins) as a play of Hotspur and his wife Kate, whom we have just seen, and the idea follows on from the prince's mockery of Francis, the waiter. (The idea that links the two would seem to be 'work'; Hal presents Hotspur as a kind of labourer, just as trapped as Francis is in his own particular *deformation professionelle*, and just as liable to be made funny from the point of view of the tavern's play-scene.) Hal, as he says, is 'of all humours that have showed themselves humours since the old days of goodman Adam to the pupil age of this present twelve o'clock at midnight'.[83] That is, in a timeless unlocatable theatrical space (as the tavern at this moment becomes) all the impulses and potentialities of human being are playable; this is comedy's scope.

But the form their play eventually takes reminds us of the limits put on play in the terminus of identities that power can fix. To see Hal as a 'developing character', to read the play as *bildungsroman*, is to sentimentalise it, in that the matrix of knowledge, power and character has been his from the beginning, as has its necessary consequence for the vice figures, in their eventual cancelling by the realisation of this matrix in law and death. Hal introduces this idea to Falstaff in their very first scene: 'now in as low an ebb as the foot of the ladder, and by and by in as high a flow as the ridge of the gallows'.[84] His first statement alone, 'I know you all . . . ',[85] undercuts any sense we might have of the 'freedom' of his 'holiday humour', and is perhaps completed by the final lines of the improvised 'play'; 'I do, I will'.[86] Hal's 'I', his 'know/do/will' does not develop in the play (at least not in terms of his 'personality'), it is always there; what the play presents is its working out in a set of agons, often interrupted, always ultimately deferred. The play extemporary turns into a contest of fixing Falstaff's identity, a conflict in which Hal's bare do/will must trump Falstaff's fanciful eloquence.

BARDOLPH. My lord, do you see these meteors? Do you behold these exhalations?
PRINCE HAL. I do.
BARDOLPH. What think you they portend?
PRINCE HAL. Hot livers, and cold purses.
BARDOLPH. Choler, my lord, if rightly taken.
PRINCE HAL. No, if rightly taken, halter.[87]

In *Henry V* of course Hal does fix the meaning of Bardolph's challenging physiognomy with a judicial 'halter'.[88] Whatever the play of reading and naming to which Falstaff and Bardolph give rise, their identities are always predicated by their bodies, the physical realities that give the play a baseline for its elaborations of character. In the first part, Falstaff's physicality disrupts 'honour', contradicting fame's death-defying definition of identity, with an assertion of the bodily real against the 'counterfeits' of glory, a kind of counterfeiting made present to us by the multiple impersonations of the king that confuse the battle scene.

> To die is to be a counterfeit, for he is but the counterfeit dying, when a man thereby liveth, is to be no counterfeit, but the true and perfect image of life indeed.[89]

Falstaff is implicitly in conflict here with Hotspur, whose attributes Hal will take over when Falstaff is shed. In part two, the same is true of his scenes with the Lord Chief Justice. In both cases, the *agon* with Hal is indicated, but deferred – Falstaff moves further and further away from the values that accrue to Hal. 'I do, I will' is more and more clearly signalled.

While in part one the body's resilience was celebrated in Falstaff's refusal to die in battle (its reality opposed to the counterfeit eternity of Fame) in part two Falstaff's insistence on youth is countered by the Justice's explicit attribution to him of 'the characters of age'.

> Have you not a moist eye, a dry hand, a yellow cheek, a white beard, a decreasing leg, an increasing belly? Is not your voice broken, your wind short, your chin double, your wit single, and every part about you blasted with antiquity?[90]

The play ends of course in the interlude-style transaction by which Hal rejects Falstaff, and, in a politically more significant though usually underplayed move, acknowledges the Justice. A stable alliance between a strong monarch and the rule of law gives Shakespeare his image of an ideal form of political power. But Hal is also creating a final 'play'. If the Justice acquires an allegorical stature – 'you are right Justice'[91] – then Falstaff's identities are reduced to the bare fact of his bodily life, and that life seen at its starkest estimation – 'I know thee not, old man'.[92] This completes the 'play extemporary'; it is the final move in Falstaff's and Hal's competition to describe Falstaff, to give his character. Hal fixes this in a public ceremony, a necessarily public act of self-definition, which at once celebrates and confirms his own power.

In part one, the identification of power with self-presentation is worked out in the conflict between Hal and Hotspur (first implicit and then acted out as combat – when Shakespeare requires a one-to-one fight, it is always to dramatise a conflict of identities). Hotspur is 'the theme of honour's tongue'.[93] He demonstrates a certain rhetorical mastery in his scenes with the King, but this is seen as limited, even self-destructive. His first excuse for not returning the prisoners demanded by the King is a specious but well-turned 'character' of the foppish messenger sent to demand them. This may sway the otherwise reliable Blunt, but Hotspur destroys his advantage with his next rhetorical setpiece, an extravagant 'character' of Mortimer's bravery, easily contradicted by the King's typically deflationary statement that no such battle took place. Left alone, Hotspur re-makes events and people in a set of dizzying but essentially self-generated flights of fancy. 'He apprehends a world of figures here' says Worcester, 'But not the form of what he should attend'.[94] To say that Hotspur sees a world of figures, that is, of rhetorical tropes and devices, is the politician's response to a speech of Hotspur's that seems to develop and confirm the equally technical rhetorical metaphor of the King's – that Hotspur is the theme, the set subject matter, 'of honour's tongue', of a rhetorical setpiece by an allegorical figure. Allegorical *personae* are, as we have seen, rhetorically · self-generating, in that their most complete utterance is a statement of the grounds of their being; they 'speak' their 'selves'. Hotspur is the theme of honour's tongue, and honour is the theme of Hotspur's tongue. Which is uttering, and thereby giving being to, the other? This circularity is expanded on in Hotspur's assertion that he will rescue 'drowned honour' (but untenderly, 'by the locks') and then, peculiarly, despoil and impersonate her – 'he that doth redeem her thence might wear/Without corrival all her dignities'.[95] But it is Hal who eventually wins and wears Hotspur's 'fame' and 'honour'. The 'form' to which Hotspur has insufficiently attended (in the platonic sense, the reality behind but apart from these exciting 'figures') is the reality of practical politics. Hotspur's mastery of, his inwardness with, the rhetorical modes of honour and fame must be won from him and put to work for the 'form' of power politics, the basic reality that the plays acknowledge.

Hal explains this to his father; Hotspur is (again like Francis, the waiter) a kind of employee, a 'factor' to 'gross up' deeds of which Hal can finally claim ownership.[96] Hal's task in this – to fabricate an identity consonant with, indeed identical to, the operation of absolute individual power – is complicated by the circumstances of his father's usurpation. He has to be seen to come from the nowhere of the tavern, not simply, as he puts it to his father, for the surprise effect, for the impressive management of self-presentation, but to cut himself off from his father's dubious claims, to have his kingship justified by his own suddenly manifest virtues. Henry wants his son to be more like Hotspur, in that such an identity would be more fitting to what the King refers to as Hal's 'princely heart'.[97] But Hal knows the issue is more complicated: in view of the usurpation, claims to an instinct genealogically accountable 'princeliness' are of doubtful validity. Hal must construct a fame-derived identity in order to justify his inherited identity. His claim to be himself, to be king, must be justified by both systems, those of feudal genealogy *and* of individual 'fame'. It is a recurrent problem for the renaissance ruler, and one that builds a kind of pathos into a play like *Henry V*. Falstaff's last battlefield oration offered his own solution to the problem – sack engenders courage, and it is the presence of this, not of Henry's blood, in Hal's veins, that makes Hal what he is.[98] Falstaff's account of his own special fathering of Hal is neat, but it reminds us of the failure of the body-based tavern world to come up with anything to counter these 'historical' systems of value. In the end Falstaff can only make a necessarily doomed attempt to superimpose himself on them, to claim surrogate roles.

The *Henry IV/V* plays use a fame-derived presentation of character to present people as an epitome of their deeds, but they demand also a recognition, beyond these 'figures' of the 'form' that determines their use and meaning – power. Knowledge of individual character is the crux of the play's politics. Warwick in a carefully presented piece of 'glossing' explains Richard's prescience of retribution, that motor of a tragic reading of events, to the anxious Henry IV:

> There is a history in all men's lives,
> Figuring the nature of the times deceas'd;
> The which observ'd, a man may prophesy
> With a near aim, of the main chance of things . . ..[99]

'Miracles', as the two worldly wise prelates who open *Henry V* remind us, 'are ceased;/And therefore we must needs admit the means/How things are perfected.'[100] The trilogy presents 'the means' by which a successful absolute ruler achieves and maintains the loyalty of his subjects. Henry V knowingly stakes his historical identity on the repossession of France. If he fails, he tells his court, they should:

> Lay these bones in an unworthy urn,
> Tombless, with no remembrance over them.
> Either our history shall with full mouth
> Speak freely of our acts, or else our grave,
> Like Turkish mute, shall have a tongueless mouth,
> Not worshipped with a waxen epitaph.[101]

But the chorus, in his prologue to the play, has already informed us of the King's success.

Henry's role in this play is a series of self-presentations all rhetorically skilful — even, perhaps especially, the mock-modest 'wooing' of the already contracted Katherine — and all successful, equally so with both 'audiences', his loyal subjects and posterity, as represented by the spectators. Henry fixes the terms of his own memory: he has created an identity consonant with his 'blood' (that of Edward III, both as an heroic 'type' and precursor and as the source of his father's claim to the throne) and projects it out of time, into history. The means by which this is 'perfected' is of more interest to Shakespeare than an accurate estimation of contingent fact. Its political meaning is as a model of absolutist practice; fame is itself a political counter of which an aspirant to power should gain control.

In *Richard II* the action puts at stake those 'monuments' in which history and identity inhere. Richard's actions, as York points out, destroy the genealogical principles of which the dying Duchess of Gloucester, like the women in Richard III, preserves an impotent memory. More specifically, he has, Bolingbroke claims,

> From my own windows torn my household coat,
> Raced out my impresse, leaving me no sign,
> Save men's opinion and my living blood,
> To show the world I am a gentleman.[102]

But Bolingbroke's own actions render the signs of monachy meaningless, by demonstrating its vulnerability to unsanctioned power. Once both these processes are underway, the characters are reduced to memorialising their own stories, shaping them into tragic or explanatory mnemonics by means of rhetoric and ceremony.

This foregrounding of theatrical spectacle composes events into emblems which invite reading but refuse an immediate disclosure of meaning. 'Sorrow's eye,' Bushy tells the Queen:

> glazed with blinding tears
> Divides one thing entire to many objects,
> Like perspectives which, rightly gazed upon,
> Show nothing but confusion; eyes wary,
> Distinguished form.[103]

' . . . you did make him misinterpret me . . . '.[104] Bolingbroke complains to Bushy and Greene. The 'perspectives' we have on events are partial and contradictory. Microcosm and analogy are the play's characteristic devices – 'model' is a recurrent term which can cover both. We are invited to find the meaning of moments in the play by seeing them as 'models' of something else – of historical moments later than or anterior to the action, or of ideas whose abstract and 'timeless' presentation allows them to be read not as political concepts but as moral or even sacred values (kingship, good government, England). As history the play has meaning chiefly in reference to an ominous futurity, perhaps in the two cycles (one as yet unwritten), perhaps as 'model' of contemporary crisis (for this of course is how Elizabeth read it on the eve of Essex's rebellion: 'I am Richard II, know ye not that?').[105] Richard himself can be seen to pass out of history. Like *Richard III*, the play moves towards a presentation of the monarch alone, constructing an interiority in the aftermath of his destruction, willed or unwilled, knowing or unknowing, of his social and historical identity. The newly deposed Richard is greeted by his queen, the prime see-er and memorialist of the play's tragic patterning, as

> the model where old Troy did stand!
> Thou map of honour, thou King Richard's tomb,
> And not King Richard.[106]

Richard is tomb, map, model of Britain's history, back through Brute to a legendary link with Troy, an antiquity exceeding even that of the encounter's setting, 'Julius Caesar's ill-erected tower'. But Richard-as-monument, as the queen recognises, is different from a new Richard, posited by the King in the deposition scene. Bolingbroke tries to render meaningless Richard's most spectacular emblematic act, the smashing of the mirror.

RICHARD. Mark, silent king, the moral of this sport:
How soon my sorrow hath destroyed my face.
BOLINGBROKE. The shadow of your sorrow hath destroyed
The shadow of your face.
RICHARD. Say that again.
'The shadow of my sorrow'? Ha let's see.
'Tis very true, my grief lies all within,
And these external manners of laments
Are merely shadows to the unseen grief
That swells with silence in the tortured soul,
There lies the substance . . .[107]

A claim to interiority – to an asocial, ahistorical, ultimately undepict-able but substantial *real* self is unusual in Elizabethan presentations of historical figures but crucial to such otherwise dissimilar plays as *Richard III*, *Richard II* and the two parts of *Henry IV*. Talbot had located the substance of which *he* was shadow in the English army. As in many of Shakespeare's uses of this idea, 'power' is the substance, character – the presentable signs of identity – the 'shadow'. Talbot, exemplary English hero, realises that his substance lies outside himself, in something closer to a generalised idea of England; he is not a claimant to any absolute personal power, his substance is larger than himself. Hotspur operates the figures of character enticingly but baselessly, without attention to the 'form' of power. Richard is left, as he persistently reminds us, with the task of locating his substance when shadow/sign/figure has been cancelled, or forcibly reinterpreted. In the world of the play the problem is not of course personal to him. This interiority is, paradoxically, untenable in conditions of absolute privacy. Claiming substance within gives Richard a strong if temporary power position – it motivates Aumerle's rebellion almost immediately – and we will see how these self-generated rituals and mnemonics remain lodged in the historical memory of the later cycle, and to what effect.

Richard's speeches explore it in a carefully focused and purposeful way.

if I turn mine eyes upon myself,
I find myself a traitor with the rest.
For I have given here my soul's consent
T'undeck the pompous body of a king;
Made glory base, and sovereignty a slave;
Proud majesty a subject, state a peasant.[108]

The improvised ceremonial by which Richard has 'unkinged' himself is in effect an appropriation of the power codified in ritual to himself alone. This challenges the claim to power Bolingbroke seeks to establish for himself. Richard, as he observed at his entrance is 'both priest and clerk'[109] in a set of ritual models of power set up to contradict and divert Bolingbroke's attempt to re-character him by means of an extorted public confession. Bolingbroke is a consummate self-stager in his own eyes and, as we shall see from later descriptions of public pageantry, in the immediate context of this play. But the micro-societies of Richard's rhetorically projected interior would seem to admit Bolingbroke no reality, no 'substance'. Richard claims even the role of traitor for himself, in an allegorical narrative where glory, sovereignty, majesty and state are of himself and under his sway – his 'I' can remake them, diminish them to merely human status of *personae*, and lower class *personae* at that.

Like many of Shakespeare's protagonists, Richard is unable to take on a stoic fullness and self-sufficiency of identity in the face of defeat, a definition of the self as against a political praxis now seen as outside.

> Thus play I in one person many people,
> And none contented. Sometimes am I king,
> Then treasons make me wish myself a beggar,
> And so I am. Then crushing penury
> Persuades me I was better when a king:
> Then am I king'd again, and by and by
> Think that I am unking'd by Bolingbroke,
> And straight am nothing. But whate'er I be,
> Nor I, nor any man that but man is,
> With nothing shall be pleas'd till he be eas'd
> With being nothing.[110]

The player metaphor suggests the vanity/emptiness of such praxis when unsuccessful, when its proponent loses the reality of power. For Richard, the attempt to create an interior world is finally defeated by the incursion into it of the name Bolingbroke, a name which in its achieved and indivisible identity renders all Richard's attempts to establish identities for himself to nothing, just as the fact of isolation and imprisonment defeated his preceding attempt to model a kingdom in and for himself. The incursion of actual representatives of Bolingbroke's power into the cell forces silence, and internalisation of speech onto the groom who visits Richard ('What my tongue dares not, that my heart will say')[111] but in destroying Richard's internalised 'patience', his unrealisable stoicism, it marked the limits of his complicity, underlines the violence of Bolingbroke's acts, in a way that the assassin Exton is left to memorialise.

Richard manages to construct an enduring power position (enduring, that is, through 'fame') in a play where the signs of political identity have been crucially and irrevocably deranged. The immediate effect of Exton's deed, the new king tells him, is to write, 'a deed of slander with thy fatal hand/Upon my head and all this famous land'. The blood Exton spilt is, as he says at the time, both 'valour' personal to Richard and 'royal blood', extra-personal, the ritual marker of identities sacramentally passed on. 'Both have I spill'd'.[112] His blasphemous and wasteful spilling changes the blood to something else – the ink of a deed (in legal pun) which redefines Bolingbroke's identity as charactered in the text of history – a slander, he calls it. Richard himself – finally an unkinged self, in the material fact of an inert and singular body – is presented in a confinement both literal and metaphoric. He is returned to Bolingbroke at the end of the play as 'Thy buried fear'.[113] To bury Bolingbroke's fear (in the sense of what frightens him) is to return not simply to his presence but to *within* him that 'fear' which we can see as from now on internalised – buried in Bolingbroke.

To see Richard as a poet King (and thus somehow ineffectual) is to attempt to exempt him from the rest of the play, from its rhetorical and ritual procedures – to exempt him (and perhaps poetry itself) from an always present, always re-present-able stucture of political praxis. There are obviously links here with *Hamlet*, which I will pick up in Chapter 4. Richard's interiority is not of a special self-exempting kind – it is a powerful rhetorical construct, a reconstruction of the language of power put up for grabs by his and Bolingbroke's transgression of a hierarchical, genealogically transmitted, absolutism. If Bolingbroke ends the play written, compromisingly, into the text of history, Richard has established for himself a position outside that text, beyond it, and so somehow with power over it, rather than in its power. This both parallels and contrasts with Henry V's similarly extra-textual larger-than-the-signs existence, as predicated in that play. Henry stands almost as a mirror opposite to Richard – wholly successful, so wholly, heroically, externalised.

The real Henry, to whose representation play and theatre are, the chorus tells us, inadequate, is not, like the real unrepresentable Richard of Bordeaux of the deposition scene, a private interiority, but an historical emblem, the epitome of his own deeds. '. . . Warlike Harry, like himself' should

> Assume the port of Mars, and at his heels,
> Leashed in like hounds, should famine, sword, and fire
> Crouch for employment.[114]

The chorus articulates a shaping of event into history. His main ploy is to convince us that events are greater than can ever be conveyed to us by means of writing. A superficial similarity to Brecht's *'V-effekt'* might remind us that in its operation on the audience the chorus's presentation is the polar opposite to alienation;[115] it disorientates us, and confuses our sense of scale in order to enforce an imaginative complicity, to make impossible any estimation of events but its own. The chorus works a trick of perspective by which not obviously heroic or romantic events – the marriage contract, for example – are placed above and beyond any of the means of signification that the theatre affords. The immensity of events cannot be comprehended by representation, so our imaginations are enlisted instead. The metaphor is apt. The imaginative scope the audience seems to be offered is actually limited to imagining movement and space.[116] We are mobilised, recruited to follow the King to France. By drawing our attention to the provisionality of representation, Shakespeare instates Henry's story in the real. The chorus offers us a privileged participation in this 'reality', an exhilarating illusion of closeness to the event. He orchestrates the successive climaxes of the historical effect, the illusory presence of the historical to which Nashe and Heywood pay tribute.

However much the play multiplies 'monuments' – names, emblems, memorials, badges, from St Crispin's day to Fluellen's leek – it simultaneously seeks to deny the textuality of history. *Henry IV part two* begins with a prologue by Rumour, who is, in conventional allegory, Fame in her unfavourable aspect. 'Which of you' he/she asks the audience, 'will stop/The vent of hearing when loud Rumour speaks? . . . But what need I thus my well-known body to anatomize/Among my household?'[117] So the theatre is the house not of fame but of rumour. The last chorus of Henry V, by picturing Shakespeare, sets him in a slightly ludicrous unheroic contrast to the heroes whom he has, after all, presented to us.

> Thus far, with rough and all-unable pen
>> Our bending author hath pursued the story,
> In little room confining mighty men,
>> Mangling by starts the full course of their glory.[118]

The modesty topos is not used personally here, but to devalue textuality itself, in order to create an effect of the *real* presence of the heroic. The epilogue to *Henry V* must refer us, finally, back to the stage, and in doing so, it reinterprets the tetralogy by placing it in a moralised relation to the absolutist argument of the trilogy.

> Henry the Sixth, in infantbands crowned King
>> Of France and England, did this King succeed,
> Whose state so many had the managing
>> That they lost France, and made England bleed:
> Which oft our stage hath shown . . .[119]

This reinterpretation of the earlier work – or, rather, the imposition of a new frame on its own consideration of the fame/survival idea – sets up a chronological sequence that counters to some extent our sense of another chronology, the development across the writing of the plays of a particular set of ideas. In both chronologies, *Richard II* acts as a point of origin – as the presentation of the crime from which the 'divine retribution' reading of events can stem, and as the laying out of the counters of feudal and individual identity, their conversion by the action of the play and in Shakespeare's reflection on it into the material of a struggle to relocate power and meaning.

In *Richard II*, *Henry IV* and *Henry V* history becomes self-presentation; fame is in the control of the successful monarch, and a well-managed self-presentation to each concentric circle of 'audience' – for this is how all other classes are represented – is the way to fame and success. The allegiance of others is there for the monarch to win and control if he can; feudal barons and the less knowable 'many' are alike in having a simply presented choice between loyalty and treachery, a choice determined by the monarch's personal convincingness. But this political use of 'self' simultaneously creates a problematic interiority. Richard II, Richard III, Henry V and for that matter Bale's *King Johan*, are credited with an interiority, a metaphoric space different from the space of action, a space which is their own, from which their actions come. King Johan makes his crucial decision – to give in to the Pope – off-stage. He enters to describe how he came to arrive at this course of action, a choice that becomes clear once he's 'out of play', outside the sinister (to Bale) play world of the interlude.

> I have cast in mynde the great displeasures of warre,
> The daungers, the losses, the decayes both nere and farre,
> The burnynge of townes, the throwynge downe of buyldynges,
> Destruction of corne and cattell, with other thynges,
> Defylynge of maydes and shedynge of Christen blood,
> With suche lyke outrages, neyther honest, true nor good.
> These thynges consydered, I am compelled thys houre
> To resigne up here both crowne and regall poure.[120]

England's landscape and his inner space coincide. The virtuous biblical monarch revolves his country's good – the play's historical space is here given its only fixed identity, continuous with the good ruler's cares, outside the scope of the play. Like Horestes's emblematised interiority, it would seem to confirm these figures' right to determine the end of the play, a right more thoroughgoingly confirmed by the complex systems of textual, religious and/or historical authority which their 'fame' figures dramatise. Shakespeare's historical figures are expansions of this interiorisation of decision, an interiorisation clearly consequent on a secular absolutist presentation of political praxis, the creation of the Tudor monarch not as 'a' but as 'the' political individual.

That interiority is necessarily limited – it cannot be presented as complete, private, space. The ruler's interiority is a space he can never inhabit. It is a space in which an historical world is reflected. The power of the ruler is the power to know but to only *be* known as the most successful of these figures, Henry V, is known, as a self-made icon, a schema of virtuous deeds. Henry V, alone for the first time in the play, constructing a mental space for himself in the form of a prayer, finds like these other kings, like Johan, that such space is occupied by history, by known or projected fact.

> Not today, O Lord,
> O not today, think not upon the fault
> My father made in compassing the crown!
> I Richard's body have interred new,
> And on it have bestowed more contrite tears
> Than from it issued forced drops of blood.
> Five hundred poor I have in yearly pay,

Who twice a day their withered hands hold up
Towards heaven, to pardon blood: and I have built
Two chantries where the sad and solemn priests
Sing still for Richard's soul. More will I do,
Though all that I can do is nothing worth,
Since that my penitence comes after all,
Imploring pardon.[121]

In Henry's case, a punitive premonition of divine revenge for his father's crime tellingly contradicts the hard-headed pragmatism of the rest of the cycle. These figures experience their selfhood only fleetingly, and then to reflect back on the history which has constructed their identities for us.

Notes

1. Cicero, Orator, *XXXVII*, 128.
2. Julius Caesar Scaliger, *Poeticae Libri Septem* (1561) I. XIII, p. 20.
3. Ibid., I. XVI, p. 24.
4. Ibid., I. XIV, p. 22.
5. Ibid., III. XX, p. 104; for Cicero see Chapter 1, pp. 30.
6. Scaliger, V. I, p. 174.
7. Ibid., V. I, p. 174.
8. Ibid., VII. III, p. 346.
9. Spenser, *The Faerie Queene*, ed. A. C. Hamilton (London, 1977) 'A Letter of the Authors expounding his whole intention in the course of this worke'. p. 737.
10. For Scaliger reference see this chapter, n. 8. For discussion of Pickering's *Horestes*, and a comparison to Scaliger, see this chapter, pp. 60–4.
11. Prudentius, *Psychomachia*, 726–33.
12. Ibid., 891–2.
13. Ibid., 900–2.
14. Ibid., 50–1.
15. Ibid., 66–71.
16. Ibid., 310–27.
17. Ibid., 18–20.
18. Ibid., 902–3.
19. Ibid., 823–41. Revelation, XXI, 15.
20. Macklin Smith deals with some of these issues in *Prudentius' 'Psychomachia'; a re-examination* (Princeton, 1976). See pp. 109–67. C. S. Lewis's reading of the poem in *The Allegory of Love* may well have popularised the 'psychic struggle' reading of the poem. See Smith, pp. 111–2, Lewis, pp. 60–1, 66–73.
21. *Psychomachia*, 755–7.
22. Ibid., 741–5.

23. Ibid., 904.
24. Ibid., 640–3.
25. 'Youth' in Peter Happe (ed.), *Tudor Interludes* (Harmondsworth, 1972) ll. 15–31, p. 116.
26. Ibid., l. 65, p. 117.
27. 'Wit and Science' in Happe, *Tudor Interludes*, ll. 344–60, pp. 195–6.
28. For an account of the social context of *Wit and Science*, and of its centrality to the St Paul's repertory, see Reavley Gair, *The Children of St. Paul's; the Story of a Theatre Company 1553–1608* (Cambridge, 1982) pp. 87–91.
29. *Wit and Science*, ll. 373–85, p. 196.
30. *Youth*, ll. 704–18, p. 136.
31. The number of players required and the doubling necessary is often referred to on the title page and in the stage directions of the plays.
32. See Francis Hugh Mares, 'The Origin of the Figure called "The Vice" in Tudor Drama' in *The Huntington Library Quarterly*, Volume XXII 1958–9, pp. 11–29.
33. 'King Johan' in Peter Happe (ed.), *Four Morality Plays* (Harmondsworth, 1979) ll. 1–21, pp. 317–8.
34. Ibid., ll. 106–10, p. 321.
35. In Jill Mann, *Chaucer and Mediaeval Estates Satire; The Literature of Social Classes and the 'General Prologue' to the 'Canterbury Tales'* (London, 1973).
36. 'King Johan', ll. 314–63, pp. 330–2.
37. Ibid., l. 631, p. 343.
38. Ibid., ll. 840–1, pp. 352–3.
39. Ibid., l. 415, p. 334.
40. Ibid., ll. 1056–7, p. 362.
41. Ibid., l. 1091, p. 363.
42. Ibid., l. 1783, p. 393.
43. Ibid., ll. 1582–3, p. 384.
44. Ibid., ll. 2033–45, p. 404.
45. Ibid., l. 1106, p. 364, ll. 2191–99, p. 410–1.
46. Ibid., ll. 2193–220, p. 410–11.
47. Ibid., l. 2319, p. 415.
48. Ibid., l. 2579, p. 425. See also Foucault's interpretation of judicial dismemberment in *Discipline and Punish* (Harmondsworth, 1977) p. 3–31.
49. 'King Johan', ll. 2671–7, p. 429.
50. Marie Axton presents the evidence in an introduction to her edition of the play in *Three Tudor Classical Interludes* (Cambridge, 1982) pp. 29–30.
51. See Axton, *Three Tudor Classical Interludes*, pp. 25–7.
52. *Horestes*, in Marie Axton (ed.) *Three Tudor Classical Interludes*, ll. 207–17, p. 101.
53. I use 'function' here in its narratological sense, as developed in structuralist accounts of simple narrative. See Afterword, pp. 207–8.
54. See n. 10 and n. 25 above.
55. *Horestes*, ll. 805–916, pp. 126–8.
56. In her introduction to *Three Tudor Classical Interludes*, pp. 25–6.
57. Ricardo J. Quinones gives an account of humanist ideas of fame and history in 'Time and historical values in the literature of the Renaissance', in C. A. Patrides (ed.), *Aspects of Time* (Manchester, 1976) pp. 38–56. See also

Edwin B. Benjamin, 'Fame Poetry and Order of History in the literature of the English Renaissance', in *Studies in the Renaissance*, Vol. VI (1959) pp. 64–84.

58. *Horestes*, ll. 227–301, pp. 101–4.

59. Ibid., p. 108, p. 121.

60. Ibid., ll. 871–3, p. 127.

61. Frances Yates gives an account of the building and of the classical derivation of these theatres in *Theatre of the World* (London, 1969). Her account of the Elizabethan theatre's relation to 'Theatres of Memory' reflects suggestively on Heywood and Nashe's account of the history play.

62. Thomas Heywood, *An Apology for Actors* (London, 1612; reprinted New York, 1973) [B4r].

63. *The Works of Thomas Nashe*, edited by Ronald B. McKerrow and F. P. Wilson (Oxford, 1958) Vol. I, p. 212.

64. Heywood, *Apology* B(v).

65. Ibid., A2(v).

66. Nashe, *Works*, l. 5, p. 211.

67. The most influential statement of the 'naturalist' position (and of the reading of Heywood that supports this) is B. L. Joseph's in *Elizabethan Acting* (Oxford, 1964) pp. 1–3. But see also Lise-Lone Marker's 'Nature and Decorum in the Theory of Elizabethan Acting' in David Galloway (ed.), *The Elizabethan Theatre II* (Ontario, 1970) pp. 87–107 for carefully historicist explanation of the terms Heywood and others use.

68. Heywood, *Apology*, C3(v).

69. Quoted in *The Race of Time – three lectures on Renaissance historiography* by Herschel Baker (Toronto, 1967) p. 46.

70. Heywood, *Apology*, B3(r)–B3(v).

71. See n. 69.

72. Katherine Duncan-Jones and Jan Van Dorsten (eds), *A Defence of Poetry in Miscellaneous prose of Sir Philip Sidney* (Oxford, 1973) p. 115.

73. After him *Vther*, which *Pendragon* hight,
       Succeeding There abruptly it did end,
       Without full point, or other Cesure right,
       As if the rest some wicked hand did rend
       Or th'Authour selfe could not at least attend
       To finish it: that so vntimely breach
       The Prince him selfe halfe seemeth to offend,
       Yet secret pleasure did offence empeach,
    And wonder of antiquitie long stopt his speach.
    (*Faerie Queen*) II, x. 68, p. 270.)

74. See Margot Heinemann, *Puritanism and Theatre* (Cambridge, 1980) pp. 31–38.

75. Dr Nowell was the Dean of St Paul's (1560–1602). See Gair *The Children of St. Paul's*, pp. 113.

76. *The Dramatic Works of Thomas Heywood* (London, 1874, reprinted New York, 1964) Vol. I, pp. 275–8.

77. Ibid., Vol. I, pp. 287.

78. Ibid., Vol. I, pp. 317–8.

79. *The Three Parts of Henry the Sixth*, edited by G. B. Harrison (London, 1959) *Henry the Sixth, Part One* II. ii, pp. 68–9.

Rhetorical Character: History and Allegory

80. Ibid., IV. vii, p. 113.
81. *Henry VI pt. III*, IV. vi, p. 338.
82. Heywood, *Dramatic Works*, Vol. I, p. 183.
83. *The First Part of King Henry the Fourth*, edited by P. H. Davison (Harmondsworth, 1968) II. iv. 91–4, p. 81.
84. Ibid., I. ii. 36–8, p. 51.
85. Ibid., I. ii. 193–215, pp. 56–7.
86. Ibid., II. iv. 466, p. 93.
87. Ibid., II. iv, 312–18, p. 88.
88. *Henry V*, edited by A. R. Humphreys (Harmondsworth, 1968) III. vi. 96–104, pp. 110–11.
89. *Henry IV pt. I*, V. iv. 113–18, p. 147.
90. *Henry IV pt. II*, I. ii. 182–6, p. 66.
91. Ibid., V. i. 102, p. 149.
92. Ibid., V. v. 50, p. 158.
93. *Henry IV pt. I*, I. i. 80, p. 49.
94. Ibid., I. iii. 77–9, p. 64.
95. Ibid., I. v. 119–205, p. 64.
96. Ibid., III. ii. 147–50, p. 110.
97. Ibid., III. ii. 17, p. 106.
98. *Henry IV pt. II*, IV. iii. 85–122, pp. 127–9.
99. *The Second Part of King Henry the Fourth*, edited by P. H. Davison (Harmondsworth, 1977) III. i. 76–9, p. 101.
100. *Henry V*, I. i. 67–9, p. 63.
101. Ibid., I. ii. 229–34, p. 72.
102. *The Tragedy of King Richard the Second*, edited by Kenneth Muir (New York, 1963) III. i. 24–7, p. 91.
103. Ibid., II. ii. 14–20, p. 77.
104. Ibid., III. i. 9–18, pp. 90–91.
105. See Marie Axton, *The Queen's Two Bodies: Drama and the Elizabethan Succession*, p. 2 (London, 1977). Heinemann, *Puritanism*, p. 39.
106. *Richard II*, V. i. 11–13, 2, p. 125.
107. Ibid., IV. i. 289–98, p. 122.
108. Ibid., IV. i. 246–51, p. 121.
109. Ibid., IV. i. 173, p. 118.
110. Ibid., V. v. 31–41, p. 142.
111. Ibid., V. v. 97, p. 144.
112. Ibid., V. v. 114, p. 145.
113. Ibid., V. vi. 84–5, p. 147, V. vi. 81, p. 147.
114. *Henry V*, prologue, lines 4–8, p. 59.
115. See for example the illustration Brecht gives in his 'Basic Model for an Epic Theatre', *The Street Scene* (1938), or its theoretical elaboration in *A Short Organum for the Theatre* (1949). Both are translated in John Willet, *Brecht on Theatre* (London, 1964.)
116. See, for example, the chorus to *Henry V*, act II, lines 1–24, pp. 94–5.
117. *Henry IV pt. II*, 'Induction' lines 1–22, p. 51.
118. *Henry V*, V. ii. 1–16, p. 152.
119. Ibid., epilogue, lines 1–4, p. 169.
120. 'King Johan', lines 1705–12, pp. 389–90.
121. *Henry V*, IV. i. 285–98, pp. 128–9.

3

Shakespeare: Character as Political Praxis

To put together texts ranging from Pickering's *Horestes* and Bale's *King Johan* to the Shakespeare cycles is to recognise a continuity between the allegorical drama and the later renaissance theatre often seen as somehow superseding it. Such a continuity can be seen to lie in an approach to character, and in the assumptions about the place of the subject in dramatic practice — the very things which are normally taken, of course, to mark a 'break' between the mediaeval and the renaissance (a break which, oddly, would have to be located in the middle of Elizabeth's reign). This 'break' seems to be more a matter of what post-eighteenth-century criticism has wanted to do with first 'Shakespeare' and then 'his contemporaries' than it has to do with the theatrical and literary assumptions available to the writer's own period. By approaching Shakespeare via rhetorical accounts of character, by placing the 'substantive' as anachronistic, we can open up in the plays a complex, flexible and precise presentation of the identifying practices of which 'transactional' character consists. The plays are not 'about' character, they are plays *of* character, presenting action and conflict through it.

While character and action are traditionally, if often problematically, discrete in Western thought, character and language come to seem distinct in a later, quintessentially modern development. The notion of a unique self beyond language, of the mysterious power of 'great' art to transmit a sense of such selves, is, as I shall argue in a later chapter, the grounds of a re-evaluation of Shakespeare in the late seventeenth and eighteenth centuries. Shakespeare criticism continues to operate in this anti-rhetorical mode. For the rhetorical tradition, within which the historical Shakespeare worked, character is a kind of language, and language a kind of action, a social praxis. A post-eighteenth-century approach to the representation of the human — as most powerfully exemplified by the 'genius' of Shakespeare — redefines character, regards language and action as entities discrete both from character and from each other, and thus poses the relation between the three as problematic, even fraught, requiring the 'critical' task of interpretation, that is, of temporary resolutions within particular readings. The *locus classicus* of the character controversy in Shakespeare studies is L. C. Knights's attack on A. C. Bradley's *Shakespearean Tragedy* (1904) in his 'How Many Children had Lady Macbeth?' (1933). The relation to language of a certain concept of character is at issue here. Bradley feels able to say that his study is not concerned with the language of the plays:

> What may be called, in a restricted sense, the 'poetry' of the four tragedies – the beauties of style, diction, versification – I shall pass by in silence. Our one object will be what, again in a restricted sense, may be called dramatic appreciation; to increase our understanding and enjoyment of these works as dramas; to learn to apprehend the action and some of the personages of each with a somewhat greater truth and intensity, so that they may assume in our imaginations a shape a little less unlike the shape they wore in the imagination of their creator.[1]

Knights, in keeping with a general movement towards 'close reading' and 'practical criticism', picks up on this and proposes in its place a reading of the plays as kinds of dramatic poems, in which close attention to language is privileged.

> We are faced with this conclusion: the only profitable approach to Shakespeare is a consideration of his plays as dramatic poems, of his use of language to obtain a total complex emotional response. Yet the bulk of Shakespeare criticism is concerned with his characters, his heroines, his love of Nature or his 'philosophy' – with everything, in short, except with the words on the page, which it is the main business of the critic to examine.[2]

Knights seems to confirm the divide between the action and characters of a play on the one hand, and its 'language' on the other. The effect in his own piece quickly becomes apparent in a difficulty in describing the structure and dynamics of a play, just as the effect of Bradley's approach is a reconstitution of the text in terms culturally distant from its own. The upshot of the controversy would seem to be that thinking about character and thinking about language are two distinct things, a position consonant with an anti-rhetorical idea of character, but unhelpful when it comes to considering Shakespeare's own context and his practice as a writer.

However familiar the Bradley/Knights material might be, it retains its interest in that this and other basic assumptions behind it remain largely unquestioned. Contemporary Shakespeare studies still tend to fall into on the one hand textual close reading, where 'character' in its modern meaning is ignored and/or taken for granted, and, on the other, into character study of a morally assertive kind (however ideologically diverse the moralities asserted). Character, again, is itself unexamined. Reading 'character' as a discourse with a knowable history in identifiable texts is to suggest an alternative reading of those texts, a reading in which the distinctions I have sketched above do not operate exclusively. Character is a special use of language, of all the languages of the stage, the plentitude of which Shakespeare persistently reflects on. And language is conceived of as a praxis – as purposive action. Such action is of necessity political; the human subject, as constructed in these purposive linguistic praxes, in this rhetoric, is in relation to other human subjects, and that relation is ultimately the reality of the state.

Thus, to invoke a concept like rhetoric is, though historicist, more than simply a matter of labelling an object of the past, and so neutralising it by enforcing its pastness. I wish neither to recover terms and then demand that we 'apply' them, nor to engage on an archaeology of Elizabethan psychology, theological concepts of the self, or whatever; such things are locally relevant, but my overall purpose is to consider some dominant practices of reading and writing, some central facts of the life of literary and theatrical texts. To place them in the context of a discourse to which these distinctions are either alien, or made in wholly different ways, is to find the means both to local illuminations of the texts and to re-opening some basic questions about the history and 'theory' of drama.

In these plays, individuation takes place within the framework of ideas that I have outlined in previous sections, as a system of 'fame'. Individuated figures, named and known as themselves, tend to reflect on the conditions of their fame – the action (in the sense of plot) tends to be developed out of such considerations, and the player's action (in the sense of his mastery of rhetorical languages, verbal and non-verbal) is used to present it as 'character'. When seen in the context of an English rhetorical tradition of drama, plays like the Shakespeare history cycles reveal both the interaction of different modes of rhetorical character – allegorical and *persona*/estate as well as historically individuated – and the ends to which that essentially Tudor tradition develops such interaction; towards a grounding of textual authority in the recognition of power, towards the mutual validation of power and textually-established 'truth', and towards a re-making of the audience-as-subject, this last being the aim to which all rhetorical practice tends.

These considerations still operate in other later Shakespeare plays, perhaps to a surprising extent. An idea like 'fame' can allow one to reclaim aspects of plays which from the point of view of more modern ideas of character seem puzzling, even inert. Reading with post-romantic expectations reshapes the plays in terms of which aspects of them respond to such reading, and so seem lively or exciting, and which do not. This is not simply to apply an historically 'past' idea with a view to explication; it is to use it to free a reading of the plays from the limiting preconceptions of that later mode of character and the even more limiting tripartite compartmentalisation of character criticism, language criticism and action/staging/structure, into which Shakespeare criticism tends to classify itself. *Measure for Measure*, for example, given the scope of comic fictions, is shaped out of the implications of rhetorical character language and power in a perhaps freer and even more thoroughgoing way than the English histories. The Duke seeks to 'know' his subjects, 'to practise his judgement with the disposition of natures'[3] as he puts it of Angelo, to assign their identities in an even more thoroughgoing way than did those earlier avatars of the renaissance monarch. But he finds that he himself is 'known', that 'characters' of him that he would wish to reject are circulating in the underworld of Vienna. The ultimate quasi-divine power, to know but not be known, is denied him. The second half of the play consists of his slow, sometimes farcically complex, rebuilding of his personal power, a mobilisation of his knowledge of others towards the staging of a second coming, climaxing in the public destruction of his false knower, Lucio. Modern humanist readings of the play, in seeking to ascribe clemency to the Duke, find this moment a problem but in the terms of renaissance politics 'slandering a Prince' indeed 'deserves it',[4] for truth and power, as we have seen, must be the mutually validating basis of an absolute monarchy, and character language is the dangerously double-edged tool by which they try to establish control over other definitions of the human.

In this process the Duke becomes invisible, nameless, unknowable. He is only called Vincentio in the cast list, in a part of the play which can never be 'played'. His enigma is not grounded in 'personality', it is that of an extreme intensification of the paradox of the ruler, the unknowable knower. In soliloquy the Duke constructs not an interiority but a sententious knowledge of universals.

It is typical of Shakespeare that we see the Duke's power 'built' (over the second, more controversial part of the play). The 'problem' presented by *Measure for Measure,* and by the three plays I deal with in this chapter, *Troilus and Cressida, Antony and Cleopatra* and *Julius Caesar,* centres in 'character', however understood. To conceive of character rhetorically is to shift the grounds of the problem (from like/don't like, approve/disapprove). They are plays of character as a political praxis, which develop conflict (conflicts larger than soluble problems) out of a combatively deployed character language. *Troilus and Cressida* explores fame in problematic conjunction with the non-individuating language of 'common' identities. *Antony and Cleopatra* elaborates fame into the grounds of an *agon,* not only of opposed selves, but of opposing discourses of the self. *Julius Caesar* opposes differing systems of personal ethics, the different parameters offered by the classical settings of these plays, to extend the Elizabethan Shakespeare's interest in the politics of self-hood.

I   *TROILUS AND CRESSIDA*: 'COMMON COMMENTARIES' AND 'TRUTH'S AUTHENTIC AUTHOUR'

Both parts of the plot of *Troilus and Cressida* – the Greek generals' attempt to persuade Achilles to fight, and Troilus's wooing of Cressida – turn on ideas of personal fame. They find their resolution in a confirming of identities already known to the audience. This is the only Shakespeare play whose sources enjoyed an established literary reputation. Chaucer's *Troilus and Criseyde* and, among many other versions of the Troy story, Homer's *Iliad,* are assumed to be present to the audience, as part of the text of fame in which those characters inhere. We watch Achilles and Cressida become 'themselves', become what we know of them – Shakespeare's awareness of a literary-textual 'fame' tradition, establishing them as the 'already known', allows him to foreground all the separate counters of those 'known' identities.

The plot dynamic of the scenes in the Greek camp is provided by Hector's challenge to single combat, seen by the commanders as a trial of fame/reputation, and delivered by Aeneas, the figure most explicitly and uncritically committed to those values. Fame is in crisis in *Troilus and Cressida*, even if, as an ideology, it is not explicitly or even implicitly questioned.

For Hector, as he is careful to point out, fame/reputation is the decisive factor in opposing the return of Helen to the Greeks, rather than any sense of her 'worth', or of ' ... the hot passion of distempered blood' like Paris's and Troilus's.[5] But in any case Fame, as the 'already-known', predicates the outcome of the council scene for us – as in Cressida's attempt to walk out of Pandarus's garden or Diomedes's to leave Cressida's tent, their attempted withdrawals only make more immediate to us these figures 'place i' the story'.[6] The Greek commanders have, since the beginning of the play, faced a similar threatened withdrawal – Achilles, in so many accounts the exemplar of heroically achieved fame – is refusing to *be* Achilles.

The effect of this is an ambiguous audience response, and thus produces a generic ambiguity – comedy, tragedy or tragicomedy? For the audience the experience of the play is that of waiting for known heroic identities to be constructed and assumed, but it also involves the shocks of comic non-heroic categorisations of character that would seem to pull in an altogether different direction. The effect is simultaneously to remind us of the closedness of individual identities already known to us, and to present us with moments in which they are still open. It both confirms us in the knowledge granted to us in the survival of literary and historical texts, and suggests the complex relation of knowledge and ignorance in those moments as lived. The anonymous author of the preface classifies the play for us generically in his telling parodies of its language. It is 'passing full of the palm comical: for it is a birth of your brain that never undertook anything comical vainly ...' 'Were but the vain names of comedies changed for the titles of commodities', serious men engaged in law and business would rush to secure them, for 'they are so framed to the life that they serve for the most common commentaries of all the actions of our lives ...'.[7] Just as he has picked up the word 'clapper-clawed', to describe what might have (but has not) happened to the play at the hands of 'the vulgar',[8] so he seems to be developing Ulysses's stress (in the defence of 'degree') on 'communities' and 'commerce'.[9] Comedy is commentary in that it presents common – not heroic – realities. It is about 'our' lives, it exists in the present, not in that continuum of time of which heroic history makes us aware. It is also a commodity – it acknowledges, as tragedy often does not, its existence as a transaction between actors and audience, as, in Shakespeare's case, a commercial transaction. That we jib at this account of the play, and maybe blame its self-styled 'never writer' for misrecognising Shakespeare's work, is part of the effect *Troilus and Cressida* articulates. In its insistence on the passage of time, and on the role of individual fame, the play sets up a non-comic discourse against the common commentaries of urban comedy, of the *personae*-defined identifications offered to us in the always-present of comic playing. Menelaus, Paris and Helen — cuckold, lecher and whore — make immediate to us and irredeemable to themselves a paradox of identity which Troilus, Cressida and Pandarus must 'act out' and which Ulysses and Nestor must harness to bring about their final if equivocal construction of Achilles. On the temporal linear level, to which the play's insistence on foresight, memory and prophecy gives us access, the play is a history, and in that it is a history of defeat, a tragic history. But at the cross-section of its on-stage present that history is comic commentary, where figures place themselves and each other as representations of general aspects of the 'actions of our lives'.

In the garden scene, when Pandarus has finally succeeded in bringing Troilus and Cressida together, each makes a vow that is also a gamble on their historic identity. Troilus projects himself to the future as an exemplar, a type of 'truth'. Cressida makes a risky bet on her own 'truth', with her 'name' as collateral. So Pandarus impatiently wraps up the thing as a bargain — Troilus has after all initiated all this with the demand that his 'truth' be 'affronted with the match and weight' of an accredited exchange. Pandarus puts himself down as guarantor. All three say 'Amen'.[10]

Each gamble is subtly different in kind. Troilus presents himself as a reliable component in his favourite rhetorical device, the elaborated simile. In depending on equivalence, the simile turns on the valuation of each of its components. Troilus claims that his name will provide a transcendently unquestionable counter for future similists. As 'truth's authentic authour to be cited' he will validate, even 'sanctify', not only his own current discourse, but any of which his name becomes a part. He is, he asserts, 'as true as truth's simplicity',[11] and it is this claim which initiates the oaths and nudges the other two into their less authoritative self-placings.

This is consonant with Troilus-as-hero seeking survival in fame — in the 'virtuous fight'[12] of his contract with Cressida, 'truth' can be simply projected *as* his historical identity, he can *be* truth. Cressida's fame, and Pandarus's, is to lose individuality, to become by-words. Pandarus *becomes* pandar, a linguistic pillorying in the term for go-between.

Shakespeare dooms Chaucer's delicately ambiguous manipulator to a catastrophic decline. Pandarus, in their first scene together, promises Cressida, 'a token from Troilus'. 'By that same token, you are a bawd'[13] she replies. The token is token of a scurrilous way one *could* name this well-placed Trojan courtier, if one wished. And in the last couplet of the garden scene Pandarus turns to the audience, steps into the comic present, to take on his common title.

> And Cupid grant all tongue-tied maidens here
> Bed, chamber, Pandar to provide this gear![14]

The *personae* are classifications of social behaviour and visible characteristics, but they are also denotations of kinds and usage of language. The cross-over effect of this dipping into the common provides a focus on two recurrent issues. Specifically to the play, what are we to make of Cressida? More generally, what in Shakespeare is the relevance of and idea of character to the languages different figures speak? What kind and what degree of differentiation operates here?

Where Troilus is addicted to the construction of complex analogy, the main currency of Pandarus's and Cressida's speech is a flippant colloquial prose. Taken at its crudest level, this creates a distinction between the Petrarchanising hero-lover, his duplicitous courtesan/mistress and their bawd. Such broad distinctions of kinds of language rely on a notion of the fitness of kinds of rhetorical device and degrees of complexity in their use of different categories of *personae*, and can be seen to operate in Shakespeare to produce basic categorisations of character in terms of class, sex, age and so on. The issues on which a more modern critical language is likely to focus – metaphorical fields of reference, intensity of effect, density of 'imagery' and so on – do not distinguish character in any particularly marked way.[15] Rhetoric however does, if in terms of general categories. Cressida's language would seem at times to confirm a courtesan-like placing of her. 'Prithee tarry/You men will never tarry' (to Troilus)[16] and 'One cannot speak a word/But it straight starts you' (to Diomedes)[17] speak of a knowingness that marks her as 'common' – knowing too much ('you men'), and too easily known. In Pandarus the effect is more marked, a feebleness in his attempts to make romantic or heroic phrases ('love, love nothing but love')[18] offsets the too recognisable language of pandarism which at the very end of the play allows him to make direct if bitter contact with those of his colleagues of 'the hold door trade'[19] who inhabit the immediate context of the performance. These are the linguistic effects by which the *personae* identifications work, fix themselves disturbingly as an available perspective, a common commentary, on the linear heroic-historical narrative. They are not of course placings of Cressida or even Pandarus once and for all, not stereotypes so much as 'parts' of the kind that one man or woman in his/her time play many of, parts which in this play are juxtaposed to the time-bound identifications of heroic fame. The conjunction of the two allows Shakespeare to open up a space in which Cressida's identity, and so the whole process of the identifying practices involved, can be explored and interrogated.

Is there an intrinsic Cressida, outside the general social/erotic interaction on which her 'private' soliloquies so puzzlingly insist? Cressida lays claim to 'truth' by opposites, by threatening herself with a reputation for falsehood.[20] She cannot claim an 'authentic' identity, let alone determine its survival as Troilus sets out to (and succeeds in so doing — we know the story even as we watch this). She works by opposites. Her 'wager' is an affecting amplification of a trick of self-presentation obvious in her from the beginning. Her first and her last soliloquy are oddly impersonal, constructed from generalisations, common knowledge, of what men and women are.[21] We may of course be more inclined to ask whether there is an intrinsic Troilus, as to a modern audience a consciously elaborate rhetoric (simile always insists on conscious artifice in a way that metaphor does not) and an insistence on simplicity and truth contradict each other — we are more likely to attribute 'sincerity' to Cressida's casual edgy prose. We must, I think, take Troilus at his own valuation; this is precisely the problem, that he succeeds in establishing a self-valuation and Cressida does not. The two lovers exist in two distinct rhetorical modes, possess, in this sense, irreconcilable characters.

Ulysses claims to 'know' Cressida as soon as he sees her —

> Fie, fie upon her!
> There's language in her eye, her cheek, her lip;
> Nay, her foot speaks. Her wanton spirits look out
> At every joint and motive of her body.
> O, these encounterers, so glib of tongue,
> That give a coasting welcome ere it comes,
> And wide unclasp the tables of their thoughts
> To every ticklish reader, set them down
> For sluttish spoils of opportunity
> And daughters of the game.[22]

This 'character' shocks us by its insistence on the innerness to Cressida of what is ascribed to her — 'language *in* her eyes . . . her wanton spirits *look out* . . .'. But this 'language' is created by reading as much as in writing/speaking, as Ulysses has pointed out in his immediately previous encounter with Achilles, a self-contradiction encapsulated in one of his slippery metaphors. Cressida may 'wide unclasp the tables of her thought . . .' but it is Ulysses who 'sets down' the would-be authoritative character disclosure. Cressida's identity as 'daughter of the game' is written on her, and this is justified simply in that it can be done — that she presents an unclasped 'table'. Her arrival in the Greek camp precedes Hector's, and coincides with Ulysses's re-making of Achilles. It is part of a sequence of parades, assessments, sizings-up. Another of the 'comm . . .' words that suggest non-individuation occurs in the stage direction at the end of the parade of Trojans which Pandarus wants to use to bring Troilus's individual pre-eminence to Cressida's eye — 'Enter common soldiers'. Pandarus draws Cressida's attention away from them — 'asses, fools, dolts; chaff and bran, chaff and bran; porridge after meat. I could live and die in the eyes of Troilus. Ne'er look, ne'er look . . .'.[23] This 'parade' parallels Cressida's presentation to a line-up of the Greek commanders. Looked at rather than looking, she is to be kissed, Ulysses suggests, 'in general'.[24] Troilus's singularity is to be emphasised in the first parade, in the second Cressida has, in Ulysses's eyes, lost hers — she is, in all senses, 'common'.

The two embassies of the Greek commanders to Achilles and, more pervasively, the impersonation games with which Achilles fills the vacuum of inaction follow a similar pattern. Patroclus imitates the commanders for Achilles, Thersites does so first for him and then for Ajax. The effect of all these scenes is reductive, tending to *personae*-like sketches of the 'common' or 'general'. Agamemnon is a pompous braggart, Menelaus a cuckold, Nestor a dotard, Patroclus an 'effeminate' lecher, and so on.[25] The players must present 'characters' of these figures without any narrative action (they are not doing anything to dramatise their identities), so what then do such characters amount to? Thersites's and Patroclus's playing reflects on this. As a result, Thersites seems to acquire a kind of authority — this may indeed be all there is to them. In identifying himself as 'envy' Thersites becomes the other face of 'fame'.[26]

Ulysses presents an awareness of this other side of 'fame' to Achilles:

> Time hath, my lord, a wallet at his back,
> Wherein he puts alms for oblivion,
> A great-sized monster of ingratitudes.
> Those scraps are good deeds past, which are devoured
> As fast as they are made, forgot as soon
> As done. Perseverance, dear my lord,
> Keeps honor bright.[27]

We are dependent for what we are on the applause of others, and this must be continually won in our presentation of ourselves, our definition of ourselves against a threatening 'oblivion'. This is a nightmare inverse of 'fame', of a kind logically derivable from *Henry V*, but never explicitly stated within it. Achilles is his own weapon. But he is also, in Thersites's most insulting phrase, 'thou picture of what thou seemest and idol of idiot-worshippers'.[28] This, implicitly, is Ulysses's estimation of him too. Ulysses — who imitates Patroclus's imitation — has the clearest and most purposive grasp on all these counters of identity. However much he reassures the other generals that Patroclus's performance is 'ridiculous and silly action' and not 'imitation'[29] in a true sense, the characters he reproduces, portraits in 'action' and rhetorical device, may well be hard to distinguish from the action of the players who take those very roles. Is there a real heroic identity possessed by the generals (something to make them more than pictures of what they seem), to which Patroclus's performances are self-evidently false? Ulysses thinks not, and uses his knowledge, his knowledge of character, to establish by the end of the play the basis of Greek success, of an heroic validation of these figures.

The moment that clinches the identity of the 'false' Cressida is elaborately witnessed and read, by Troilus, Ulysses, Thersites and ourselves. It echoes the garden scene in a pattern of pairing and threatened division, both as enacted by the 'lovers' and as developed in Cressida's language. When she tried to leave in the earlier scene she claimed:

> I have a kind of self resides with you;
> But an unkind self, that itself will leave
> To be another's fool.[30]

Which self is leaving which? The self created by love of Troilus stays with him, but it is both 'kind' (like) the self that leaves, that exists independent of Troilus, and 'unkind', in splitting off. What then is the third 'self'? Does it include the second in the first? The effect is deliberately ambiguous – none of these selves are nameable, none of them are Troilus's ('another's') but there is a consciousness of departure, of divided being, among Cressida's selves. How then can she be said to betray Troilus, when she has no single self (as he claims he has) to 'give'? Her doubleness is carefully worked out here not as a simple opposition between *real* and *false* selves, but as an impossibility of the authenticity to which Troilus lays claim. It is this that shocks him when he sees her with Diomedes. The principle of 'unity' itself has been undone for him, and he identifies that unity of word and meaning in 'authenticated' discourse – 'if souls guide vows, if vows be sanctimony/ . . . This is not she.' It was. Cressida's awareness of division, her ability to 'be' within it, is for him a 'madness of discourse' pushing him to a 'bifold authority' (a contradiction in terms, for 'truth's authentic authour') in that it forces him to recognise the complicating fact that this 'is, and is not Cressida'.[31]

Troilus resolves this by adopting the heroic identities of the battlefield, 'in characters as red as Mars his heart/Inflamed with Venus',[32] Cressida is left in ambiguous division. 'One eye yet looks on thee/But with my heart the other eye doth see'.[33] How does an eye see with a heart? In this complex (if also banal) compartmentalisation of herself Cressida pursues to a logical conclusion the doubleness she presented in her first scene; she claims realities of feeling existing apart from a banal and contradictory social language, but has no language which might locate those feelings for us, even as transient 'affects'. She presents a 'common' non-individuated sense of herself, even when alone. Her 'character' is not determined by herself, but by our knowledge of one action.

Her language and Troilus's allows for remarkably few points of contact. Their conjunction (unlike that of Antony and Cleopatra or Romeo and Juliet) needs a go-between, if only that provided by the perspective of our prior knowledge; fame constructs them as a couple. In this highly worked rhetorical play – first and foremost a play of 'character', thus understood – their love is a foreknown defeat, to set against the partial victory of Ulysses's design on Achilles. When Cressida evokes the effect of time on 'mighty states characterless . . . grated to dusty nothing'[34] she picks up an idea recurrent in the play, and most often associated with Ulysses or Nestor.[35] The idea of figures or characters that point to a larger undefinable thing is used by them with a confidence in an ability to *know* that Cressida's prescience of time denies her. Time, and 'oblivion', destroy the 'characters' by which we know — to live in time is to live in different characters (play many parts), to be fixed in one or to be forgotten. Cressida's dividedness is a way of living in time, of traversing the discontinuities of a complex historical moment. Nestor and Ulysses feel that control over the characters gives them control over a thing to which the characters refer, and this is true in the world of the play, for those with the rhetorical skill to operate it. 'There is a mystery in the soul of state',[36] Ulysses warns Achilles, and Achilles is known by it — the 'state' *is* knowledge, power, and as long as its 'characters' exist the likes of Ulysses can operate it. This notion of the state has replaced the power/truth nexus of Tudor absolutism as the authority of the play. As Troilus learns, and Cressida already knows, there is nothing to authenticate self in either public or private spheres. There is instead the state-intelligence, the knowledge of others urged on Henry IV by Warwick,[37] put in action as a principle of power, existing for Ulysses as a self-regulating, self-justifying force. Shakespeare uses the structures of command given him by his story to present to his Inns of Court audience an intriguingly 'other' yet tellingly accessible formulation of the rhetorical praxis of power.

II   *ANTONY AND CLEOPATRA*: TRIUMPHS AND BLEMISHES

Perhaps the most disturbing thing about *Troilus and Cressida* is that the characters of the participants are not in their own control. The signs, the 'tokens' by which they are known, the names given them, are ultimately the property of that 'knowledge' made present to the audience in Shakespeare's time-dominated manipulation of the fame *topoi*, the knowledge that operates within the play as Ulysses's controlling 'state'. Paradoxically this makes the play more acceptable to certain kinds of modern critic than those plays where participants consciously and purposively operate 'character'. *Antony and Cleopatra*, like the other plays in this section, lies outside the theatrical mainstream — there have, at least in this country, been remarkably few successful productions. Even *Troilus and Cressida* seems to have lost the currency given it by two famous Royal Shakespeare Company productions,[38] and none of these plays, though unquestionably 'great' in literary-critical terms, has ever been as central to acting tradition as are say, *Hamlet, Lear, Romeo and Juliet*, or even (though again, without much recent success) *Othello*. Character, as these plays insistently develop it, is not to be easily understood in post-Stanislavskian terms.

That Antony and Cleopatra first 'play', then combatively build and finally must try to establish their identities *as* 'Antony' and 'Cleopatra' (finally perhaps as 'Antony and Cleopatra') is not a clue to some deficiency in their 'real selves' (immaturity, as a certain kind of English critic would probably call it) but their being in the play, the play's action, their praxis in its world.

Like the English histories, *Antony and Cleopatra* is a series of *agons* of character, of conflicts sometimes literalised in physical combat, of literal battles sometimes decided by projections of character in reputation and fame. The conflict between Octavian on the one hand and Antony and Cleopatra on the other is realised and resolved posthumously – the play holds out its resolution to its final moments, the final fixing and reading of identities. Octavian's interests are moral in the strictest sense – he wishes to fix Antony according to a notion of personal *mores*, to represent him, even to himself, as defective within a certain definition of his being and so, ultimately, defeated both inside and out. There is no question but that absolute power is Octavian's aim from the start. We can see the process at work in a speeded-up form in the case of Lepidus. Lepidus seems reasonable and diplomatic in his first few scenes. He works hard to deflect the imposition of a politics of *mores*. First he tempers Octavian's discourse of 'natural vice', of 'composure' (natural composition) and 'blemish' by invoking a relativising metaphor of 'appearance', of seeing and interpreting:

CAESAR. You may see, Lepidus, and henceforth know
   It is not Caesar's natural vice to hate
   Our great competitor. From Alexandria
   This is the news; he fishes, drinks, and wastes
   The lamps of night in revel; is not more manlike
   Than Cleopatra, nor the queen of Ptolemy
   More womanly than he; hardly gave audience, or
   Vouchsafed to think he had partners. You shall find there
   A man who is th' abstract of all faults
   That all men follow.
LEPIDUS. I must not think there are
   Evils enow to darken all his goodness;
   His faults, in him, seem as the spots of heaven,
   More fiery by night's blackness, hereditary
   Rather than purchased, what he cannot change
   Than what he chooses.[39]

Then, when Antony comes to Rome, he tries to persuade Enobarbus to tone down Antony's 'private stomaching', to 'entreat your captain/to soft and gentle speech'.[40] But after his drunkenness on Pompey's ship, Lepidus becomes simply the butt of ridicule, mocked in elaborated comic character by the commonsensical Menas and Enobarbus. The next thing we know, he has been wiped out, slandered (re-charactered) and then killed. The logic of this, and something of the play's metaphorical procedures where character is concerned, can be seen in the comments of the servants who introduce the banquet scene. Their 'character' of the drunken Lepidus opens with the remark that 'Some o' their plants are ill-rooted already, and least wind i'the world will blow them down'.[41] That this can be taken to refer to the political future of most of the banqueters as well as to their alcoholic intake does not mean (as undergraduate essays can suggest of the relation between Antony and Cleopatra's 'adultery' and their downfall) that the link between the two is causal. The character applies to more than Lepidus's drunkenness by virtue of the set of relations predicating *control* — reason's control over appetite, self's control over circumstance, men's control over women, Romans' over 'barbarians' the ruler's over the ruled — which map out that specifically classical discourse of self and world within which Octavian is shown to operate. This whole sequence in the play, reaching its theatrical climax in dance and song, is an expansively metaphoric presentation of what it is, as the servants finally put it, 'To be called into a huge sphere, and not to be seen to move in't'.[41] Lepidus's error lies in what is 'seen' of him, and this is token of his inability to operate the power-language of the play.

Octavian's moral mode is thus more subtle than a presentation of cause and effect, and less 'principled' than a personal disapproval. It is wholly an aspect of his political praxis. It is an attempt to fix a character on his opponents and to project one for himself, using more specifically Roman means of course than Hal used towards not dissimilar ends. Every aspect of his post-Aristotelian model of the achieved self would mark Antony out as a loser, if that discourse were to be as successfully imposed on him as it was on Lepidus.

This idea of a model of the self which people must be seen to be acting out, to be judged and 'placed' in accordance with, returns us to self-representation, to the (to us) problematic relation of acting to the self. The assumption that Octavian and his adversaries share is that the self is acted, that is, put in play and observed — it is not a separate concealed entity to which such 'play' can give us only partial and delusive access. In theatrical terms, the effect is a kind of confidence in the staging of 'selves', an extrovertly theatrical arena in which everything can be read as 'significant action'. 'Look . . . /How this Herculean Roman does become/The carriage of his chafe'[43] says Cleopatra of Antony in an early scene. 'Observe how Antony becomes his flaw,/And what thou think'st his very action speaks/In every power that moves',[44] says Octavian to Thidias, the skilled rhetorician he sends to persuade Cleopatra. Octavian wishes to present Antony's military defeat as 'flaw', as inherent and visible mark. Such ideas are finally focused in a notional metatheatre, like the parades and impersonations of *Troilus and Cressida* – the 'triumph' in which Octavian intends to 'stage' a defeated Antony and Cleopatra for Rome. Antony warns Cleopatra of this as their defeat becomes obvious, and the dynamic of the final section of the play is given by her attempt to counter it.

Cleopatra is, as one of the Romans puts it to Enobarbus, 'a most triumphant lady, if report be square to her'.[45] As a conversational prelude to Enobarbus's description of her at Cydnus, the play's most famous rhetorical set-piece (precisely that, a fixing of Cleopatra's fame in terms she stage-manages), it marks Cleopatra out as mistress of the play's most compelling mode of character, self-staging as celebration, as a demonstration of control over all the various characters available to one figure. In terms of Roman character politics, Octavian and his court's interpretation and operation of the 'dispositions' of others, Enobarbus's portrait of triumphant luxury and rule is a decisive error, as his questioners hint in returning to the proposed marriage to Octavia – can Octavia's 'beauty, wisdom, modesty . . . settle/The heart of Antony'?[46] Clearly not, and the point, like Lepidus's drunkenness, is more than merely personal. Like all Shakespeare's Roman women, Octavia is the bearer of male values and the channel of social relationship between men. In relation to Antony she is both symbol and test of the larger set of correspondences, all predicating 'control', of which Octavian is master and by which Antony can only stand condemned. Cleopatra in Octavian's triumph would represent the imposition of all these categories of (in Roman eyes) a necessary control – on an historical level, of Roman over barbarian, on the allegorical level, to which triumphs always tend, of the male/the 'higher' rational soul/the virtuous state over the female/the lower faculties of the soul/the anarchy of 'affections' – like Spenser's Acrasia, brought back by the knight of Temperance to Gloriana's court.[47] 'Her life in Rome would be eternal in our triumph' says Octavian, in one of those tellingly ambiguous circularities to which the play's diction tends. The triumph may only have the fleeting life of theatre, but she is to be fixed eternally 'in' it as 'in' Rome, given a place in that ideology whose triumph it is. Further, her life (her survival) would be 'eternal in *our* triumph'; it would confer 'triumph'[48] on Octavian, give 'life' to *his* fame. One might set this against the 'scene' Antony and Cleopatra 'play' (the terms are hers) on his departure for Rome. After subverting Antony's heroic self-presentation to underline his theatricality, to impose the comedic *persona* of a *miles gloriosus* on him, Cleopatra shapes the conventions of allegorical identification into a personal meditation on the conditions of their fame.

CLEOPATRA. How this Herculean Roman does become
　　The carriage of his chafe.
ANTONY. I'll leave you, lady.
CLEOPATRA.　　　　　　　　Courteous lord, one word.
　　Sir, you and I must part, but that's not it:
　　Sir, you and I have loved, but there's not it:
　　That you know well. Something it is I would –
　　O, my oblivion is a very Antony,
　　And I am all forgotten.
ANTONY.　　　　　　　But that your royalty
　　Holds idleness your subject, I should take you
　　For idleness itself.[49]

Such oblivion is not the threat to identity of its counterpart in *Troilus and Cressida*. Cleopatra forgets and is forgotten, but Antony's name is the condition of such forgetfulness, and such oblivion must be in a sense a return and not a loss. Cleopatra recapitulates this figure (or rather her eunuch does, speaking for her) in the fiction of her death presented to the defeated Antony.

　　　　　　The last she spake
　　Was 'Antony! most noble Antony!'
　　Then in the midst a tearing groan did break
　　The name of Antony; it was divided
　　Between her heart and lips: she render'd life,
　　Thy name so buried in her.
ANTONY.　　　　　　Dead, then?
MARDIAN.　　　　　　　　Dead.[50]

Burying, like 'oblivion' in the earlier scene, is simultaneously a loss and a preserving here; one 'name' is lost in, and so preserved by, the identity of the other, here in a context where the burying is to become all too literal. In response to Cleopatra's oblivion speech Antony proposed an equivalent allegorical *persona* for her, and in doing so illuminates the mode and condition of the lovers' rhetorical action. Cleopatra, in setting up the play of oblivion and idleness, may appear as an allegorical figure like the Idleness who diverts Redford's Wit from the pursuit of the lady Science, or like one half of the binary choice offered to Hercules, Antony's ancestor and type, the choice that leads away from active virtue.[51] Idleness, in an ideology of fame, leads to oblivion, to the erasure of identity. But Antony recognises that Cleopatra, more Hal than Falstaff, has this *persona* in her power, a power identified with her 'royalty'. Both lovers operate the various characters — moral placings and comedic *personae* every bit as belittling as those into which we see Pandarus and Cressida shrink — with a confidence that the play presents as personal power. Their names represent the termini of these 'play' identities, the point of ultimate control from which they operate in the world the play so expansively maps.

The play's diction, its almost uniquely fluent juxtapositions of 'common' and rhetorically elaborate language is an aspect of the protagonists' multiplication of identities, of the bewildering and glamorous confidence with which they move from one self-presentation to another — we are most aware of this quality of the play's language when one or other of the lovers is named or charactered. But, as the play goes on, the circle of action available to Antony and Cleopatra becomes smaller.

Defeat seems to unmake these selves — in this context Antony and Cleopatra can recognise neither their own selves nor each other. Antony sees his identity slipping away, changing ceaselessly and uncontrollably like clouds or water.[52] As in the 'poor player' analogy, an action that fails leaves character an emblem of vanity.[53] Antony may see himself as a maddened Hercules, but Cleopatra proposes another 'type' for him — Ajax.[54] Ajax's madness, comically developed in the servant's account to Cressida, is seen by Shakespeare as a confusion of 'humours' and impulses, an uncertainty as to his own identity.[56] Antony acknowledges this 'type' in preparing for death — 'the seven-fold shield of Ajax cannot keep/The battery from my heart'.[56] Cleopatra armed him for their last victory; here he disarms, in recognition of an Ajax-like uncertainty, the 'madness' of a self de-composing itself. Armour, a hard but physically articulated casing, becomes one of the components of military action that the play shifts between literal and metaphorical reading, as a buildable and deconstructable self. When Antony's actions first become unpredictably discontinuous, Enobarbus reflects on the play's dominant ideas of behaviour and being.

> I see men's judgements are
> A parcel of their fortunes, and things outward
> Do draw the inward quality after them
> To suffer all alike.[57]

The last point encapsulates exactly what Octavian wants to be seen to do, to effect the internalisation of defeat that this discourse of the self proposes. But Enobarbus also, in denying the existence of an independent, unswayable, 'inward quality' offers a carefully anti-stoic placing of the play's sense of character and self. There is, in other words, *no* separate and inner self – 'fortunes' are determining realities. The obverse of this is that identity can as well be remade as dismantled and it is Cleopatra's exploitation of this that shapes the play towards its conclusion.

Another aspect of military conflict becomes assimilated to the mark/seal character metaphor; the wounds to which the aptly named Scarus gives the character of readable signs ('I had a wound here that was like a T,/But now 'tis made an H'[58]) are not only the memorials of a heroic fame-conferring action, they are problematically metaphorised in the love-plot, as memorials of a different kind. Octavian, according to Thidias:

> knows that you embraced not Antony
> As you did love, but as you feared him.
> CLEOPATRA.   O!
> THIDIAS. The scars upon your honor therefore he
> Does pity, as constrained blemishes,
> Not as deserved.
> CLEOPATRA.   He is a god, and knows
> What is most right. Mine honour was not yielded,
> But conquered merely.[59]

Cleopatra's 'conquer'd' picks up an idea of enforced dominance that conditions relationships in the play on the largest and smallest scale. That her reputation is a mark made not by but on her, developed in this case in terms of Caesar's favourite ideas of 'blemishes' on the moral life, is a recurrent notion in Shakespeare's accounts of women's 'character'. In the earlier poem, *The Rape of Lucrece*, it is worked out with an obsessive complexity. Cleopatra's 'O!' economically leaves open her own reaction to this particular development of the play's 'Roman' discourse — it neither engages in it nor opposes it. But in her later scenes with Octavian and his emissaries we can see her 'play' the submissive role the Romans require — 'I hourly learn/A doctrine of obedience'.[60] She even decorates it, in the complex dissimulations of the treasure scene, with mocking impersonations of Roman femininity:

> O Caesar, what a wounding shame is this,
> That thou vouchsafing here to visit me,
> Doing the honor of thy lordliness
> To one so meek, that mine own servant should
> Parcel the sum of my disgraces by
> Addition of his envy. Say, good Caesar,
> That I some lady trifles have reserved,
> Immoment toys, things of such dignity
> As we greet modern friends withal; and say
> Some nobler token I have kept apart
> For Livia and Octavia, to induce
> Their mediation.[61]

She 'learns' these discourses to have them in her power, to use them to her own ends. To see this as treacherous is to lose track of Cleopatra's mode of resistance, to fall into Antony's confusion or into the complacency of the Roman ideology. Thidias after all had badly miscalculated, and ended up with the 'wound' metaphor literalised, on his own back.

The mark/stamp/wound idea tends to describe something done rhetorically but it also suggests a physical domination. Thidias's use of it subtly shifts between the two, as an attempt at imposing Octavian's politics of *mores*. Cleopatra's honour is after all a rhetorical construct, and as such is more under her control than Thidias realises. The 'blemish' idea however would seem to present it as a passive woundable entity, a vulnerable 'composure' like those which Octavian elsewhere tries to ascribe to Lepidus and Antony. Thidias seeks to make rhetorical imprints on Cleopatra, and so re-character her as submissive, 'conquer' her rhetorically by leading her to acknowledge that she is already 'conquer'd' by men. The metaphor is used with a similar ambiguity in *The Rape of Lucrece*:

> For men have marble, women waxen minds,
> And therefore are they formed as marble will;
> The weak oppressed, th'impression of strange kinds
> Is formed in them by force, by fraud, or skill.
> Then call them not the authors of their ill,
>   No more than wax shall be accounted evil
>   Wherein is stamped the semblance of a devil.[62]

The immediate context of this is rhetorical. It describes Lucrece's maid who receives and responds to the 'impression' of Lucrece's grief without fully knowing what it is. This is presented as on the whole a good thing, especially since the marble metaphor has recurred earlier several times as index of the rapist Tarquin's unreceptive cruelty. Shakespeare goes on to develop the idea in ways that move from its immediate context to bring it closer to the central concerns and narrative of the poem – this wax-like receptivity means that women 'carry' the print of what men have done to them – Lucrece, not Tarquin, bears the shame of the deed (or is at least Shakespeare's focus for presenting it). This is unjust, we should pity her, but it is generally and inevitably so. Character, as the poem elaborately articulates it, is the rhetorical formulation of an act, written in and read as particular fame, and in women's case this tends to be done *to* rather than *by* them. When Cleopatra calls herself 'marble-constant' she is directly reversing this – she listens to the conventionally scurrilous characters of women offered her by the clown, but this like her final fantasy of the burlesquing Roman comedians seems to mark a distance between the characters imposed on her and her choice for herself.[63] The last stage of the play attests to her final 'triumph'. Octavian must confront her staging of herself, her construction of her self as her own monument, and must acknowledge 'A pair so famous'.[64] It is a resolution to parallel Lucrece's, but where the waxen Roman lady dies in acknowledgement of the complex male power structures played out around her, even within her, to the point of denying her an autonomous identity (dies *to* acknowledge them), the marble Egyptian dies to disrupt exactly those values, to triumph in the play's politics of character and fame.

III   *JULIUS CAESAR* : REBELLION AND INTERIORITY

The shift of focus in *The Rape of Lucrece*, from Tarquin's anticipation of the rape to Lucrece's reaction to it, is bridged by a transference from one to the other of one of the poem's allegorical models of the self – as a castle, with servants, and a lady running it, suddenly besieged and, in Lucrece's case, sacked. The allegories that map out Tarquin's and Lucrece's 'selves' are interchangeable from one to the other, and continuous with the political praxis that gives the story its context and overall dynamic. The lady is in the first instance Lucrece, the castle her sleeping body, the servants her blood, disturbed by Tarquin's hand on her breast. Then it is Tarquin's soul, spotted by his act. But it is also still Lucrece – literally, as the mistress of the house into which Tarquin tricked his way, as his 'spotted' victim.[65] This is not of course to say that Lucrece is Tarquin's soul. But it is to point out the complex and non-substantive way in which she is Lucrece. Both participants are fragmented into allegorical *personae* of values and 'affections', *personae* who engage in battles, sieges, the life of a great house, but tending to destruction, not rebuilding – allegorical models of the self familiar from Prudentius, Spenser and allegorical drama. Such metaphors operate in this poem just as they do in Prudentius and Spenser, though here within the frame of inset narratives, narratives that act as figurative expansions of points in the story overall. The continuity between these allegories of self and the literal narrative should remind us of the alienness of a sense of a private bounded self to allegorical discourse. The various ladies are all 'Lucrece', the battles all aspects of the battles fought by the male figures, the destruction of the house is always the same crisis for Rome, because all are expansions of conflicts within that classical discourse of power with which Shakespeare here, as in his Roman plays, is specifically engaged.

Aspects of the action of the plays can also function allegorically. Armed combats often represent *agons* of identifying practices. Enclosures – Richard II's dungeon, Cleopatra's monument, Richard III's tent – are termini in the plot, but markers of metaphorical limits and space also. In *Julius Caesar*, Brutus's household serves to mark off an imperilled line between retirement and political action. Brutus's emergence into the conspiracy has its 'type' in a figure who turns up at the end of *Lucrece*; the fame of Tarquin and Lucrece re-characters *that* Brutus, persuades him to throw off his role as 'fool', and become instead a revenger and founder of the republic. The first half of *Julius Caesar* centres on how and why the later Brutus makes a parallel move.

Cassius offers Brutus, as Ulysses offers Achilles, 'mirrors' to a true latent self. Here both Brutus and Cassius identify it as 'inner', possessed privately by Brutus but not divulged in action or open speech.

> since you know you cannot see yourself
> So well as by reflection, I, your glass
> Will modestly discover to yourself
> That of yourself which you yet know not of.[66]

'Characters' of Brutus, of Rome and of Caesar form the main thrust of Cassius's persuasion. In a soliloquy he acknowledges his purpose in terms that contradict those he uses to Brutus himself:

> Well, Brutus, thou art noble; yet I see
> Thy honorable mettle may be wrought
> From that it is disposed; therefore it is meet
> That noble minds keep ever with their likes;
> For who so firm that cannot be seduced?[67]

So Brutus's potential for action, 'that of yourself which you yet know not of', is not a 'hidden worthiness' which the conspiracy activates, but something to which his statically 'noble' qualities must be 'wrought'. Cassius avows himself engaged on the rhetorical task of shaping malleable human material against its intrinsic disposition. The speech marks out Cassius as without that kind of interiority (it cannot be acted 'in character' in a modern sense). His description of his actions seems impersonally explicit, jarringly self-belittling in its Iago-like definition of the 'noble' as existing only elsewhere. But where this seems to place Cassius as instrumental, to set up a distinction of focus between Brutus's self and Cassius's operation on it, it also directs attention to the idea of the 'noble' – is it extrinsic or intrinsic, can it only exist in privacy, must it, to have political effect, be 'wrought/From that it is disposed'?

The play marks a careful set of microcosmic limits around Brutus – interiority, a self-scrutiny described with unusual and important explicitness in his first extended speech, his marriage, his household, represented by Lucius and re-established in the tent scene, Caesar's court, Rome, world history, the universe of pagan philosophies. Brutus is presented in and through all these, and the same crisis replicates itself across all of them. He takes on to himself the idea of rebellion, internalises it:

Between the acting of a dreadful thing
And the first motion, all the interim is
Like a phantasma, or a hideous dream.
The genius and the mortal instruments
Are then in council, and the state of a man,
Like to a little kingdom, suffers then
The nature of an insurrection.[68]

The metaphorical/literal shift in the reading of action is set up here in ways clearly consonant with the presentation of the storm, with the idea of sickness that colours Cassius's account of Caesar, and with the condition of the conspiracy itself.[69] As in *Antony and Cleopatra* the Aristotelian notion of the correspondences of different aspects of the human, mapped on one axis of peace in achieved control, is present to the play's Romans, but where in that play an attempt to impose it is eventually thwarted, here it is centred on one man, seen to be attempting to remake it from within himself.

The republican Brutus figures comparatively little in the play, acting as a marker of genealogical identity, of 'Roman blood' rather than as the later Brutus's 'type' in the pattern of fame. It is on this sense of Roman identity, rather than on any oath, that Brutus depends to keep the assassination plot together. The plotters are thus not, in a strict sense, conspirators; they have not bound themselves together in some implicitly subversive form of micro-society by taking an oath that over-rides their fealty to the state. Brutus uses allegorical personification to express his horror at the idea of such a new social entity coming into being. He shifts the literal disguises of the plotters into a metaphorical statement of the 'unmasking' process of psychomachia:

O conspiracy,
Sham'st thou to show thy dang'rous brow by night,
When evils are most free? O, then by day
Where wilt thou find a cavern dark enough
To mask thy monstrous visage? Seek none, conspiracy;
Hide it in smiles and affability:
For if thou path, thy native semblance on,
Not Erebus itself were dim enough
To hide thee from prevention.[70]

The rebellion is instead to be a spontaneous assertion of an already existing identity, corporate though experienced individually:

> do not stain
> The even virtue of our enterprise,
> Nor th' insuppressive mettle of our spirits,
> To think that or our cause or our performance
> Did need an oath; when every drop of blood
> That every Roman bears, and nobly bears,
> Is guilty of a several bastardy
> If he do break the smallest particle
> Of any promise that hath passed from him.[71]

This careful characterisation of the act of rebellion allows Brutus to follow it through, to contain it within all the microcosmic limits put round his selfhood without essentially disturbing any of them. His impolitic plainness of rhetoric after the assassination is an expression of the same desire to see it as a confirming, not a remaking, of identities, and thus an act that should speak for itself. Antony is unwisely underestimated by the plotters because of that very aptitude for 'play' which gives him at least temporary access to rhetorical control.[72] Antony creates the character of an avenging Caesar:

> Caesar's spirit, ranging for revenge,
> With Até by his side come hot from hell,
> Shall in these confines with a monarch's voice
> Cry 'Havoc', and let slip the dogs of war[73]

and destroys Brutus's attempt to fix the meaning of the assassination, its character and that of those involved in it.

Different figures in *Julius Caesar* are worked out in the different rhetorical modes by which they operate, and by which they account for their actions and their relation to each other. They all thus have fixed and distinct values, which they can invoke, successfully or mistakenly, in projecting political action, or can construct into equations in which each can further define the other:

> If I were Brutus now, and he was Cassius,
> He should not humor me.

or:

> Was that done like Cassius?
> Should I have answered Caius Cassius so?
> When Marcus Brutus grows so covetous

> To lock such rascal counters from his friends,
> Be ready, gods, with all your thunderbolts,
> Dash him to pieces![74]

There is no stable source of 'authority' in this excitingly flexible paradigm of political action, no one figure's personal system can be used to 'place' our reading of the others. As different figures at different times realise, their actions are projected to an unknowable posterity, are thus given up to open-ended reading. The two most fully developed are Brutus and Caesar; both pursue modes of operating 'character' that define their political value while making it impossible for them to act successfully themselves.

Ben Jonson's creative mishearing of one line in the play as 'Caesar never did wrong without good cause' is a witty exaggeration of a tendency in Caesar's self-presentation. The line in fact reads

> Know, Caesar doth not wrong, nor without cause
> Will he be satisfied.[75]

Jonson's impulse to deride it may reflect on the singlemindedness with which Shakespeare's Caesar arrogates to himself the authority (power-as-truth) which the play refuses to locate in any single position, a refusal that thus produces a dangerously compelling but unplaceable figure. Caesar, like Pandar, becomes a by-word; his citation of his own name is not simply a projection of fame/reputation but the coinage of a rhetoric appropriate to a new kind of being, of which he is the first (and, Brutus hopes, the last). It would perhaps be most simply placeable as a Jonsonian monomania. But, in contradistinction to Brutus, this allows Caesar *no* private space, no interiority, and this dooms him. Firstly, that it makes him just as prey as Brutus is to be rhetorically 'wrought' by flattery – the play's rhetoricians are identified with the fluency of, on different microcosmic levels, bodily humours, the mob, the storm, and an epicurean, uncontrolled universe, as against the stasis of the self of which Brutus and Caesar represent opposite but complementary polarities. Secondly, it allows him no space to acknowledge the things that might preserve him. Personification allegory for Caesar is a process of externalising, of emptying out the self:

> I rather tell thee what is to be feared
> Than what I fear; for always I am Caesar[76]

And, later,

>   Danger knows full well
>   That Caesar is more dangerous than he.
>   We are two lions littered in one day,
>   And I the elder and more terrible,
>   And Caesar shall go forth.[77]

'Caesar's spirit' is the final construction/externalisation that survives
the man, and fills Brutus's privacy in the tent before Phillipi.
Nonetheless, the play allows Brutus a measure of success, limited but
real triumphs in his attempt to live by a politics of virtue. His quarrel
with Cassius defines this ambition in him against the pragmatism and
casual emotionalism of his co-commander. Brutus's struggle to impose
an integrity on ordinary military conduct, his complex attempt both to
define himself against and to control Cassius's 'humour', and the
double victory of stoic principle over the news of Portia's death (itself
a kind of stoic martydom) all mark the emerging status of a single
figure living by a definite code. The scene is a difficult one for modern
audiences, but it becomes easier, I think, if we see it not as about 'the
conspiracy' and therefore about how it couldn't last (for Brutus no such
thing has ever existed anyway), but as a scene about how Brutus could
have/might still arrive at a version of individual power based on a
version of the self different from, implicitly better than, Caesar's.
Similarly the repeated presentation of his self-control seems heartless/
fake in terms of post-Romantic assumptions, but it is necessarily first
private and then public, as Brutus has committed himself to an
integrity of life that assumes the same values apply to both. It is not as
if he were 'false' to a discrete private sphere in which Portia existed,
she herself, as she reminds him, is through her father a public symbol of
ancestral Roman values.[78] Their privacy is recapitulated and her loss
underlined by the presence of Lucius in the subsequent tent scene,
perhaps even in Brutus's solicitude for the sleeping boy's lute. Their
marriage is a space in which (knowingly and with her collusion)
conservative Roman values are re-inscribed and enacted. Her suicide,
like Lucrece's, preserves and encodes them, as do Brutus's reactions to
the news.

At the end of the play the four protagonists – Antony, Octavian,
Cassius and Brutus – are fixed in individually telling positions. Cassius
has 'misconstrued everything' – committing suicide after a mistaken
reading of the progress of the battle, crowned with a victory wreath
after death, confronted like this by Brutus, perhaps as an emblem of the
vanity of one committed to action when that action has failed. Brutus

however has managed to build around him the most successful of the play's micro-societies — 'I found no man but he was true to me',[79] he says, surrounded by loyal soldiers. In these final scenes his monosyllabic rhetoric finally finds its place. Antony marks him out as exceptional:

> This was the noblest Roman of them all.
> All the conspirators save only he
> Did that they did in envy of great Caesar;
> He, only in a general honest thought
> And common good to all, made one of them.
> His life was gentle, and the elements
> So mixed in him that Nature might stand up
> And say to all the world, 'This was a man!'[80]

As a 'man', in simple integrity of being, Brutus upholds the virtues that in action he has been seen to attempt to subvert. He can thus be exempted from the opprobrium that must fall on the other rebels. His internal 'state' (he did himself imagine it as a kind of monarchy, after all) has remained in exemplary order. Thus, even in defeat, his interiority retains its values (unlike Cassius's and later Antony's). After its destruction in Antony's rhetoric, the notion of an 'inward' nobleness, distinct from external 'honour', is recouped by the play, recognised by Antony himself, even granted limited success.

Notes

1. A. C. Bradley, *Shakespearean Tragedy* (first edn 1904, repr. London, 1976), Introduction, p. xiii.
2. L. C. Knights, 'How Many Children had Lady Macbeth?' (1933) in *Explorations* (London, 1946).
3. *Measure for Measure*, edited by J. W. Lever (London, 1965). II. i. 162–3, p. 76.
4. Ibid., V. i. 521, p. 149.
5. *Troilus and Cressida*, edited by David Settler (New York, 1963) II. ii. 169, p. 88.
6. *Antony and Cleopatra*, edited by Barbara Everett (New York, 1964) III. xiii. 46, p. 129.
7. *Troilus and Cressida*, 'The Epistle to the Reader: A Never Writer, to an Ever Reader. News', 3–12, p. xli.

8. From Thersites's description of an heroic combat which is also, in another light, an undignified scrabble for reputations (equally a matter of actors and audiences). Ibid., 2, p. xli, V. iv. l, p. 172.
9. Ibid., I. iii. 103−8, p. 67.
10. Ibid., III. ii. 175−209, pp. 113−4.
11. Ibid., III. ii. 170, p. 113.
12. Ibid., III. ii. 173, p. 113.
13. Ibid., I. iii. 292−3, p. 62−3.
14. Ibid., III. ii. 212−3, p. 114.
15. A point made by Ann and John Thompson in the conclusion to *Shakespeare, Meaning and Metaphor* (Brighton, 1987) pp. 208−11.
16. *Troilus and Cressida*, IV. ii. 15−16, p.130.
17. Ibid., V. ii. 97−8, p. 162.
18. Ibid., III. i. 116, p. 105.
19. Ibid., V. x. 51−6, p. 183.
20. Ibid., III. ii. 184−97, p. 114.
21. Ibid., I. iii. 298−305, p. 63; V. ii. 106−111, p. 163.
22. Ibid., IV. v. 54−63, p. 143. Ulysses also presents us with a 'character' of Troilus, a straightforwardly 'heroic' character, but then we learn that his source is Aeneas, that unquestioned proponent of fame. Ulysses's 'character' of Cressida is his own; what might have been an authoritative fixing of the two, to get them settled before the resolution of the more public plot, simply reminds us of the different rhetorical systems by which they are known, IV. v. 95−112, p. 145.
23. Ibid., I. ii, 248−53, p. 61.
24. Ibid., IV. v. 21, p. 141.
25. Ibid., I. iii. 14−184, pp. 68−9; III. iii. 38−74, pp. 116−17.
26. Ibid., II. iii. 21−2, p. 90.
27. Ibid., III. iii. 145−51, p. 120.
28. Ibid., V. i. 6−7, p. 153.
29. Ibid., I. iii. 149−50, p. 68.
30. Ibid., III. ii. 149−52, p. 112.
31. Ibid., V. ii. 134−43, p. 164.
32. Ibid., V. ii. 161−2, p. 165.
33. Ibid., V. ii. 104−05, p. 163.
34. Ibid., III. ii. 189−90, p. 114.
35. Ibid., I. iii. 324−5, p. 74.
36. Ibid., III. iii. 201−2, p. 122. Ulysses, as he explains it, seeks also to characterise this 'mystery' as 'divine', as beyond what 'breath or pen can give expressure to'.
37. See Chapter 2, p. 77.
38. Peter Hall's (Stratford, 1960) and John Barton's (Stratford, 1968).
39. *Antony and Cleopatra*, I. iv. 1−15, p. 57.
40. Ibid., II. ii. 1−9, pp. 67−8.
41. Ibid., II. vii. 1−2, p. 93.
42. Ibid., II. vii. 14−16, p. 93.
43. Ibid., I. iii. 83−5, p. 56.
44. Ibid., III. xii. 34−5, p. 127.
45. Ibid., II. ii. 190−1, p. 75.

46. Ibid., II. ii. 247–8, p. 77.
47. *The Faerie Queene*, Book III, Canto I, Stanza 2.
48. *Antony and Cleopatra*, V. ii. 65–6, p. 169.
49. Ibid., I. iii. 84–93, p. 56.
50. Ibid., IV. xiv. 29–34, p. 156.
51. See Chapter 2, pp. 51–2.
52. *Antony and Cleopatra*, IV. xiv. 1–14, p. 155.
53. See, for example, *Macbeth*, V. v. 23–8.
54. *Antony and Cleopatra*, IV. xii. 43–7, p. 153; IV. xiii. 1–3, p. 154.
55. *Troilus and Cressida*, I. ii. 19–30, pp. 52–3.
56. *Antony and Cleopatra*, IV. xiv. 37–9, p. 156.
57. Ibid., III. xiii. 31–4, p. 128.
58. Ibid., IV. vii. 7–8, p. 146.
59. Ibid., III. xiii. 56–62, pp. 128–9.
60. Ibid., V. ii. 30–1, p. 170.
61. Ibid., V. ii. 159–70, p. 176.
62. *The Rape of Lucrece* in 'Narrative Poems', edited by William Burto (New York, 1968) 1240–46, p. 62.
63. *Antony and Cleopatra*, V. ii. 240, p. 180; V. ii. 272–7, p. 181; V. ii. 216–21, pp. 178–9.
64. Ibid., V. ii. 359, p. 185.
65. *The Rape of Lucrece*, 435–48, pp. 107–8, 715–28, p. 117.
66. *The Tragedy of Julius Caesar*, edited by William and Barbara Rosen (New York, 1963) I. ii. 67–70, p. 39.
67. Ibid., I. ii. 308–12, p. 47.
68. Ibid., II. i. 63–9, p. 57.
69. Ibid., I. ii. 100–31, pp. 40–1; I. iii, pp. 48–54; II. i. 261–70, p. 65, 310–4, pp. 67–8.
70. Ibid., II. i. 77–85, p. 58.
71. Ibid., II. i. 132–40, p. 60.
72. Ibid., II. i. 181–91, p. 62.
73. Ibid., III. i. 270–4, p. 86.
74. Ibid., I. ii. 313–5, p. 47.
75. From *Timber*, quoted in Brian Vickers (ed.), *Shakespeare: The Critical Heritage*, Vol. I, 1623–1692 (London, 1974) p. 26. *Julius Caesar*, III. i. 47–8, p. 78.
76. Ibid., I. ii. 211–2, p. 43.
77. *Julius Caesar*, II. ii. 44–8, pp. 69–70.
78. Ibid., II. i. 292–7, p. 66.
79. Ibid., V. v. 35, p. 132.
80. Ibid., V. v. 68–75, p. 134.

4

Acting and Empathy on the Elizabethan Stage

I 'NO THEATRE, NO WORLD': ACTING AND SPECTATING AS ANALOGIES FOR HUMAN BEING

The most famous English imitation of Theophrastus, Sir Thomas Overbury's collection of *Characters*, contains in its expanded version of 1615 a character, probably by the playwright John Webster, of 'An excellent Actor'. The terms of Webster's praise are familiar from rhetorical tradition – 'Whatsoever is commendable in the grave Orator, is most exquisitely perfect in him; for by a full and significant action of body, he charms our attention: sit in a full Theater, and you will thinke you see so many lines drawne from the circumference of so may eares, whilst the *Actor* is the *Center*'. The actor uses this power to invoke 'nature' ('she is often seen in the same Scaene with him') and 'by his action he fortifies morall precepts with example; for what we see him personate, we thinke truely done before us'.[1] The force of 'personate' here seems to relate to 'action' in the preceding clause. To personate is to use the resources of one's person to present, not another being in a Stanislavskian sense, but a thing *done*, action in this sense. The player's 'action', his ability to use non-verbal signals as part of a rhetorical mode, makes generalised ideas of the human ('morall precepts', notions of right or wrong *mores*) into concrete example. In such action he 'personates' generalities by giving the audience a 'center' in his individual presence, a centre he holds by a complete and vivid 'semioticisation' of his person, his visible being, 'a full and significant action of body'. The initial effect of this is to 'charm' but it also articulates aspects of human being in the most immediate way – it makes 'precepts' into 'things truely done before us'.

Webster's defence of the actor is couched in rhetorical terminology similar to that used by Nashe and Heywood in similar projects.[2] Like theirs, the thrust of his piece is a defence of the actor's profession, and his method is to emphasise specialised skill, in the context of a purposive use of rhetoric. But the largest claims for the importance of acting can be made by analogy – the stage is like the world, acting is like being. Reflections on acting and spectating are metaphorically extensible to the most basic experience of the human, as being and knowing, acting and judging, and so theatre itself is understood as a metaphorical restatement of the most urgent realities of human life. This ultimately is the grounds of its defence.

The issue of character is the issue of the construction of the subject in spectatorship as well as in performance. Like the theoretical theatre of the *Poetics*, the historical theatre of the English Renaissance defines itself in terms of its effect on the audience – character, in whatever mode, cannot be understood without such consideration, but within a rhetorical mode it is meaningless except in terms of its power to 'new mold'[3] the hearts of the spectators, the power Webster's actor so amply displays. In this chapter I will approach the question of what acting and character are in English renaissance theatre through recurrent analogies of the effect of theatre, and through the use of the theatre as an analogy of life in the world.

Actors and Parts

The 'induction' to John Marston's play *Antonio and Mellida* opens with the players 'with parts in their hands, having cloaks cast over their apparel'.[4] 'We can say our parts', says the player to present 'Piero', 'but we are ignorant in what mold we must cast our actor's'.[5] 'Actors' means 'participants in the action', characters in that sense. 'Whom do you personate?' 'Alberto' asks him, and on receiving the reply, describes the action suited to Piero's tyrant *persona*:

ALBERTO. O, ho; then thus frame your exterior shape
   To haughty form of elate majesty
   As if you helt the palsy-shaking head
   Of reeling chance under your fortune's belt
   In strictest vassalage; grow big in thought
   As swoll'n with glory of successful arms.
PIERO. If that be all, fear not, I'll suit it right.
   What cannot be proud, stroke up the hair and strut?
ALBERTO. Truth. Such rank custom is grown popular;
   And now the vulgar fashion strides as wide
   And stalks as proud upon the weakest stilts
   Of the slight'st fortunes as if Hercules
   Or burly Atlas shoulder'd up their state.[6]

The induction moves in and out of the theatre-as-world analogy to expand on the paradoxes of character that the players encounter – everyone, Alberto says, can assume the action that denotes Piero as a tyrant, so what is its special value? Balurdo plays an indeterminate role, 'the part of all the world',[7] the fool, who like Shakespeare's Ajax, is everyone and no-one. Antonio is 'an hermaphrodite, two parts in one',[8] both Antonio, and Antonio-as-amazon. Galeatzo has a 'humour ... to be describ'd by signs and tokens. For unless I were possess'd with a legion of spirits 'tis impossible to be made perspicuous by any utterance'.[9] This unsuccessful prince and suitor can find no stably defining self-presentation in Marston's competitive court-world. But Alberto and Feliche have probably the most difficult tasks. Alberto's two roles both in their different ways represent neglected virtue – the non-person of the exiled prince, Andrugio, and the scorned lover, another victim of the court, who lacks 'the outward stamp of opinion'[10] and is thus in that context uncharactered. Feliche worries at the role of a stoic philosopher, so internalised, so 'impregnably fortress'd with his own content' that the player can find no way into it 'neither able apprehension to conceit, nor what I conceit gracious ability to utter'.[11] All nonetheless strive to find fitting action, fitting epithets and to 'dispose my speech to the habit of my part'.[12] The induction is not, of course, documentary evidence, though it seems likely to offer more basic data than many commentators seem willing to allow. It explores the meaning of playing a part, on stage and in life, in ways that establish many of Marston's concerns in the play. It presents this informal rehearsal as microcosm of action and character in the world. Like most direct accounts of Elizabethan stage practice, this scene is discounted as evidence by stage-historians, as too unlike versions of staging required by modern critical conception of how the texts should be read. It may represent the crude practice of the boy players by whom it was first performed, but *Shakespeare's* players, it would seem, must have been doing something else, probably consonant with the post-Stanislavskian practice of the modern English actor, but somehow unrecorded at the time.[13] In the context of Elizabethan ideas of character there seems no reason to assume that Marston is doing any more than wittily expanding on commonplaces, with the necessary concision of a theatrical presentation of back-stage practice, but with an appeal to the audience's knowledge that this was in some sense what actors *did*. Central to Marston's sense of what is interesting about the process of acting is the notion of a 'character'. The most intriguing aspects of its construction are conventionality – the rules for construction and reading – and multiplicity – the number of apparently contradictory 'characters' available to one player, even across sexual difference. And there is also the problem of interiority, of asocial selves – what is the 'action' of the philosopher, the exile, the man without 'the stamp' of his immediate society?

If there is a distinction to be drawn between the rhetorically schooled boy players and the professional rhetoricians of the adult theatres, it may be in the degree of complexity with which similar effects – of discontinuity, interiority, disguise, misfitting and so on – could be exploited. Webster's character also focuses on the multiplicity of the actor's roles – we may 'take him (at severall times) for many of them'.[14] This basic idea is developed later in the passage: 'All men have beene of his occupation: and indeed, what hee doth fainedly that doe others essentially: this day one plaies a Monarch, the next a private person. Heere one acts a Tyrant, on the morrow an Exile; A Parasite this man to-night, t[o]-morrow Precisian, and so of divers others'.[15] The fragmentation into *personae* and/or elaborated characters of a single person's life is a *topos* that English renaissance dramatists return to persistently. Webster gives two versions of it here. The first describes a tragic action, two versions of the change in identity consequent on a fall from power. What is it for Richard II or Antony, to seek to be 'a private person'? Is it possible for them? In seeking it, what do they become? The other, the change of a parasite into a precisian (or Puritan) is a comic juxtaposition of the *personae*, with perhaps a hint of the underlying 'hypocrisy' (or actorliness) of one who could be both.

Such partial identities (referred to as 'parts', of course) are, while within the scope of one person, in themselves essentially discrete. This may perhaps be touched on in Webster's equation of the player with the painter. Portraiture is an often-used analogy of rhetorical character presentation; character descriptions in plays tend to be vividly pictorial, not only in their use of 'fitting' visual detail, but in their shaping into a visual unity, a Horatian *'ut pictura poesis'*,[16] whether allegorically iconic (Henry V as the chorus presents him)[17] or comically detailed (Hotspur's 'Popinjay' messenger[18]). Each 'character' is a portrait, recognisable, distinct and self-contained. But what does it mean that, like portraits, one painter may produce many, and that none could be said to represent the 'whole' of the 'sitter' (who can thus equally well be said to produce a multiplicity of 'characters' of his or her self)?

'To square out a Character by our English levell', according to the

1622 edition of the Overbury collection, 'it is a picture (reall or personall) quaintly drawne, in various colours, all of them heightened by one shadowing. It is a quicke and softe touch of many strings, all shutting up in one musical cloze: It is wit's descant on any plaine song.'[19] These analogies stress the relation between multiplicity and singleness in the construction of a set-piece character – names, fit detail, (physical, linguistic and behavioural) and ingenious analogies are many, but they point to one unifying principle or 'theme'. When developed in plays, this kind of character acquires further multiplicity, in its relation to other modes of identification, to the elaborate language of 'significant action', to the very act of playing. The 'reall or personall' distinction is a legal distinction, between litigation addressed to a person, for compensation, for example, as opposed to litigation for a specific (so 'real') item of property.[20] 'Personal' implies the validation of individual identity, 'real' the validation of some transferable goods – 'real' meaning by derivation, royal, the crown being the ultimate legal source of any 'right' to land or property. The distinction is made in the preface lightly and in passing – it is hardly a 'clue' to the characters, but it does suggest allusively, as do the comparisons to painting and music, that the notion of knowable identities, predicated on one system, is alien to the 'character' mode. Does the character deal in transferable properties, or personal identity? Are such identities 'personal' or are they validated and/or defined by 'real' power? The allusive and the problematic are part of the pleasures offered by character writing (dramatic and non-dramatic) in the early seventeenth century. Character effects make 'pictures' that are often discontinuous with each other and/or contradictory to other information, other character ideas that we are given. They may be pictures produced in action only momentarily and within the framework of another adopted role – in a disguise, most obviously, but in anecdote too, in allegorical vignettes and metatheatrical presentations like Marston's induction – the very plenitude of these devices is a virtuoso test of the Elizabethan actor, a test of fluidity, crispness and control. Modern actors, searching for Stanislavskian wholeness or 'character' blur and make unnecessarily puzzling such moments in Shakespearian texts – they are, quite rightly, seen as an embarrassment to 'correct' modern acting, thus rendering a role like Edgar in Lear almost unplayable. How to find a Stanislavskian 'line-through' *that*? Character is then the defining aim of the Elizabethan actor, the source of his most startling (useful or dangerous?) effects, but it is *rhetorical* character, as I have described it so far. The effects which this lends to the sophisticated writer are evident in the complexities, the 'richness' in character, of the most ambitious Elizabethan plays. An awareness of the source and process of these effects does not 'alienate' or distance an audience, it articulates the audience-player relation in a way which intensifies such effects. Webster's use of character-effects, like Marston's, is often an exploitation of such discontinuities, such contradictions of information and action, of self-assessment and satirical vignette. In *The White Devil* and *The Duchess of Malfi* this is elaborated into an aesthetic of the unknowable, into melancholic darkness in the second case, or into a resistant and anti-melancholic self-staging in the first. These are two polarities of the use of character as problematic, both amply represented in Shakespeare, and both more relevant to attempts to account for the complex 'actorliness' of these plays than modern metaphors of 'depth' and 'roundness'.

The character of the 'excellent actor' ends up problematising itself. It concludes with an attack on a rival, anti-theatrical, writer of characters and a reflection on character-writing as a mode of moral judgement – 'I valew a worthy Actor by the corruption of some few of the quality, as I would doe gold in the oare; I should not minde the drosse, but the purity of the metall'.[21] This follows logically on from his consideration of what the actor does, in that, by classing actors and orators together, Webster places acting and rhetorical character-drawing as aspects of the same thing. What, then, is the validity of presenting *as* individual what is to be understood as general? Webster's last statement raises just this question. Indeed, for all the orthodoxy of his basic approach to 'the actor', his formulations open up issues explored more thoroughly elsewhere in his work. The validity of the character mode, developed in set-piece speeches or piecemeal throughout a play – and one must assume worked out in the player's 'action' – is made paradoxical in this rhetorical character of a character-producing rhetorician. Webster makes the familiar point about the representation of historical figures, but he inflects it in a new way: 'a man of deepe thought might apprehend the Ghosts of our ancient *Heroes* walk't againe, and take him (at severall times) for many of them'.[22] For Nashe or Heywood the effect of this is extrovert and purposive, it recruits the audience into the heroic historical world. For Webster it is an effect of introspection, even melancholy. The dead come again not to a social group, but to a pensive *individual* ('a man of deepe thought') and they come not in the eternal life of fame, but as 'Ghosts'. Similarly his prefatory verses to Heywood's *Apology* bear witness to the role of morality in his development of the fame trope –

not as the thing 'conquered' or annulled, but as a transforming reality decisive in its fixing of moral identities:

> Be therefore your owne iudgement your defence
>   Which shall approue you better than my praise,
> Whilst I in right of sacred Innocence,
>   Durst ore each guilded Tombe this knowne truth raise.
> "Who dead would not be acted by their will,
> "It seemes such men haue acted their liues ill."[23]

So death finally fixes identities partial and transitory in life – the excellent actor acquires a paradoxical identity, only perceptible in the parts he had played, the multiple death involved in the death of one performer – 'I observe, of all men living a worthy Actor in one kind is the strongest motive of affection that can be: for when he dies, we cannot be persuaded any man can does his parts like him'.[24] 'In one kind' points to a degree of specialisation – the 'kind' or 'type' in which an actor would tend to specialise provides another analogue of the problematic relation of individuality to the common, a problematic focused for him, as for Shakespeare, by the players' arts of action and character, out of which, like many renaissance writers, they frame a model of human life and mortality.

Watching and Judging

Ralegh's madrigal 'What is our life?' develops the life-as-theatre *topos* along two different though equally traditional lines.

> What is our life? A play of passion,
> Our mirth the music of division,
> Our mother's wombs the tiring houses be,
> Where we are dressed for this short comedy,
> Heaven the judicious sharp spectator is,
> That sits and marks who still doth act amiss,
> Our graves that hide us from the searching sun,
> Are like drawn curtains when the play is done,
> Thus march we playing to our latest rest,
> Only we die in earnest, that's no jest.

A play, in its brevity and insubstantiality, is an emblem of the transience of life. 'Only we die in earnest, that's no jest'; in death we return not to the off-stage professional life of 'the tiring houses' from which we came, but to something more final. In Ralegh's conceit neither play nor life devalues the other; 'our mirth the music of division', is both an undercutting equivalence (so that is what mirth amounts to) and an enhancing diagnosis (so that is the experience of human mirth – both music and division, for one is the foundation of the other). In identifying the audience of his 'play', however, Ralegh draws on an older tradition, in which plays, far from bearing the taint (however subtle) of vanity, are an image of the urgency with which we must scrutinise and carry out our every act. As in the Prudentius *Psychomachia* and its later metatheatrical analogues,

> Heaven the judicious sharp spectator is,
> That sits and marks who still doth act amiss.[25]

Does the 'vanity' idea infect the notion of heaven's spectatorship? does it trivialise heaven to present it as one of those critical spectators often mocked in plays as one of the playhouses' most recognisable types, as part of the essentially fictive life that theatre calls into being? The poem observes a fine if fittingly insubstantial balance. It allows both the sense of a metaphysical reality behind the scenes *and* an intimation of nothingness, and weights the balance only slightly towards the second.

Heywood's development of similar ideas in his prefatory poem to the *Apology* takes the absorption of 'heaven' into the idea of theatre (an effect of the conversion of the idea from religious *topos* to secular conceit), towards an assertively positive but startlingly paradoxical conclusion. He marks his initial statement of the world-as-theatre idea with the marginal note 'So compared by the fathers' (i.e., of the Church). But his final note underlines a more heterodox conclusion:

> If then the world a Theater present,
> As by the roundnesse it appeares most fit,
> Built with starre-galleries to hye ascent,
> In which *Iehove* doth as spectator sit,
> And chiefe determiner to applaud the best,
> And their evill actions doomes the rest,
> To end disgrac't whilst others praise inherit.
>> He that denyes then Theaters should be
>> He may as well deny a world to me.

'No Theater, no world', affirms Heywood.[26] The traditionally Christian idea of heaven's spectatorship can be seen in its application to the Elizabethan secular theatre to confer a god-like role on the human audience. Or, at least, in transferring the idea from God, it uses this structure to describe human spectatorship, to account for that particular theatre's construction of the audience-as-subject. Thus god-like practices of judgement become the responsibility of a human audience, and a notion of theatre emerges in which human self-judgement – on an individual or social level – is the main dynamic of spectatorship.

There are many renaissance accounts – in stories, commentaries and plays – of how theatrical action and character work on the audience, and what notion of an audience they require. The cultural centrality of theatre, as much as an analogue of life in the world as of a rhetorical praxis in its own right, depends on a sense of theatre as the most powerful and complex development of rhetorical languages, thus conferring on theatre a status which turns the idea of judgemental spectatorship from religious analogy into human fact. Theatre is an arena of intense affective forces, and renaissance attempts to describe it tend to account for and justify the use of those forces from within a framework of rhetorical terminology and common analogies. Modern notions of empathy are, by virtue of the post-romantic psychopathology that they require, both too simple and too mysterious to help us understand this. Many of the effects (the affective forces) that we would class under a consideration of empathy are in play, but in a different relation to each other and used to different ends. The rhetorical model is of course complicated and modified to the demands of a new context, public secular urban theatre, conceived of on the most ambitious scale.

The third book of Heywood's *Apology* presents definitions of theatre in terms of its purpose and effect. The 'use' of different forms of theatre is, in familiar rhetorical terms, a re-making of audience-as-subject, presented within the context of Heywood's argument as a recognition of proper social praxis – 'sometimes of Curtesans, to divulge their subtelties and snares, in which young men may be entangled, shewing them the means to avoid them'.[27] Sometimes 'Playes are writ with this ayme, and carryed with this methode, to teach the subiects obedience to their King, to shew people the untimely ends of such as have moved turmults, commotions, and insurrections, to present them with the flourishing estate of such as live in obedience, exhorting them to allegeance, dehorting them from all trayterous and fellonious stratagems'.[28] As these two examples show, Heywood's argument is angled towards city authorities, his aim to establish the theatre as a city institution, to counter claims for its disruptive effect and to win civic status for actors. As we have seen, the identification of the audience with particular social groupings, the articulation and justification of the institutional identities in which they participate, provides the dynamic of Heywood's own history plays, where similar ideas to those of the *Apology* are worked out in more complex dramatic form. The mechanism of response required here is essentially the same as that of emulation/fame, but its effect is societal rather than individual. To respond individually would be comically inappropriate. Heywood may ask 'why should not the lives of these worthyes, presented in these our dayes, effect the like wonders in the Princes of our times?',[29] but his audience is not an audience of princes. The citizen and his wife in Beaumont's *The Knight of the Burning Pestle* (1607), express some unease at what they are likely to see at the private theatre they have accidentally ended up at, and two of Heywood's history plays are instanced as the kind of entertainment that they would prefer.

> I'm a stranger here: I was ne'er at one of these plays, as they say, before: but I should have seen *Jane Shore* once, and my husband hath promised me any time this twelve month to carry me to *The Bold Beauchamps* . . . .[30]

Beaumont's play turns on a joking literalisation of 'emulation' – Rafe, the apprentice, encouraged by his master and mistress, takes part in the play as a heroic grocer in search of great deeds, the knight of the title. Heroic individuation can only be properly empathised with by a being with equal scope for action, the 'English Prince' at the top of the hierarchy within which Heywood's theoretical construct of a theatre works, who is thus its ultimate audience. Others, as we have seen in the case of Shakespeare's Talbot and Henry V, and the play's orchestration of audience response to these figures, find a proper place in relation to them – the model of social relations the plays construct is not simply 'on stage', it is enacted through audience response (emulation/ reverence/exhorting and dehorting), through the play's construction of the audience as a particular kind of society. But we must not assume that, outside the special task which Heywood's *Apology* sets itself, the effects to which these devices work are necessarily *confirmatory* – of a social order, or moral system. The conception of the text which they imply can be mobilised to higher degrees of complexity; it is available to a broad range of ideological project, a flexibility consequent on its avowal of power relations, its consciousness of identifying systems. The *Apology* locates such power relations with a cautious, conventional and non-specific conservatism. Individual plays present them in much more problematic and questionable forms.

Empathetic response to the fame-derived individual is ruled out for all but a few exceptional, ideal, perhaps strictly fictional, individual audience members. The plays are more likely to address their audience through the 'common' codes of social identity. The audience are nonetheless often seen as experiencing some kind of individuating revelation in the play. For Heywood, comedy is 'the imitation of life, the glasse of custome, and the image of truth';[31] 'custome', the general non-individuated realities of social life, is revealed in comedy, but the effect of the mirror good theatre holds up to the audience can be sharply, even sensationally isolating. In a mirror, one sees oneself; one tends also (and surely this is the force of the mirror analogy in its classical mediaeval and humanist history) to be surprised by what one sees. The mirror gives us something we cannot question, but the revelation is a shock, whether pleasant or unpleasant, as it is given to us as 'other', as outside our selves. It makes us aware of a boundary on the self — this is perhaps the most crucial of all those otherwise unacknowledged things that mirrors confront us with. By using the mirror as an analogy for a play's relation to its audience, for its mimesis of the human and construction of the audience as human (as observing subject, and as that which is observed), renaissance theatre presents a different account of its processes than either the arena of the *psychomachia* (which it takes over and modifies, absorbs, as we have seen, into its notion of human spectatorship) and the modern 'empathy' (with which it shares some effects and for which of course it still provides some written scenarios). The renaissance theatre is a mirror-effect in that it offers its audience a shocking (perhaps), implicitly otherwise unobtainable sense of itself as human (as Shakespeare's protagonists constantly and persuasively remind each other, no-one can see their own face unaided, so we are all helplessly in thrall to offered accounts of our identity).

Shakespeare makes the point more forcibly than Heywood does, for Hamlet, who gives the following version of the *topos* has even more at stake in the matter. 'Anything so overdone is from the purpose of playing, whose end both at the first and now, was and is, to hold as 'twere the mirror up to nature; to show virtue her own feature, scorn her own image, and the very age and body of the time his form and pressure'.[32] Nature here is of course human nature, as the mirror reflects those who look into it. Virtue present in such nature is given feature, made identifiable, as in Prudentius's justification of his *Psychomachia*, made known to itself and so strengthened. Scorn, more wittily, gets its own reaction back to fix its identity in that unbecoming facial image – audience response is itself called into play, provocatively turned back on itself by the skilled player. The last statement is more puzzling – 'the time' is perhaps also personified, given gender (his) and a 'body', even the conventional (old) 'age' – so, as with virtue and scorn, personification is aptly used to describe the construction in mirror/ stage as a visible human image of the otherwise unseen and unseeable (ourselves, here de-personalised, seen as our historical moment, not as our experience of ourselves as individuals). The more immediate meaning of 'age' is as the contemporary moment in which the audience exists, given back to it in a knowable 'form'. Pressure is an odd idea of how a mirror receives an image and gives it back; it seems to derive instead from the character metaphor, which works also through 'form'. The mirror works through the players' rhetorical skills, which, as Hamlet acknowledges, work towards the 'purpose of playing', the showing of the audience back to itself, through the articulation of character devices.

Personification, abstractions, and a generalised sense of 'time' are, like Heywood's 'custome', a reminder that the components of what the mirror shows are not in themselves individuated or personal. 'The purpose of playing' is not, as in empathetic theatre, to offer us, the audience, individual figures with whom we can 'identify', but rather to give us back something we would not otherwise know as ourselves. The mirror idea focuses the common truths of 'custome', but leads us to identify them as our reflection. This perhaps lies behind the fondness of the Elizabethans for stories of individuals tricked into self-declaration by the powerful effect of playing. Heywood tells two such stories as examples of the extreme effect of the actor's art, as individuations of the social and moral force such art can have.

At *Lin* in *Norfolke*, the then Earle of *Sussex* players acting the old History of Fryer *Francis*, and presenting a woman, who insatiately doting on a young gentleman, has (the more securely to enjoy his affection) mischievously and secretly murdered her husband, whose ghost haunted her, and at divers times in her most solitary and private contemplations, in most horrid and fearful shapes, appeared, and stood before her. As this was acted, a townes-woman (till then of good estimation and report) finding her conscience at this presentment [sic] extremely troubled, suddenly skritched and cry'd out Oh my husband, my husband! I see the ghost of my husband fiercely threatening and menacing me. At which shrill and u'expected [sic] outcry, the people around her, moov'd to a strange amazement, inquired the reason of her clamour, when presently un-urged, she told them that seven years ago, she, to be possest of such a Gentleman (meaning him) had poysoned her husband, whose fearful image personated itselfe in the shape of that ghost: whereupon the murderess was apprehended, before the Justices further examined, and by her voluntary confession after con-demned. That this is true, as well by the report of the Actors as the records of the Towne, there are many eyewitnesses of this accident yet living, vocally to confirme it.[33]

The stage, particularly for Shakespeare, has an enticingly paradoxical relation to the concealed, to history's only partially recorded crimes (as in the first history cycle and in *Richard II* and *Richard III*) and, as here, to crimes concealed, as a dungeon or grave, in guilty memory. Hamlet has heard such stories as Heywood's, and puts them successfully to the test.

Mirrors and Man: *Hamlet I*

A recurrent theme in defences of theatre like Nashe's and Heywood's is its effect on the melancholy and sloth to which idle young men are prone. Rosencrantz and Guilderstern report back to Claudius and Gertrude after Hamlet has outlined for them his notion of a world theatre centred on the human, but in which the human is itself meaningless, nothing but a 'quintessence of dust'. Rosencrantz has already, in conversation with Hamlet, reduced his melancholy to face value. The action of the players, he says, can reanimate the sick prince, by restoring his capacity for 'delight'.[34] Claudius and Gertrude both like the idea, but the players' art is recuperative in a larger sense than they realise. Playing, for Hamlet, brings 'is' and 'seems' together – it externalises the hidden, the buried, the secret, re-orders that which his knowledge first of 'incest' and then of murder has put 'out of joint'. His rhetorical and theatrical exploration of this disjunction offers him both the means and the obstacle to that exposé, that public 'show' and staged destruction, which mark revenge as a theatrical, a rhetorical, act.

Hamlet's welcoming of the players marks a resolution to the displacement of man from the imagined world stage that his 'melancholy' sketched for Rosencrantz and Guilderstern – the stage with, as so many commentators have pointed out, a distinct resemblance to the Elizabethan theatre, to its metatheatrical extension as an arena of scrutiny and judgement in which both the human and the divine participate.[35] The players are masters of the rhetorical representation of the human, in ways that Hamlet celebrates on their entry by listing and wittily elaborating the *personae* available to them, and which he must try to control in his anxiety that representation be perfect, that it does not fail and so present instead (so show in the mirror) another of the 'antic' parodies of the human which people his speeches. They must not act like those that 'neither having the accent of Christians, not the gait of Christian, pagan, nor man, have so strutted and bellowed that I have thought some of nature's journeymen had made men, and not made them well, they imitated humanity so abominably'.[36] The split between 'is' and 'seems' is posited in the play as a crisis in a discourse of the human – the players, in their control over its terms, offer at least a temporary resolution. Hamlet's advice to the players is an Horatian presentation of issues of discretion and control, of a seemly as opposed to a disordered image of 'man'. Like his memory of his father, and his evaluation of Horatio, the players represent the temporary or marginal resolution in such an image that is all the play seems to allow.

The effect of Hamlet's play is a heightened and more specific acting out of the 'mirror' analogy for audience response. Theatre is an arena of recognition and self-judgement; it returns to the audience a view of itself-as-other, and by doing so marks, identifies, re-characters it. In doing so it is both mirror and stamp. This hybrid analogy for the impact of rhetorical 'charactering' underpinned the advice to the players, and is then repeated and developed in Hamlet's interview with his mother.

His self-appointed task in the 'closet' scene is a continuation of the project of the play scene. As his soliloquy tells us, the 'mirror' of the play has given Claudius back his crime, to lodge itself in his newly apparent 'conscience', to fix his identity irredeemably in the face even of himself and 'heaven'.[37] Similarly Hamlet sets up for Gertrude 'a glass/Where you may see the inmost part of you'.[38] This has been part of the Gonzago play as well – the elaborate protestations and vows of the player queen (conceivably the short speech which Hamlet has inserted into an already determined scenario) have acted as such a mirror, but one to which Gertrude allowed herself only a wittily guarded response.[39] He approached this meeting with her in a strikingly stagey speech, aptly so in view of the preceding scene: Hamlet is full of the triumph of his mousetrap's rhetorical affects. But his Lucianus imitation is interrupted by a sense of a necessary control – a 'discretion' like that he enjoined on the passion of the players: 'let not ever/The soul of Nero enter this firm bosom' – Nero being notorious not only as the murderer of his mother but as one of those Roman emperors whose incorporation of real violence into their stage shows provided renaissance commentators with some morally ambivalent illustrations of the power of theatrical representation.[40] Here the independent force of 'words' must be harnessed carefully, kept from spilling over into a violence that would break the Ghost's injunction not to 'let thy soul contrive/Against thy mother aught'.[41] His rhetorical mirror, the obsessive charactering of Gertrude's acts, and of her former and her present husband, succeeds in imprinting on the 'penetrable stuff' of Gertrude's heart the signs of a guilt of which no previous utterance of hers had given any inkling.[42] Hamlet's first speech was triggered by his mother's distinction of the 'common' and the 'particular', but he diverted her attempt to make him either justify or resign his own particularity by choosing another more casual opposition in her question as the basis for his reply – 'is' as opposed to 'seems'. Gertrude made no real distinction between the two, but Hamlet uses them as the basis for a flamboyant riddling disruption of the court's fluent pragmatic and at that point wholly confident language. The gap he opens up now opens up for Gertrude and Claudius too.

The idea of theatre thus introduces into *Hamlet* a model of the human, a discourse of character, to be reflected on and problematised over the whole of the play. The Hamlet story allows Shakespeare to articulate some of the basic suppositions of rhetorical theatre, to present the skills and effects of this theatre at its most developed. In doing so it provides us with the means to reconsider the notion of empathy, particularly in the inset or ecphrastic 'scene' it shares with *The Rape of Lucrece* – Hecuba's grief at the fall of Troy.

The speech of the players that inspires Hamlet to try out some character effects on Claudius is 'Aeneas' tale to Dido'. Polonius gets bored when the player moves out of narrative to rail against fortune, but it is a necessary shift in his rhetorical strategy to instate himself as spectator of something he has never seen, to put himself thus inside the narrative, and so construct a position which he can then invite us to share with him. 'But who – ah woe – had seen the mobled queen'. He then makes Hecuba visible to us, offers us a painterly character of her.

Had we seen her (which we now in a way have) we would (as he has) rail thus on fortune – so he *has* seen her; so have an audience of the gods. They weep, he weeps, perhaps Dido weeps (the speech is addressed to her and she weeps, though for a different reason, at the end of the equivalent narration in Virgil).[43] If he is really good the audience should weep. Hamlet is impressed. The player skillfully creates circle within circle of 'audience' to an imaginary event, superimposing one on the other (the theatre audience, Dido's court, the Danish court, himself, the gods) by giving all access to a rhetorically created subject position – 'but who' – and leading us to a reaction – 'ah woe' – which pre-empts its actual object – 'the mobled queen', who then becomes its character, the character of woe, of human loss. It means something different to all of them, of course, but it allows all those differences to come together in some idea of a godlike 'audience' whose overview we can even as human individuals momentarily share. *'Sunt Lacrimae rerum'*, as Virgil's Aeneas realised, when he himself confronted a picture of Troy.[44] Shakespeare's Lucrece finds a conveniency to herself in pictured characters of the same figures: ' . . . the power of Greece/For Helen's rape the city to destroy',[45] as her husband and his friends are to destroy Tarquin's regime. Lucrece's reading of the painting is a reading of its character effects, her use of it a consideration of 'action' fitting to her own story. But the narrative moves off from Lucrece to describe the 'conceited painter's'[46] command of character effect in less personal terms. The first part of this ecphrasis is presented as the perceptions of an impersonal viewer ('you', 'one'). 'Such sweet observance in this work was had/That one might see those far-off eyes look sad'.[47] The painter's 'observance' (care) puts into the work an effect of another kind of observance, of looking and being looked at. Those eyes are looking out at Troy, at the imminent revenge of a rape. Where does the sadness lie? Observance/look/see would suggest it was transferable, even if it seems unlikely to be transferred to Lucrece (given the reason for which she may be assumed to have sought out a painting on this particular subject). But she fixes, as Hamlet does, on Hecuba.

> To this well-painted piece is Lucrece come,
> To find a face where all distress is stelled.
> Many she sees where cares have carved some,
> But none where all distress and dolour dwelled
> Till she despairing Hecuba beheld,
>   Staring on Priam's wounds with her old eyes,
>   /Which bleeding under Pyrrhus' proud foot lies.

In her the painter had anatomized
Time's ruin, beauty's wrack, and grim care's reign;
Her cheeks with chops and wrinkles were disguised;
Of what she was no semblance did remain.
Her blue blood, changed to black in every vein,
　　Wanting the spring that those shrunk pipes had fed,
　　Showed life imprisoned in a body dead.

On this sad shadow Lucrece spends her eyes
And shapes her sorrow to the beldame's woes,
Who nothing wants to answer her but cries
And bitter words to ban her cruel foes.
The painter was no god to lend her those;
　　And therefore Lucrece swears he did her wrong
　　To give her so much grief and not a tongue.[48]

Her 'empathy' with Hecuba takes the form of matching painted, observable grief to her own verbalised grief. But it takes her to an observation that contradicts her initial impulse for looking at the picture.

'Show me the strumpet that began this stir,
That with my nails her beauty I may tear.
Thy heat of lust, fond Paris, did incur
This load of wrath that burning Troy doth bear.
Thy eye kindled the fire that burneth here,
　　And here in Troy, for trespass of thine eye,
　　The sire, the son, the dame and daughter die.

'Why should the private pleasure of some one
Become the public plague of many moe?
Let sin, alone committed, light alone
Upon his head that hath transgressed so;
Let guiltless souls be freed from guilty woe:
　　For one's offense why should so many fall,
　　To plague a private sin in general?'[49]

The public/private distinction she makes here is the result of a diversion of her sympathies, towards those on whom the rape is to be revenged. So the effect of the painter's skill in using character is to complicate initial reactions, to lead to a 'general' point, but one that can only be expressed as a question. Her search for other objects of

empathy leads her back to her own situation by even more
problematic means.

> She throws her eyes about the painting round,
> And who she finds forlorn, she doth lament.
> At last she sees a wretched image bound
> That piteous looks to Phrygian shepherds lent.
> His face, though full of cares, yet showed content;
>   Onward to Troy with the blunt swains he goes,
>   So mild that patience seemed to scorn his woes.
>
> In him the painter labored with his skill
> To hide deceit, and give the harmless show
> An humble gait, calm looks, eyes wailing still,
> A brow unbent that seemed to welcome woe,
> Cheeks neither red nor pale, but mingled so
>   That blushing red no guilty instance gave
>   Nor ashy pale the fear that false hearts have . . .."[50]

This is Sinon, who betrayed Troy. The painter here is trapped in a
paradox of his art — a paradox of Shakespeare's own art too, as the
plays persistently remind us. How can deceit function (that is, deceive)
and still be readable as deceit? Lucrece knows from her own experience
that she can read this 'character' *against* its constitutive signs; it returns
her to the debate in which she and Tarquin, both 'internally' and in
dialogue, were engaged before the rape. Her only recourse is to
destroy the painted signs, an act which returns us to the materiality of
both paint and flesh.

> Here, all enraged, such passion her assails
> That patience is quite beaten from her breast.
> She tears the senseless Sinon with her nails,
> Comparing him to the unhappy guest
> Whose deed hath made herself herself detest.
>   At last she smilingly with this gives o'er:
>   'Fool, fool!' quoth she, 'his wounds will not be sore.'[51]

The experience of mimesis by a defined individual is here, as in
Hamlet's case, problematic—effects like the modern idea of empathy
are involved, but their effects are partial and contradictory. What we
cannot know or feel is as sharply defined for us by such experience as

are the things that we can, that we think we know. We feel neither as 'public' nor 'private'; we are made to confront the difficult distinction between the two. We are given access to things that surprise and disturb us, are not allowed a 'safe' position, for our own experience is required as the means to interpret what we see, but what we are told about that experience revivifies it, makes it dangerously present.

So much is clear from a reading of this passage against our Elizabethan murder stories, of which *Hamlet* is simply the best known and most articulately self-reflexive. But the impersonal first section of the ecphrasis carefully recapitulates on rhetorical ideas of character so as to lead up to an epigrammatic reflection on another larger though related aspect of Shakespearian character. The harmonious and successful working of character devices leads from the expertly rendered physiognomies of Ulysses and Ajax (here, as in *Troilus and Cressida*, the opposite poles, knowledge and self-ignorance, in a story whose character content Shakespeare sees as diagrammatically fixed), to the detailed rendering of Nestor's oratory and its individual and collective effects (painting 'doing' rhetoric, in a way that points up 'actions' importance) and finally to Achilles.

> For much imaginary work was there;
> Conceit deceitful, so compact, so kind
> That for Achilles' image stood his spear,
> Griped in an armed hand; himself behind
> Was left unseen, save to the eye of mind:
> A hand, a foot, a face, a leg, a head
> Stood for the whole to be imagined.[52]

The heroic Achilles seems to have to be 'imagined' in *Troilus and Cressida* too, since the signs we are given there add up to something else. A qualitative distinction between an object of knowledge required by the text, and the knowledge granted us by the signals the text provides is an effect of Shakespearian character that I have already touched upon. That object of knowledge may be (may perhaps most often be) the heroic 'reality' of fame—the Chorus's Henry V, Cleopatra's Antony—or it may be a self, like Richard of Bordeaux's or Hamlet's (problematic selves of powerless princes). Shakespeare's 'conceit deceitful' proceeds like the painter's through an idea of 'kind', through what we take to be common or natural to particular kinds of states of being. But it leads us to an Achilles 'imaginary' in the sense that the last line of the stanza evokes in witty contrast to the older meaning (painterly, visual) of the first line. It must, to paraphrase Hippolyta's thoughtful reponse to the inadequacies of the mechanicals' play, be our imagination and not the 'imaginary work' of the text.[53] Lucrece's Trojan ecphrasis coincides with Hamlet's, as a reflection on the very idea of character.

II *HAMLET* II: CHARACTER, ACTION AND INTERIORITY

A modern reader may well describe the model of character that I have explored so far as 'external'. A simple metaphorics of 'inside' and 'outside' provided a recurrent grid for literary, rhetorical, banally colloquial accounts of human subjecthood. Individuality, in the texts I have discussed, tends to be presented as 'outside', as 'character' written in 'fame'—character, in depending on an idea of construction and perception, of writing and reading, impression and acknowledgement, is, according to this model, 'external'. This does not mean that these texts function without an idea of 'interiority', but it does mean that such a thing is essentially discrete from character, and that it is in character, not in the sense of an inner self, that our 'individuality' inheres. Interiority is a concern of the fame-defined figures discussed in Chapter 3, but its relation to their known *characters* is paradoxical, even oppositional. Nor does that interiority provide them with a discrete and ownable core of individual value—it is, rather, yet another microcosmic arena in which the *agons* of a larger praxis are recollected and repeat themselves. Shakespeare's most celebrated interiorities—Richard II, Brutus, Hamlet—are all caught, in their different ways, in a tantalising metaphorics of inner and outer.

Richard's interior world is modelled to the pattern of exterior social relations. In this play, microcosmic correspondence plays a peculiarly important structural role.

> I have been studying how I may compare
> This prison where I live unto the world:
> And for because the world is populous,
> And here is not a creature but myself,
> I cannot do it.[54]

Richard's solitude endangers the economy of comparison—there is nothing in his cell that he can use as a model of the larger world outside it (not even, one assumes, the animals and furniture Lear uses in similar straits[55]). If there is nothing to mark the difference between himself and that which is outside himself but inside the cell, then the limits of the cell and of his self are co-extensive. The cell/world comparison is unstable. His thoughts become people, who themselves think and feel, in ways that bifurcate further into paradoxes and dialectic internal to themselves

> My brain I'll prove the female to my soul,
> My soul the father and these two beget
> A generation of still-breeding thoughts;
> And these same thoughts people this little world,
> In humours like the people of this world,
> For no thought is contented. The better sort,
> As thoughts of things divine are intermixed
> With scruples, and do set the word itself
> Against the word; as thus: 'Come, little ones';
> And then again,
> 'It is as hard to come as for a camel
> To thread the postern of a small needle's eye.'[56]

Thus distancing is impossible; these are not externalised entities that Richard can rule; they represent to him his own perceptions, and the materiality of his literal enclosure defines cell/self/world not as a kingdom but as a prison.

> Thoughts tending to ambition, they do plot
> Unlikely wonders: how these vain weak nails
> May tear a passage through the flinty ribs
> Of this hard world, my ragged prison walls . . ..[57]

This is to be resolved perhaps in Richard's death speech, an ultimate escape

> Mount, mount, my soul; thy seat is up on high,
> Whilst my gross flesh sinks downward here to die.[58]

In life he returns continually to his own lack of 'content', unable to assert, in the terms of a courtly stoicism, 'my mind to me a kingdom is'.[59] The speech then shifts to a different account of unstable identity, in the metaphor of the player and the *persona*/part.[60]

But there is a world in Richard's cell, a world that he addresses his speech to—the theatre audience. The play picks this up, reminds us of our presence. No privacy is possible to Richard—only nothingness can confer that on him, only nothingness can in effect un-king him. Music sounds halfway through the speech—giving him at last an analogy, for Richard can only operate in analogies, can produce nothing from 'within' himself. The substance that he laid claim to cannot be experienced in complete privacy; it comes into being in a social arena, its effect is, in the end, rhetorical. Richard escapes into an unknowable 'nothing', but his fame leaves an indelible mark on history's text.

Hamlet's interiority is, at its simplest, accountable for in similar ways to Richard's. Its initial expression draws on two ideas familiar from the earlier play—the inner 'substance', in excess of all possible 'show', and the desire for a painless quasi-natural dispersal of physical identity—Hamlet wants his 'too too solid flesh' to 'melt' like Richard's 'mockery king of snow'.[61] Hamlet's positing of this problematic interiority, this 'substance' apart from physical being is, like Richard's, stated as a challenge, to the court of a usurper.

> 'Tis not alone my inky cloak, good mother,
> Nor customary suits of solemn black,
> Nor windy suspiration of forc'd breath,
> No, nor the fruitful river in the eye,
> Nor the dejected haviour of the visage,
> Together with all forms, moods, shapes of grief,
> That can denote me truly. These indeed seem,
> For they are actions that a many might play;
> But I have that within which passes show,
> These but the trappings and the suits of woe.[62]

However much Hamlet may disclaim 'show' and 'play', this is a formally wrought, neatly rounded, very public, speech. It establishes, as Richard's uncrowning ceremony does, a personal power position in an almost mocking relation to his enemy's self-staging, a rhetorical evasion of a concerted attempt to re-define him from outside.

As powerless prince, in, as one might put it, an 'internal exile', Hamlet's inner unshowable self is explicable in terms of the ideas I have outlined in previous chapters—his distance from an apt social praxis, his exile from 'fame', the cancelling, or at least occlusion, of his genealogical identity, either blank him out (from history, ultimately) or force him, in the playing time of the theatrical moment, into the construction of a private self. Antony, defeated, no longer Antony, desired to live 'a private man at Athens'[63] —that would be unthinkable, certainly unstageable, and the play ultimately allows no such private self. *Hamlet*, famously, focuses on just such a dilemma—what is self divorced from action? I stress that its starting point lies with the paradox of the powerless prince to avoid a misrecognition of this privacy as somehow proto-bourgeois[64]. It may be appropriable as such, but it is worked out in the play—most notably in relation to the Fortinbras plot—in terms of assumptions about princely identities, and thus is to some extent continuous with the histories (English, Roman and Trojan) of a few years earlier. The point of access that Hamlet's interiority allows to a post-romantic sensibility may perhaps lie in this sense of an exile from action, a sense of an ahistorical self. But clearer distinctions must be drawn before we can see how this operates in Shakespeare's text, as opposed to the rich texts of cultural fantasy derived from it.

As that first, very poised, public speech would suggest, this interiority is in itself a series of rhetorical strategies. Hamlet's 'centre',[65] as Polonius calls it, 'the inward man'[66] in Claudius's terms, exists by virtue of a concealment, a self-imposed privacy from the court—a silence as to that which has so far been divulged only to Hamlet and the audience. It exists chiefly in relation to Polonius and Claudius. Hamlet develops it, elaborates the mystery, in dialogues with them or with their spies. It is in this context that Hamlet's most eloquent (or at least, most rhetorically sustained) accounts of his 'particularity' take place.

HAMLET. What have you, my good friends, deserved at the hands of
     Fortune that she sends you to prison hither?
GUILDENSTERN. Prison, my lord?
HAMLET. Denmark's a prison.
ROSENCRANTZ. Then is the world one.
HAMLET. A goodly one, in which there are many confines, wards and
     dungeons, Denmark being one o'th' worst.
ROSENCRANTZ. We think not so, my lord.
HAMLET. Why, then 'tis none to you; for there is nothing either good
     or bad but thinking makes it so. To me it is a prison.
ROSENCRANTZ. Why, then your ambition makes it one: 'tis too narrow
     for your mind.
HAMLET. O God, I could be bounded in a nutshell and count myself a
     king of infinite space—were it not that I have bad dreams.
GUILDENSTERN. Which dreams indeed are ambition; for the very
     substance of the ambitious is merely the shadow of a dream.

HAMLET. A dream itself is but a shadow.

ROSENCRANTZ. Truly, and I hold ambition of so airy and light a quality that it is but a shadow's shadow.

HAMLET. Then are our beggars bodies, and our monarchs and outstretched heroes the beggars' shadows. Shall we to th' court? For by my fay, I cannot reason.[67]

Hamlet's presentation of a relativising process of 'thinking' as the basis of a private moral reality seems continuous with the ascription to himself of 'that within', but what such thinking does for him is to construct a prison—as it did for Richard. So, the hint to Rosencrantz is that such interiority, such privacy, is enforced and undesirable—an effect of Claudius's seizure of power as Richard's literal imprisonment was of Bolingbroke's. But no—Hamlet shifts the ground of their discussion. Thinking in itself knows no enclosure, makes 'infinite space'. Hamlet shifts the focus one more move inward—within thinking itself one may encounter 'bad dreams'.

Hamlet of course eventually gets the better of them, and offers them as a kind of sop for their confession of intent another elaborated disquisition on how 'thinking' makes things 'seem' to him.

I have of late, but wherefore I know not, lost all my mirth, forgone all custom of exercise; and indeed it goes so heavily with my disposition that this goodly frame the earth seems to me a sterile promontory, this most excellent canopy the air, look you, this brave o'erhanging firmament, this majestical roof fretted with golden fire, why, it appeareth nothing to me but a foul and pestilent congregation of vapours. What a piece of work is a man, how noble is reason, how infinite in faculties, in form and moving how express and admirable, in action how like an angel, in apprehension how like a god: the beauty of the world, the paragon of animals—and yet, to me, what is this quintessence of dust?[68]

Hamlet's explanation for this cosmic disillusion is on the surface commonsensically banal. He has 'foregone all custom of exercises', and his consequent lassitude 'goes so heavily' with a 'disposition' which is normally, as we are told elsewhere, 'most royal', that he has lost the ability to feel delight. However vast the cosmic map he draws, this is only, in what is both a large claim and a neat disclaimer, how it 'appeareth . . . to me'. But of course his explanation is mockingly circular. Why has he lost all his mirth? 'Wherefore I know not'.

The problem of 'reading' Hamlet's character(s) is first raised by the letter Polonius produces to show Claudius and Gertrude, a love letter from Hamlet to Ophelia, but written in a crude almost parodistic style. While the letter uses a threadbare, so 'inauthentic' language, it nonetheless strains to assert sincerity and truthfulness – 'Doubt thou the stars are fire,/Doubt that the sun does move,/Doubt truth to be a liar,/But never doubt I love . . . that I love thee best, O most best, believe it'.[69] The language of the letter collapses into hyperbole and tautology in demonstrating the impossibility of an authentic truthful language – Ophelia is left to take its assertions on trust as there is nothing 'in the writing' to back them up. A 'convincing' letter is unimaginable, given how language functions in this play: by establishing a point of reference, a mark of some trustworthy identifying praxis, in language action or 'character', in anything other than the marginal figures of players, remembered father or Horatio's stoicism, it would give a token of a knowable innerness, a congruence of feeling, word and action in Hamlet himself – which is exactly what the play wants to avoid. Hamlet has no such innerness to, in a romantic sense, 'write out of'. A crisis in language, a divorce of 'is' and 'seems', the collapse of an idea of 'man' ('Thine . . . whilst this machine is to him', the letter ends[70]), have rendered this impossible. One of the most disturbing things about the play is that it locates its statement of this crisis in exactly that area – love – where we might conventionally expect the inner authentic language to work. Ophelia becomes a kind of blank on which these failures of language, these crises in identifying praxis, can most sharply and pathetically be seen to act. Her identity simply fragments, becomes the effect of the common non-individuated discourse of popular ballads and proverbial phrasing. Whether what she says in the mad scene refers to her own experience or not is wholly irrelevant – the point of the scene is that only the simplest kind of control over reference is now available to her.

> Her speech is nothing,
> Yet the unshaped use of it doth move
> The hearers to collection. They aim at it,
> And botch the words up fit to their own thoughts,
> Which as her winks and nods and gestures yield them,
> Indeed would make one think there might be thought,
> Though nothing sure, yet much unhappily.[71]

Like Lucrece, Ophelia is 'not her own'. Or rather, her words, actions, any readable sign she presents are the property of the observer's knowledge. That they are in themselves 'nothing', but become something in reading, is the legacy of that complex and obsessive reading/spying/observation, to which her father tragi-comically devoted himself; its essential distance from 'that within', is a return of the play's persistent trope for character processes; there is 'nothing' to Ophelia, or something unknowable, something at least that eludes observation. 'I have nothing with this answer, Hamlet,' Claudius says at the beginning of the play scene, 'these words are not mine.' 'No, nor mine now,' is the reply.[72] That words, or other kinds of signs, cannot be owned, cannot be unequivocally the property of those who utter or those who receive them, is another recurrent idea in the play's riddling common-sense. Hamlet's most private utterance, his letter to Ophelia, sets our sense of their relationship in terms of just such an unownable language. The so-called nunnery scene offers another such disjunction—Hamlet's words seem to bear no relation to the situation as it has been set up for us, he deals in the common characters of a misogynistic discourse—they bear no relation to Ophelia, nor does she react to them in any other way than to class them simply as 'madness' — a 'madness of discourse' perhaps, like Troilus's. Polonius has set this part of the play in motion after Ophelia has described Hamlet's incursion into her closet:

OPHELIA. O my lord, my lord, I have been so affrighted.
POLONIUS. With what, i'th' name of God?
OPHELIA. My lord, as I was sewing in my closet,
    Lord Hamlet, with his doublet all unbrac'd,
    No hat upon his head, his stockings foul'd
    Ungarter'd and down-gyved to his ankle,
    Pale as his shirt, his knees knocking each other,
    And with a look so piteous in purport
    As if he had been loosed out of hell
    To speak of horrors, he comes before me.
POLONIUS. Mad for thy love?
OPHELIA.   My lord, I do not know,
    But truly do I fear it.
POLONIUS.   What said he?
OPHELIA. He took me by the wrist and held me hard.
    Then goes he to the length of all his arm,
    And with his other hand thus o'er his brow
    He falls to such perusal of my face
    As a would draw it. Long stay'd he so.

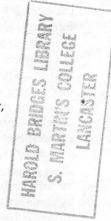

At last, a little shaking of mine arm,
And thrice his head thus waving up and down,
He rais'd a sigh so piteous and profound
As it did seem to shatter all his bulk
And end his being. That done, he lets me go,
And with his head over his shoulder turn'd
He seem'd to find his way without his eyes,
For out o' doors he went without their helps,
And to the last bended their light on me.[73]

The play's time scheme makes it difficult to put this in a cause or effect relation to any particular events. It is certainly reductive to read it as Polonius does, as a sign of love, even of madness, but what else could conventional character language tell us? What it presents is a vignette or emblem of those processes of interpretation and 'significant action' worked out overall in the presentation of their relationship. Ophelia describes the ordered signs of Hamlet's condition, the derangement of his princely identity, but he seeks to read *her* face. His wordless sigh is in a sense what he reads there—a blank (one cannot read faces in this play—only, perhaps, the ghost's). It is also, in Ophelia's hyperbolic sense of it, an emblem of personal dissolution, of that passive declension into non-being which Hamlet so famously lays claim to elsewhere.

At the beginning of the nunnery scene Polonius poses Ophelia with a book—a book she only pretends to read. This echoes Hamlet's earlier entrance with a book, a book from which he pretends to read insulting characters of old age to mock Polonius. Reading is one way of presenting interiority, or at least contemplation, on stage. Hamlet's interiority is riddling, concealed (what is he really reading?), Ophelia's is empty. Ironically it is this, Ophelia's and Polonius's little play, and not Hamlet's more ambitious spectacle, that first provokes Claudius into an acknowledgement of the gap between what is known of him, his 'painted word', and what he knows, his 'deed'. That gap, that interiority, presents itself to him as 'conscience'—a private knowledge of self.[74] Ophelia's mimed contemplation sets up an equally quizzical counterpoint to Hamlet's most famous contemplative moment.

Hamlet's soliloquies are usually triggered by his perception of some other person; they are worked out as attempts to fit together identities for that person (Gertrude, Fortinbras, Claudius, the player) fragmented by some action and character which may imply an 'interior' position, a private subjectivity, but which proceed out from that and render it unknowable in the fragmentariness and multiplicity of *personae* that the performance requires. They are redefinitions of and by Hamlet, in the face of an audience – to whom they are addressed and to whom they tend to offer some explicit pointer to the progress of the plot. Hamlet's first soliloquy grounds his desire for his own dissolution in the derangement of Gertrude's identity consequent on her marriage: the speech swarms with possible identities for her, and for himself, Claudius and old Hamlet. Hyperion, satyr, an allegorised 'frailty' that is also 'woman', Niobe, 'a beast', uncle, father's brother, father, I, Hercules – all extend, divert and clutter an extraordinary long sentence that begins with the simple question 'must I remember?' and ends with the thing remembered – 'She married'.[75] Which is really all he had to say. This, Claudius's establishment of personal power, and, when the ghost reveals it, the murder, are all 'unnatural'; the 'incest' is so in a way that Claudius carefully flaunts, in an absolutist move. His 'discretion' fought successfully 'with nature'[76] in a way that aggrandises his absolute control; Hamlet must however elide his own particularity. It is 'to nature most absurd', a 'fault to nature'[77] whose rules he, unlike Claudius, has to obey. 'To be or not to be' has no clear occasion or outcome. In picking up and extending, from the Rosencrantz and Guilderstern scene, the idea of 'dream' (an undescribed or unknowable dream) as that which challenges the subject from within whatever interiority it constructs for itself, the speech declares its continuity with those riddling and self-deprecatingly sophistical depictions of a malaise both private and cosmic. The dream represents a knowledge of a vast exterior (the after world, in this speech) encountered in the privacy, the simplest kind of withdrawal 'into' the self, of sleep. To try to trace the logical progression of the speech is to become aware how much it is in a sense thinking for its own sake, an exploration not of ideas, but of the limits on interiority.

> To be, or not to be, that is the question:
> Whether 'tis nobler in the mind to suffer
> The slings and arrows of outrageous fortune,
> Or to take arms against a sea of troubles
> And by opposing end them.[78]

'To be, or not to be' may be the first question, but is this the same question as 'Whether 'tis nobler . . .'? The second question might after all be simply a matter of stoic endurance as against action, which, if one read the soliloquy only as far as 'end them', would put into doubt which of the alternatives in the first question correspond to which in the second. 'To take arms', in a conventional and rousing image of action is equivalent to non-being—in the interior space which this soliloquy constructs, being and action are irreconcilable. What is troubling about the statement is that we know that the first alternative—'to be' in a stoic integrity of being—is outside Hamlet's scope. Hamlet sees Horatio's social position as having a potential for integrity unavailable to the court, for 'why should the poor be flattered?' Horatio's distance from a disrupted and misleading language presents the possibility of a philosopher's stoicism—he stands apart from the action 'as one in suffering all has suffered nothing,/A man that Fortune's buffets and rewards/Hast tane with equal thanks.' Hamlet wishes to internalise this quality, to 'wear . . ./In my heart's core, ay in my heart of heart',[79] but such stoic certainty is unavailable to Hamlet himself, it can be quoted or appropriated in the qualities of others. In this play, a wholeness of being, a personal integrity, is available only to marginal figures. In 'to be, or not to be' there is only the not-being which is a kind of action. Fortune has been presented as a persistent but not particularly well-armed individual adversary, but when action takes arms, *its* adversary is inhumanly and infinitely destructive; to oppose 'a sea of troubles' in individual action is to appear puny, even comical. The opposing ends the opposer, and only in that sense ends 'them'.

These opening lines present their propositions as infinitives, not as states (being or not being), personifiable abstractions (life or death), personal choices (should I or shouldn't I), nor even choices put impersonally (should we/one/you), but as open potentialities, implying no particular subject position; 'slings . . . arrows . . . take arms' suggest human agency, but in context undercut the value of such agency. 'Them' is the first marker of a human positionality, the first finite in a structure of infinitives, which it brings to an apt full stop. The 'troubles' are the human itself—'them' applies to the sea, but as we know that such 'opposing' cannot end the sea, can only end whatever there is 'to take arms', so 'them' would seem to refer to whatever can 'take arms', to 'end them', in ending itself. The next sentence keeps the idea at a careful syntactical distance—'by a sleep to say we end . . . 'Tis a consummation devoutly to be wished'. More infinitives, taking the idea of desirable non-being farther away, as hypothetical statement ('to *say* we end'), fragmented by the syntactical hiatuses in Hamlet's sentence. The most stable idea in the first half of the speech is the idea of sleep, for here the equivalences ('To die, to sleep') no longer observe even the structure of logical proposition, but take on instead a lullaby-like rhythm, instate Hamlet's fragmenting thought process as a self-lulling retreat into that most accessible and complete privacy. This is the nearest he comes to the painless 'melting', the gentle dispersal of self he earlier claimed to desire.

The second half of the speech makes more extrovert use of the positionalities and identifying practices of his 'philosophical' rhetoric.

> To die, to sleep;
> To sleep, perchance to dream—ay there's the rub:
> For in that sleep of death what dreams may come,
> When we have shuffled off this mortal coil,
> Must give us pause—there's the respect
> That makes calamity of so long life.
> For who would bear the whips and scorns of time,
> Th'oppressor's wrong, the proud man's contumely,
> The pangs of dispriz'd love, the law's delay,
> The insolence of office, and the spurns
> That patient merit of th'unworthy takes,
> When he himself might his quietus make
> With bare bodkin? Who would fardels bear,
> To grunt and sweat under a weary life,
> But that the dread of something after death,
> The undiscover'd country, from whose bourn
> No traveller returns, puzzles the will,
> And makes us rather bear those ills we have
> Than fly to others that we know not of?[80]

An acknowledgement of a human context, not only for his thought, but for his presence on stage, in 'we' and 'us', forms a bridge to a lively satirical peopling of his speech with confident personification ('the whips and scorns of time'—knowable human form of suffering for general suffering and undifferentiated human experience), with the *personae* of a mundane social world and with a final image uniting the notion of beleaguered labour with the petty but wounding attacks of fortune, to present, with an almost burlesque precision, an emblem of human life in the world as the labour of Atlas, undertaken without dignity or recognition, and undertaken in common—a peasant Atlas, as the internal image of a prince. The thought of dreaming seems to have woken him up—this is what it is 'to be'.

This suddenly accessible community of experience is the condition of his concluding statement.

> Thus conscience does make cowards of us all,
> And thus the native hue of resolution
> Is sicklied o'er with the pale cast of thought,
> And enterprises of great pitch and moment
> With this regard their currents turn awry
> And lose the name of action.[81]

If 'conscience doth make cowards of us all' then no-one *in particular* is 'a coward'—as Hamlet assured himself that *he* was not in his last soliloquy—introspection holds us all back from non-being. But that non-being is *action*—the self-contradictoriness of the sea idea is forced back on our attention by the physiognomic metaphor, by which a resolution native to us, showing in our faces as healthy colour, is 'sicklied o'er' as the result of thought/conscience. This death-like pallor is an odd way of describing the impulse 'to be' and the contrary impulse 'not to be' is odd enough as 'resolution' let alone as somehow 'native' to us. Again Hamlet's sets of corresponding prepositions have gone askew, and again the soliloquy's numbing identification of 'not to be' and action lies behind this. This statement can be read as brusquely commonsensical out of context (thinking is bad for you) but, taken with the overall tendency of the soliloquy, it returns us to the limiting conditions on Hamlet's interiority. He posits a notion of being a resistant self-hood, apart from action, private from the world, but cannot sustain this. Non-being is an inaccessible alternative—the self cannot dissolve into a sleep-like death, or a fragmentation of discourse like sleep. So he returns to life in the world, life as human, to perceive it as a more brutal kind of endurance. The only alternative to this is something that, as he puts it, has lost its name in these processes of 'conscience'. He produces that name as the last word of the speech. Its name is 'action'.

So now action is only a name, and it is hard to know what can be so named. The gap between signs and things is the space in which interiority operates in this play, and here it looms as a divorce between action and being. The outcome of the speech is only to return us to the recurrent problem of identification—Hamlet ends it by mocking Ophelia's pretended contemplation. How to identify *her*? 'Nymph' and 'Orisons' fit neither with each other nor with her. Hamlet challenges her to fill her empty interiority with remembrance of him. So the nunnery scene begins.

The action with which these central scenes of the play are concerned is a rhetorical action—so much so that when Hamlet is offered a practicable opportunity of *physical* action—finding Claudius at his prayers—he passes it over. Death (and the point is reiterated in the cases of old Hamlet and Rosencrantz and Guilderstern) somehow fixes identity in the sight of heaven. Shakespeare uses points of Christian doctrine here more as an extension of his interest in the paradoxes of character definition than as a theological argument in its own right—it offers an idea of heaven's spectatorship/judgement/ sealing of identity to coincide here with the audience's (to whom Hamlet addresses his speech over the head of a Claudius who, like Ophelia, is only miming interiority, though not here by his own choice) and with that of a presumed audience within the play. The audience's reaction is excitingly contradictory—the push towards a making open of the hidden that is the dynamic of the rhetorical action would be contradicted by an improvised and secret killing—but then what does Hamlet *want* after all? Claudius's physical death, as this scene is there to point out, is only part of it. Revenge is never a merely private act, cannot properly take place in a private space—a 'showing' analogous to that of the play scene must be involved in it.

Claudius's soliloquy projects a court of heaven that condemns him, that must condemn him—'there the action lies/In his true nature'.[82] The allegorical figures that people such a court are powerless in the face of Claudius's identification with his act—'Mine own ambition' stands for both his acquired kingship and that aspect of himself which led him to aim for it, and he is able to resign neither. Only a self-dissolution, another melting, which must come from outside, can free him from his obdurate self-hood.

> Help, angels! Make assay.
> Bow, stubborn knees; and heart with strings of steel,
> Be soft as sinews of the new-born babe.
> All may be well.[83]

But then the simple, fittingly childlike, spatial metaphor of his final couplet reminds us that words have acquired a treacherous life of their own, cannot be owned or made to bear meaning by an act of personal will; language fails even in its representation to the court of heaven.

Claudius's conscience can only represent to him the gap between sign and substance. As in his first soliloquy, this representation is what his conscience amounts to. His prayer cannot 'go' anywhere, it is merely the circumscription of an agonising ('O heavy burden'[84]) but inescapably empty inner space.

After Hamlet's journey to England, and the end of that delusive game and countergame of 'character' that makes up the central section of the play, the play seems to thin out, to display a more mannered and spectacular version of its recurrent interests. Hamlet positively takes on this thinness in the last of his self-recharacterings, the encounter with Fortinbras' army – 'from this time forth/My thoughts be bloody, or be nothing worth'.[85] Good night, sweet prince. But if the taking-on of a Fortinbras-like identity is qualified by a sense of its insubstantiality, as 'the shadow of a dream', the substance to be set against it is no longer 'within'.[86] Hamlet's interiority has been a self-qualifying and unstable construct. The shadow world of action is now set against precisely those 'common' realities which Gertrude first tried to persuade him to acknowledge. No-one is 'particular' in the grave from which the sexton retrieves Yorick's skull. Anything but Marvell's 'fine and private place', it is a busy emblem of the world. Or rather, it is imaginable as such – in the anonymity of death, one of the dead that crowd it is indistinguishable from another. The famous, great, the *personae* of social life all become indeterminate dust. In contemplating Yorick's skull Hamlet faces not simply an intimation of mortality, but a paradox, like that embodied (if one can put it that way) in the ghost, of an identity fixed and vivid in memory, and an absence of any certainty in the present to match it; 'I knew him, Horatio', but there is nothing to be known from his skull.[87] One can set this scene against 'to be, or not to be' as its externalised counterpart, a digging into the enclosing but only jokingly ownable ('Whose grave's this Sirrah?/Mine sir'[88]) to throw up (literally here) emblems of mortality, markers of that limit on the particular self set by the 'bourn' of death. Like Ophelia's madness it offers us in a culturally hackneyed but still potent 'scene' a visible 'action' of the play's concern with the 'common' and the 'particular'.[89]

Hamlet's fight with Laertes in (or around) the grave is his last 'mad' act – it is motivated by a point of style as much as by passion. Laertes's expression of feeling seems ridiculous. Words, words, words. Hamlet can simply disown these words, and implicitly all the words of his 'madness', in externalising that madness; for the first time, he describes himself as mad, not in 'self-knowledge', but as a kind of emptying out of self.

> Was't Hamlet wrong'd Laertes? Never Hamlet.
> If Hamlet from himself be ta'en away,
> And when he's not himself does wrong Laertes,
> Then Hamlet does it not, Hamlet denies it.
> Who does it then? His madness. If't be so,
> Hamlet is of the faction that is wrong'd;
> His madness is poor Hamlet's enemy.[90]

So the space between show and substance is not the space of an interiority, it is an absence of meaning, a disowning, a kind of silence. Hamlet's interiority has been replaced not by an inner stoicism ('to be') but by a move to an action which is also a giving up of self ('not to be') – for belief in Christian providence, or simply 'silence'. The silence of which Gertrude unexpectedly and movingly speaks at the end of her son's disownable words to Laertes in the graveyard scene (where Hamlet, as he says later, 'forgot myself'[91]) is fittingly institutionalised by Claudius as a 'living memorial' for the self-forgotten, and like her father unmemorialised Ophelia. 'The hour of quiet'[92] he decrees takes us back to the non-identified common reality of the grave.

This silence then is the final 'substance' of the show. 'The rest is silence', says Hamlet, dying, but Fortinbras approaches with trumpets and drums. Hamlet does not get flights of angels singing him to his rest, as Horatio hopes ('goodnight sweet prince'/'to sleep, to die'); the historical moment enters jarringly into what was, for a moment, death's silent cell.[93] Fortinbras's final 'character' of Hamlet reminds us of that exile from royal, heroic identities within which Hamlet's revenge, his privacy 'within', his silence have all existed.

> For he was likely, had he been put on,
> To have prov'd most royal; and for his passage,
> The soldier's music and the rite of war
> Speak loudly for him.[94]

It reminds us of its opposite, the ahistorical moment, the self apart from action, the unknowable interiority, which Hamlet has attempted to construct. The play takes place in a lapse of knowable character. Fortinbras's return forces identities on to figures and events (and sets up both a stage show and a narrative performance, Horatio's, to represent them) but his entrance, like these identities, jars – theatrically, in the opposition of his drums and trumpets to Hamlet's wished-for silence. The Hamlet Fortinbras affirms, like the

Hamlet Ophelia describes at the end of the closet scene is not the Hamlet of the play. The perfect courtly prince, the royal figure of feudal and military history is presented as a static icon, to remind us that what we have seen is a derangement, a slippage of 'is' and 'seems', not simply within an individual personality, but within a world, a language, an idea of 'man'. The play explores this through a rhetorical character language, a densely theatrical articulation of that language's identifying practice. Though Hamlet on some occasions locates the mystery, the unreadability consequent on this derangement 'within' himself, the experience of the play leads us from the 'particular' to the 'common' — the substance in excess of signs is an intimation, finally, of mortality, of that sense both of nothingness and of our materiality into which it develops the idea of death. It is against this that the processes of inscription, reading and memorialisation, the processes that define and assert the individual, must finally be set.

In this context, 'that within' Hamlet is not some principle of individuality, but an intuition, released in the contemplative set-pieces of the central section of the play, of its very absence. Such are the 'dreams' to which his riddling responses to Rosencrantz and Guildenstern and his famous soliloquy both refer. 'To be or not to be' articulates his fullest retreat from 'character'. It tends to the condition of an almost subjectless utterance — only the acknowledgement of the audience, as 'we', constructs a subject position and, in being both 'common' and public (to 'us'), it evades any sense of a *particular* subject, any urgent individualism, or special subjectivity. In locating being in the absence of action and action as the opposite of the theatrical moment that defines and proposes it, the speech constructs for Hamlet an impossible mental space, an inaccessible interiority, from which action cannot come, nor being inhere. Neither 'subjectivity' nor 'interiority' are available to him; they are the most unstable of constructs, and become more so the more the play moves off the map of knowable history and political praxis, of social identity and familial relationship, elaborated for us at the beginning and swiftly reaffirmed at the end.

Post-romantic readings of the play have invested in subjectivity and interiority as the hallmarks of Hamlet's 'character'. This is a kind of filling in of what the text itself insistently presents as a gap, a making particular of what is in the text non-individuated, common; it is in that sense a kind of performance, the establishment of a personal text in fruitful contradistinction to the text as recorded and received. We require our Hamlets to tread a careful middle path, demanding a charismatically 'particular' presence, but eschewing too 'sentimental' or too 'intellectual', (and thus either way too immediately knowable) a presentation of a self-hood we still prefer to see as enigmatic, as our prime theatrical symbol of the depth and mystery of individual personality. Such readings are not 'wrong' but they do make only partial and distortive use of an almost uniquely rich theatrical text—our mistake would be to identify them with that text, with discourses that construct subject-hood and interiority in different ways and to different ends. Such readings are the product of a particular idea of character—the multiplicity of possible 'Hamlets' is allowed by the very irrelevance of that idea to a text that nonetheless accommodates such multiplicity, accommodates it by virtue of its vivid actorliness, (by its refusal to specify or interiorise, by the very 'playability' of discourse which Hamlet only teasingly forswears) and by the paradoxical universality, the community of being and not being that it opens up in the silences of an insistently noisy text. 'Man' here is the enigma, not a particular man.

III HUMOUR AND MELANCHOLY: INDIVIDUATION AND CONTAINMENT

The absence of psychology from the discourse of the character that I have outlined so far may disconcert, given its centrality to the assumptions of character (less aptly called a discourse, given its anti-textual, anti-rhetorical basis) through which Shakespeare's plays are later read. Hamlet's response to Horatio's enquiry about his uncle's drinking habits may seem to instate a 'psychological' reading of the play.

> HORATIO. Is it a custom?
> HAMLET. Ay marry is't
>   But to my mind, though I am native here
>   And to the manner born, it is a custom
>   More honour'd in the breach than in the observance.
>   This heavy-headed revel east and west
>   Makes us traduc'd and tax'd of other nations—
>   They clepe us drunkards, and with swinish phrase
>   Soil our addition; and indeed it takes
>   From our achievements, though perform'd at height,
>   The pith and marrow of our attribute.

So, oft it chances in particular men
That for some vicious mole of nature in them,
As in their birth, wherein they are not guilty
(Since nature cannot choose his origin),
By their o'ergrowth of some complexion,
Oft breaking down the pales and forts of reason,
Or by some habit, that too much o'erleavens
The form of plausive manners—that these men,
Carrying, I say, the stamp of one defect,
Being Nature's livery or Fortune's star,
His virtues else, be they as pure as grace,
As infinite as man may undergo,
Shall in the general censure take corruption
From that particular fault. The dram of evil
Doth all the noble substance of a doubt
To his own scandal.

Enter GHOST.

HORATIO.   Look, my lord, it comes.[95]

Hamlet proceeds here from a discussion of the drunkenness that
provides other nations with a generalised 'character' of the Danes (one
that Shakespeare draws on again in *Othello*[96]) to outline what may seem
to be a theory of personality deformation. But that explanation
hesitates (typically for a play in which 'or' tends both to articulate and
obscure the more tantalizingly explicatory statements) between a
medical diagnosis—'their o'ergrowth of some complexion'—and an
explanation in the terms of post-Aristotelian education theory—some
over-developed 'habit'. This last effects a transition back to the
rhetorical language. Such a habit does not deform 'personality', it
'o'erleavens/The form of plausive manners', that is, in a homely, even
trivialising metaphor, it puffs up the forms of persuasive social
behaviour like badly made dough. This statement has to serve also for
the conclusion of his quasi-medical description of the 'vicious mole of
nature'. It is not clear what that destructive internal force is operating
on, ultimately. In a typical syntactical shift, 'or' intervenes before the
statement is finally concluded. The modern reader may well supply a
notion of 'personality', but the 'stamp' that the 'one defect' impresses is
an individuating mark to be perceived and read in the 'general
censure', the common social discourse of character. The hitherto

unfixed 'medical' language is transformed and limited by its metaphorisation in terms of this idea. 'Corruption' here is corruption of the individual as 'generally' known, of his character in the social sense. It puts that character 'of a doubt/To his own scandal'.

The emergence of the character/stamp metaphor as the basis of this disquisition returns to the opposition of signs to that 'which passeth show', and so helps us place 'substance' as both a physical material whose nature is changed by the 'dram of eale', and as that which is obscured, rendered doubtful by the misleadingness of apparently readable signs. The difficulty of the metaphor is symptomatic of the play, in its attempt to use a common physical metaphor to signify, to make known, a concept of unknowability. 'Scandal' and 'doubt' is, Hamlet concludes, the ordinary condition of the identifying discourses of the human, and in the play he is, of course, right.

The psychology posited by the speech depends on the familiar analogy of the self as a fortified house or castle, the model which tends to define the notion of interiority as post-classical discourses (Christian or humanist) present it. The 'o'er growth of some complexion' becomes both a 'flood' and perhaps also a rebellion (as Laertes's incursion into Elsinore is seen as an incursion like the ocean's).[97] The model of the self as castle implies an individual in charge of that castle. Where in earlier rhetorical writing that which is enthroned in the castle may represent some supra-personal quality (wisdom, in the *Psychomachia*),[98] in Shakespeare it tends to be 'I'—the subject, or, as the point of origin of praxis, the 'will'. The 'complexion' is in itself a physical property, which this metaphor places as *outside* a self that must fend it off, build the barricades of reason against it. The model of a house under siege, with an internal hierarchy to structure its own operations, represents forces we take to be inside the self (psychological), as continuous with those we take to be outside it (social, for example), and so disallows an attempt to locate the reality of the self (as we assume we all have real selves) in its very separateness and uniqueness. Psychology in its pre-modern forms thus takes its place in a structure of analogies, a set of correspondences, in which the subject ('I') occupies a notionally individuated position, centred and with the potential for control, but in which all forces and effects are outside it. Forces that we would class as 'psychological', as part of our personalities (or even as determining our personalities) are here impersonal, even interpersonal, best understood by analogies with other such forces as they operate in the cosmos, or in social life.

This makes available to Shakespeare a richness of metaphor for presenting the operations of the self – a richness of inclusive metaphor, in that the forces given verbal 'substance' are accessible to the audience, not simply the property of a *particular* self. The subject position, the 'I' from which a Shakespeare 'character' speaks is thus both separate from, anterior to his or her 'character' (in the sense of the word known to Shakespeare), and separate and at least notionally superior to the affective forces whose operation that 'I' excitingly and complicatingly confronts. A post-romantic construction of the subject would locate the reality of such forces within the individual subjectivity, thus defined as essentially distinct from the praxes of language or 'action' in which it may or may not participate. Shakespeare and his contemporaries are not somehow 'deconstructing' this notion of the individual, but we may have to in order to make sense of much of the texts, as they operate outside it, within a historically prior, though still accessible, discourse.

The idea of 'complexion' in this speech refers to the familiar theory of the 'humours', or four fluids in the body, blood, phlegm, choler and black bile, of which, though ideally held in balance, there may be some 'o'ergrowth', some disturbance of the internal economy of the body. A particular 'complexion' may then result – a new relation of these components, which will show itself in complexion in the modern sense, as in other readable signs, and will result in a particular 'temperament' associated with them – sanguine, phlegmatic, choleric, melancholic. As a medical theory of the physical constitution of 'personality', the 'humour' theory depends on an analogical mode of knowledge. That is, the four humours correspond to elemental forces – air, earth, fire and water – as well as to experienced bodily states. They provide an explanation of those states in so far as they give them a place in this pattern of analogies, locating them on a model of the cosmos which is also a model of the self. This system accounts for effects and states taxonomically rather than causally – it provides a way of knowing the body, and on this basis a system of treatment can be built.

The system holds good by virtue of a kind of commonsense applicability of the metaphors that structure it – anger makes us go red then pale, like fire, and we feel hot; persistently angry people may suffer from physical disorders that 'explode' within them, they may eventually burn themselves out. Though some of these figures of speech may be a development out of the humour metaphor, and so give us a received pattern whose origin we forget and so seem to experience spontaneously, the basis of the metaphor can be accounted for experientially. The exception here is melancholy. The black bile is a notional humour, it is not observable in the body, nor are its effects easily traced through experience.[99] It is thus a more flexible kind of metaphorical construct, a kind of free space in the humour system – both a notional category of kinds of disorder, and a disorder of the notional. Literary development fills the medical vacuum – melancholy is a kind of 'madness in discourse', a dislodgement of language (verbal, behavioural, 'character') from reality as affirmed or intuited elsewhere, and so the creation of a private space, limitingly but also expansively individual.

The humour system is a development of classical medicine, and in no way peculiar to the English Renaissance. What is of particular interest in this period is its development, especially in drama, as an account of individuation – an individuation often implicitly condemned, opposed to a unified and ordered model of the human (as self/society/the cosmos of human knowledge), but creating a free space, of 'humour' in comedy, 'melancholy' in tragedy, in which the structures of that cosmos can be reflected and put into play. In its exploration of the idea of 'the private' and of the private 'mental stuffe', as Chapman calls it, of 'pure religion',[100] later Elizabethan comedy sets a rhetorical notion of character against fashions for innerness, and so uses the discontinuities, the gaps in 'character' to construct problematic interiorities.

In the prologue to Ben Jonson's *Every Man Out of His Humour*, Asper picks on Mitis's casual use of the word humour to complain of its 'abuse', its too free usage, and he offers his own explanation.

ASPER. O, I craue pardon, I had lost my thoughts.
    Why, Humour (as 'tis ens) we thus define it
    To be a quality of aire or water,
    And in it selfe holds these two properties,
    Moisture, and fluxure: As, for demonstration,
    Powre water on this floore, 'twill wet and runne:
    Likewise the aire (forc't through a horne, or trumpet)
    Flowes instantly away, and leaues behind
    A kind of dew; and hence we doe conclude,
    That what soe're hath fluxure, and humiditie,
    As wanting power to containe it selfe,
    Is Humour. So in euery humane body
    The choller, melancholy, flegme, and bloud,

> By reason that they flow continually
> In some part, and are not continent,
> Receiue the name of Humours. Now thus farre
> It may, by Metaphore, apply it selfe
> Vnto the generall disposition:
> As when some one peculiar quality
> Doth so possesse a man, that it doth draw
> All his affects, his spirits, and his powers,
> In their confluctions, all to runne one way,
> This may be truly said to be a Humour.[101]

Humour in itself then is a 'quality' of the elements of air and water, and so can be applied metaphorically to anything 'wanting power to contain itself'. Thus, taken at its broadest possible application, it is defined by its opposition to the idea of containment. This model is, according to Asper, a model by which we can describe and so know 'the general disposition' – the overall state of an individual or the state of the human, of 'Everyman'. Its opposition to the house/room analogy offers Jonson a basic metaphorical structure for presenting mental process. In the earlier *Every Man in his Humour*, the jealous husband Kitely tells his wife of a headache by which he refers to the cuckold's horns, but which she literalises –

DAME. What aile you sweet heart, are you not well, speake good MVSSE.

KITELY. Troth my head akes extremely, on a sudden.

DAME. Oh, the lord!

KITELY. How now? what?

DAME. Alas, how it burnes? MVSSE, keepe you warme, good truth it is this new disease! there's a number are troubled withall! for loues sake, sweet heart, come in, out of the aire.

KITELY. How simple, and how subtill are her answeres? A new disease, and many troubled with it! Why, true: she heard me, all the world to nothing.

DAME. I pray thee, good sweet heart, come in; the aire will doe you harme, in troth.

KITELY. The aire! shee has me i' the wind! sweet heart! Ile come to you presently: 't will away, I hope.

DAME. Pray heauen it doe.

KITELY. A new disease? I know not, new, or old,
   But it may well be call'd poore mortalls plague:
   For, like a pestilence, it doth infect
   The houses of the braine. First it begins
   Solely to worke vpon the phantasie,
   Filling her seat with such pestiferous aire,
   As soone corrupts the judgement; and from thence
   Sends like contagion to the memorie:
   Still each to other giuing the infection.
   Which, as a subtle vapor, spreads it selfe,
   Confusedly, through euery sensiue part,
   Till not a thought, or motion, in the mind,
   Be free from the blacke poyson of suspect.
   Ah, but what miserie' is it, to know this?
   Or, knowing it, to want the mindes erection,
   In such extremes?[102]

The disease is his humour, developing uncontainably, moving like air or water through a compartmentalised and static self.

Kitely reads his wife's words as another layer of metaphor, and indeed, given the analogical process of the humour idea, it is impossible for Kitely to identify a stable 'literal' level, 'inside' himself, a reality (physical illness or mental construct, headache or suspicion) which places the other alternative as a figure of speech, or to distinguish the two as cause and effect (as in modern diagnosis). External 'fact', that his wife is faithful or unfaithful, is the only possible stabilising force, an end to the flowing of humour which is also the endless flow of an internalised discourse. Kitely's 'fantasy' cannot be put in order from within himself. It is misery to know this, in that knowing is of necessity a participation in a mental process cut adrift from external object, and so caught in the flux of the 'subtle vapour' of a discourse that is also a disease. 'Well', Kitely concludes.

           Well, I will once more striue,
    (In spight of this black cloud) my selfe to be,
    And shake this feauer off, that thus shakes me.[103]

His selfhood is of course defined as separate from this metaphorical construction of interior process. The 'I', the subject, that strives 'myself to be', confronts, in the suspicion of jealousy, a disorderly flow of 'humour', of internal discourse divorced from external 'affect'. The two models of interior life – the 'flow' model and the hierarchical, static model of the 'house' – can be seen in Kitely's speech as two models of discourse. What the soliloquy presents microcosmically is presented in macrocosm in the play as a whole – that free disorderly flow of humour is also a way of describing the action of farce. The gallants that meet in the literal house of which Kitely is, in a familiar pattern of analogies, 'the head', represent a congregation of humours, a semi-secret disorderly gathering around which the action of the play is structured. Jonson's comedies develop the idea of humours into dramatic structures in which the players present individuated humours temporarily in possession of figures defined differently by other implicitly more stable systems. 'Character' in this process becomes a fiction, operated knowingly or unknowingly but essentially split off from the 'reality' of societal identifications. The humours adopt what personae they please. In *Every Man In*, Brainworm, the observant actor of social types, goes through a series of disguises which point up the provisionality and often downright incongruity of the *personae* taken on by the humour-figures (most notably in Bodadil-as-soldier).[104] At the end of the play this seems to have been re-ordered, the households/selves re-established, the farce at an end. But as we are reminded at the end of Jonson's more complex refinement of the idea in *Every Man Out*, 'order' can only be affirmed elsewhere, outside the play, or at most, at its point of dissolution.[105] Jonson does not show his figures 'converted'; as 'actors' in a play of humours their 'action' is the playing out of a humour, at the end of which 'let them vanish, vapours'.[106] Out of their humour they are nothing, they must run from the stage. The plays end with a reminder that we are, in a double sense, their 'subject', for they are our 'mirror'. The reconstructed self must be seen to be not on the stage but in the audience.

'Humour' can thus be developed as an internalised discourse, opposed to the external discourse of character; acting in contradiction to, even imperilling, the ordered model of the self; liable to deceive or render helpless the subject, so that 'I' can only strive 'to be myself'. Though these more traditional ideas are reinforced by the structure of the play, as well as in the structure of soliloquies and in explicatory statements, 'humour' provides an accessible and fashionable way of accounting for the individuated and the anti-social. Asper complains at the end of his explanation of the humour metaphor, that

> But that a rooke, in wearing a pyed feather,
> The cable hat-band, or the three-pild ruffe,

> A yard of shooetye, or the Switzers knot
> On his French garters, should affect a Humour!
> O, 'tis more than most ridiculous.
> CORDATUS. He speakes pure truth now, if an Idiot
>   Haue but an apish, or phantasticke straine,
>   It is his Humour.
> ASPER. Well I will scourge those apes;
>   And to these courteous eyes oppose a mirrour,
>   As large as is the stage, whereon we act:
>   Where they shall see the times deformitie
>   Anatomiz'd in euery nerue, and sinnew,
>   With constant courage, and contempt of feare.[107]

Characters in the plays aspire to 'affect' humours, yet it may be hard to see, if 'humour' is an analogy anyway, that its proper application can be so strictly circumscribed. Derangement of conventional signs of behaviour and dress, a disruptive and socially self-exempting action point, as in Hamlet's case, to 'privacy', 'mystery', 'that within'. Plays tend to make the distinction between the social currency which makes these signs of the unknowable banal, all too easily known, and a genuine self-individuation, humour thought through, not just another 'character'. As the contrast between Dowsacer and Labesha in Chapman's *Humorous Dayes Mirth* would seem to show, the seriousness of Dowsacer's melancholy lies not in its persistence (he converts from it in the end) or in its consequences (it is Labesha who tries to kill himself) but in the quality of the reflections to which it gives rise, (of which, indeed, it may be said to consist). The mistake of the false humorists is to operate humour as a mode of 'character', to adopt its external signs while unable to sustain its value as an internal discourse.

Chapman's play is a comic exploration of these conflicting discourses, of humour, character and the self. It opens with the elderly Count Labervele entering 'This . . . holy Greene, my wife's close walke'[108] with a counterfeit key. His wife is a puritan:

> Faire is my wife and young and delicate,
> Although too religious in the purest sorte,
> But pure religion being but mental stuffe,
> And sence, indeed, al for it selfe,
> 'Tis to be doubted, that when an obiect comes
> Fit to her humour she wil intercept
> Religious letters sent vnto her minde,
> And yeelde vnto the motion of her bloud.[109]

The 'religious letters' of her internal discourse are a private self-generating mode of reason and choice which Labervele, a firm believer in a more old-fashioned psychology, aims to curtail by the impress of external objects. He orders his own life along strictly traditional lines:

> Shal I admit him to make farther triall?
> Ile haue a Dialogue betweene my selfe
> And manly reason to that speciall end:
> Reason, shall I indure a desolate man to come
> And court my wife, and proue her constancie?
> Reason: To court and proue her you may beare my lord,
> For perfite things are not the worse for triall;
> Gold will not turne to drosse for deepest triall:
> Before God a comfortable saying:
> Thanks gentle reason, Ile trouble you no more.[110]

The puritan contradicts the proper outward signs of social identity – 'she goes more like a milke maide than a Countesse, for all her youth and beautie'[111] – and the arbiter, the comic organiser of the play, Lemot, sets out to explore this intriguingly novel self-individuation. Like her husband, he banks on the force of outward objects, challenging her to test her inward 'constancy' against the incursion of sense

FLORILA. You are an odde man I see, but first I pray tel me how kissing is the best proofe of chast Ladies.

LEMOT. To giue you a reason for that, you must giue me leaue to be obscure and Philosophicall.

FLORILA. I pray you be, I loue Philosophie well.

LEMOT. Then thus Madam; euery kisse is made as the voice is by imagination and appetite, and as both those are presented to the eare in the voyce, so are they to the silent spirites in our kisses.

FLORILA. To what spirit meane you?

LEMOT. To the spirites of our bloud.

FLORILA. What if it doe?

LEMOT. Why then my imagination, and mine appetite working vpon your eares in my voyce, and vpon your spirites in my kisses, pearcing therein the more deeply, they giue the stronger assault against your constancie.

FLORILA. Why then to say, proue my constancy, is as much to say, kisse me.

LEMOT. Most true rare Ladie.

FLORILA. Then prooue my constancie.[112]

But as the play goes on it becomes clear that the puritan's innerness remains undisturbed. If outward signs – or dress, or behaviour – or external objects, like jewels or kisses, are separate from an essential inner self, then they can be played with and manipulated at will. As in other plays of the period (Middleton's for example) puritanism is a form of licence, in that the divorce of signs from 'that within' allows a disowning of the merely exterior and validates self-directed asocial behaviour. These can be classed as deceit/disguise or rebellious exhibitionism – the fascination of the theatre with puritanism lies partly in the identification of this kind of divorce of inner and outer as a kind of actorliness – and the actor Richard Perkins points out in a prefatory poem to Heywood's *Apology*:

> Still when I come to playes, I love to sit,
> That all may see me in a publike place:
> Even in the stages front, and not to git
> Into a nooke, and hood-winke there my face.
> > *"This is the difference, such would have men deeme,*
> > *"Them what they are not: I am what I seem."*[113]

In the world of readable signs it is the actor, not the interiorised and thus implicitly covert puritan, who 'is' what he 'seems'. Though the puritan's behaviour can be labelled in this way as 'hypocrisy', it remains a powerful re-orientation of the idea of the self – Chapman's puritan remains unconverted, secure in a mode of operating behaviour which not even the witty Lemot can out-manoeuvre.

Chapman's play of humours is organised in a freer way than Jonson's. Lemot sets out to

> sit like an old King in an old fashion
> play, hauing his wife, his counsel, his children, and his foole about
> him, to whome he will sit and point very learnedly as foloweth;
> My counsell graue, and you my noble peeres,
> My tender wife, and you my children deare,
> And thou my foole –
> COLINET. Not meaning me sir I hope.
> LEMOT. No sir, but thus will I sit, as it were, and point out all my
> humorous companions.[114]

The actual king in the play is thus displaced by the arbiter, the knower of humours. The King is shown on his entrance to be the victim of an internal rebellion:

KING. Why sound these Trumpets, in the Diuells name?
CATALIAN. To shew the King comes.
KING. To shew the King comes?
  Go hang the Trumpetters, they mocke me boldly,
  And euery other thing that makes me knowne,
  Not telling what I am, but what I seem,
  A King of clouts, a scarcrow, full of cobwebs,
  Spiders and earewigs, that sets Iackdawes long tongue
  In my bosome, and vpon my head,
  And such are the affections of loue
  Swarming in me, without commaund or reason.[115]

The body/self/kingdom model may be affirmed here to set against Florila's puritanism, but it is in spectacular disarray, emblematised further by Lemot's message to the Queen that a jealous rival was about 'to take from him [the King] in traiterous fashion,/The instrument of procreation'.[116] Alarmed by such violence to the body politic, the Queen joins the flow of the deceived and humorous towards a chaotic congregation at Verone's ordinary.

The end of the play is a masque and lottery – neither king nor wit is at the head of Chapman's comic structure, but Fortune. As Verone's pregnant maid plays her in the masque, Fortune takes accommodatingly physical form to instate the regenerative body of comedy against the ordered male body of king and kingdom. Both the king and the melancholic Dowsacer, unlike the puritan Florila, return to order at the end, their humours dispersed, the model of control implied by humour theory re-established, 'is' and 'seems' united in social identities. The king, unkinged by the 'affections of love' had come in search of the notoriously private Dowsacer, Labervele's son. Objects – a picture of a woman, a sword and some fashionable clothes – are laid out to prompt Dowsacer's meditations ('Indeed the sence doth still stir up the soule, and though these objects do not worke, yet it is very probable in time she may; at least, we shall discern his humour of them').[117] The king and his court then withdraw to observe the result.

Dowsacer's starting point is a text from Cicero – 'What can seems strange to him of earthly things/To whome the whole course of eternitie,/And the round compasse of the work is knowne?' Dowsacer admires the sentiment, but not Cicero himself, 'but yet I marvaile much/How it should spring from thee . . .', from work, ambition, social and political praxis; – it should have sprung from privacy, withdrawal, contemplation.[118] Like Hamlet's (which they antedate and may have influenced) Dowsacer's contemplations open up a sense of the cosmic, the extrapersonal, as intuited in solitude – they hold a mirror to a vast exterior. Also like Hamlet's, the scope of Dowsacer's meditations is the gap between 'is' and 'seems' – it is of this that the objects remind him. Labervele, uncomprehending of the fashions for interiority that seem to have possessed his household, hopes that the picture 'make him more humane, and sotiable' 'Nay,' responds the king, 'Hee's more humane than all we are'[119] – asocialness creates a space in which the human can be more inclusively experienced.

As the very presence of these objects may remind us, by their contrast with Florila's inwardness, Dowsacer's interiority is circumscribed and controlled, rather as the scene is qualified in the play as a whole by the eventual reimposition of hierarchies, of the human as the social, in accordance with the model that the currently disordered king reminds us of on his entrance. The 'is/seems' disjunction is not pursued to any particularly radical end – Dowsacer (again unlike Florila) approves of a mutually validating system of class differentiation in behaviour and dress, and reaffirms the value of character and sign.

LABERVELE. I would not haue my friend mocke worthy men,
    For the vaine pride of some that are not so.
DOWSACER. I do not here deride the difference of states,
    No no in shew, but wish that such as want shew
    Might not be scorned with ignorant Turkish pride,
    Beeing pompous in apparel, and in mind:[120]

At the end of the scene the beauty of Martia reorders the 'chaos' of Dowsacer's humour, the image of the beloved occupying the centre of self/kingdom, and reordering it. A similar pattern is developed in Shakespeare's *Twelfth Night*, where the notional Viola-as-female (projected beyond the end of the play, but not seen since 'her' entrance) occupies a similarly notional space, as 'Orsino's mistress and his fancy's queen'.[121] The play's often remarked on 'lyrical' quality is partly a product of its graceful and very complete metaphorisation of action: – Olivia is the 'soul within the house'[122] on which Viola, who 'acts', even 'personates', Orsino's woes, makes her rhetorical impress – and melancholy is again a kind of lapse of the knowable, the social world re-sorted into households at the end. Sebastian's remark, that Olivia cannot be mad, or she could not run her household, works by analogy rather than diagnosis. By bringing the soul-as-chatelaine idea back to our attention, it reminds us of the temporariness of farcical disorder. Olivia's loss of control over house/self/world, her recognition that 'ourselves we do not owe'[123] (that is, own), releases her into the remaking of 'character', the loss of fixed subjecthood, which the play presents as the experience of love. The discourse of fancy, melancholy, madness, the flow of humour, is finally contained and ordered, and again that order is unimaginable, projected outside the play.

Malvolio may be taken by Maria for 'a kind of puritan',[124] but his interiority when witnessed is pathetically empty. Alone he rehearses modes of social behaviour to himself, he lives entirely within the outward character of his occupation. That is why his 'gulling' is so cruelly self-entrapping – he is the last person in whom one could detect any depth of melancholy or madness, but the deceit that Maria engineers foists the derangement of identifying signs on a man who has nothing within at all, so traps him in the character of a social self-presentation, foists humour on a man as static and organised as the social forms he exists to uphold. Florila, or the ladies that have such a good time at Mrs Allwit's christening party (in Middleton's *A Chaste Maid in Cheapside*)[125] represent the fascinating but also threatening buoyancy of a puritan sense of self. Melancholy opens up a notional space in which the world is reflected. The effect of interiority is, most obviously in Hamlet, produced by the gap of 'is' and 'seems', that sense of a 'substance' in excess of signs, which Shakespeare characteristically explores. Shakespeare's most powerful effects often depend on deflection of audience attention away from knowable signs to an unknowable but notional 'larger' entity. That this effect is often worked out through character does not mean that such an entity is a 'real' self, in a post-romantic sense, though it may well be that such a device can partially accommodate the importation of such a sense of self through the secondary texts of performance and commentary. It may be an heroic self, or something inter-personal – the state or (as in *As You Like It*) gender. Webster may well imitate this effect in his own problematisations of character. But all these effects are the product of the same discourse of the human, the same rhetorical assumptions, the same model of the self. Ideas of melancholy and humour accommodate a social and private behaviour to it, but as Chapman's Florila indicates, however sketchily, the later Elizabethan period sees the emergence of a discourse of the self that radically redraws this model. The purity of pure religion, and the reason why it was to a bewildered Labervele just 'mental stuffe', is its independence of outward signs and its assumptions of an authority coming not through an established social hierarchy, but directly to the individual, from God. Heywood's adversary, 'I. G.' writes in his 'refutation' of *the Apology*:

> The first and last history concerning trecherous murthers committed by untrusty wives upon their husbands, hee applyeth to playes, because at plaies their first discoveries were intimate.
>
> But it was farre otherwise, for these bloody-minded wives lay long in their sinnes without repentance, God for a great while using mercy and patience towards them: But when he saw them to persist in their inflexible stubburnnesse, that instead of suing to him for grace and remissions of their sinnes, they provoked him to greater anger, and instead of coming to the temple there to pray, to haunt Sathans Sinagogue there to see sport and feed their pleasures: hee even tooke them napping in the Divells Sanctuary: that where they thought to conceive much mirth from vanity, there they might be prickt in conscience, and receive the beginning of their sorrow, at last to bring them to repentence, that God might save their soules, though in his justice hee brought their bodies to destruction.[126]

The theatre has no particular power in this story, it is simply a location, if an evil one, in which and in opposition to which God's own design on the individual women's consciences finally comes to fruition. The writer's opposition to Heywood is a clash between two different models of the human – in Heywood's world-as-theatre the power of judgement is activated within rhetoric, and externally and socially expressed, while in I. G.'s biblical narrative of God's anger, all happens inwardly, between the women and their God. The privacy and interiority of the puritan writer allows no function for theatrical communication, while Heywood, conversely, takes over the judgemental role from God and attributes it to the effect of the mirror held up to the women's nature. His examples are, he says, 'familiar' in the sense of domestic – to bring theatre's power home to us, to remind us how close hidden crimes and secret subversions (both murderers are women, and so rebels against the 'heads' of their households) can be. To be an audience is thus to be excitingly, even dangerously, implicated in revelations of human potential; there is something rather suspicious, Heywood and his supporters hint, about those who are afraid to openly participate in this. In the tradition which Perkins and Heywood seek to defend, acting is revelation, not disguise, a mirror, not simply 'sport' and theatre is not 'Sathans Sinagogue', but a model of God's judgement, made over (blasphemously, in I. G.'s eyes) to the

170 Character: Acting and Being on the Pre-Modern Stage

human agency, the audience, that through the mirror's power are both observers and observed, judges and judged. What Perkins, either as actor or as a rather exhibitionist audience member 'seems' is exactly what he is – all is extroverted, nothing internalised, as the puritans troublingly and threateningly internalise their moral sense. The derangement of outward signs is a radical challenge to a society that orders itself round the heirarchical placings of a readable discourse, as is the insistence on an unreadable, inspirational interiority, a private knowledge of divine reality. This short circuits the dominant discourse of authority more abruptly than Hamlet could: humour is an inner discourse by virtue of an exterior affirmed elsewhere, but the mental stuff of Protestant interiority flows beyond the containment of an established hierarchy and its identifying practices.

Page 170

1. *The Complete Works of John Webster*, edited by F. L. Lucas (London, 1927), Vol. IV, 'An Excellent Actor', p. 42.
2. See Chapter 2, pp. 64–9.
3. Heywood, *Apology*, [134r].
4. John Marston, *Antonio and Mellida*, ed., G. K. Hunter (London, 1965), Induction, p. 4.
5. Ibid., 3–4, p. 4.
6. Ibid., 7–19, p. 4.
7. Ibid., 29, p. 5.
8. Ibid., 68, p. 7.
9. Ibid., 115–17, pp. 8–9.
10. Ibid., 27, p. 5.
11. Ibid., 99–101, 104–6, p. 8.
12. Ibid., 54, p. 5.
13. See, for example, Peter Thomson in *Shakespeare's Theatre* (London, 1983), p. 117.
14. Webster, 'An Excellent Actor', 11–12, p. 43.
15. Ibid., 19–23, p. 43.
16. Horace, 'Poetry as Picture', *Ars Poetica*, 361.
17. *Henry V*, prologue, 4–8, p. 59.
18. *Henry IV*, pt. 1, I. 3. 30–68, pp. 58–9.
19. *The Overburian Characters* (Oxford, 1936), p. 92.
20. *Oxford English Dictionary*, repr. 1970. 'Personal', sense 6.
21. Webster, 'An Excellent Actor', 35–7, p. 43.
22. Ibid., 10–12, p. 43.
23. Heywood, *Apology*, [a2v].
24. Webster, 'An Excellent Actor', 23–6, p. 43.

25. In the *Penguin Book of Elizabethan Verse*, edited by Edward Lucie Smith (Harmondsworth, 1965), p. 216.
26. Heywood, *Apology*, [a3r–v].
27. Ibid., [F4r].
28. Ibid., [F3v].
29. Ibid., [B3v].
30. Francis Beaumont, *The Knight of the Burning Pestle*, edited by Michael Hattaway (London, 1969), Induction 50–3, p. 14.
31. Heywood, *Apology*, [Fv].
32. *The Tragedy of Hamlet, Prince of Denmark*, edited by Harold Jenkins (London, 1981) III. ii. 19–24, p. 288.
33. Heywood, *Apology* [Gv].
34. *Hamlet*, I. v. 46, p. 218.
35. See Anne Barton, *Shakespeare and the Idea of the Play* (London, 1962), p. 159.
36. *Hamlet*, III. ii. 31–5, p. 289.
37. Ibid., III. iii. 36–71, pp. 314–6.
38. Ibid., III. iv. 18–19, p. 319.
39. 'The lady doth protest too much, me thinks.' Ibid., III. ii. 225, p. 301.
40. Ibid., III. iii. 384–5, p. 319.
41. Ibid., I. v. 85–6, p. 220.
42. Ibid., III. iv. 36, p. 320.
43. *Aeneid*, I. 462.
44. Ibid., IV. 30.
45. *The Rape of Lucrece*, in *Narrative Poems*, edited by William Burto (New York, 1968) 1368–9, p. 139.
46. Ibid., 1371, p. 139.
47. Ibid., 1385–6, p. 140.
48. Ibid., 1443–63, pp. 142–3.
49. Ibid., 1471–84, pp. 142–3.
50. Ibid., 1499–512. p. 144.
51. Ibid., 1562–8, p. 146.
52. Ibid., 1423–9, p. 141.
53. *A Midsummer Night's Dream*, edited by Stanley Wells (Harmondsworth, 1967), V. i. 208–11, p. 114.
54. *Richard II*, V. v. 1–5, p. 141.
55. *King Lear*, III. vi.
56. *Richard II*, V. v. 6–17, p. 141.
57. Ibid., V. v. 18–21, p. 141.
58. Ibid., V. v. 111–12, p. 145.
59. The first line of Edward Dyer's poem, from Rawlingson MS 85. in the *Penguin Book of Elizabethan Verse*, edited by Edward Lucie Smith (Harmondsworth, 1965), pp. 112–3.
60. *Richard II*, V. v. 31–41, p. 142, quoted in Chapter 2, p. 81.
61. Ibid., and *Hamlet*, I. ii. 129, p. 187. The Arden edition, used elsewhere in this book, gives 'solid' as 'sullied'.
62. *Hamlet*, I. ii. 76–86, pp. 183–4.
63. *Antony and Cleopatra*, III. vii. 15, p. 126.
64. Francis Barker makes such an identification in *The Tremulous Private Body*.

65. *Hamlet*, II. ii. 159, p. 245. The literal meaning, as Polonius uses it, would seem to be as the centre of the earth.
66. Ibid., II. ii. 6, p. 237.
67. Ibid., II. ii. 239–65, pp. 250–1.
68. Ibid., II. ii. 295–308, pp. 253–4.
69. Ibid., II. ii. 242–3, pp. 242–3.
70. Ibid., II. ii. 121–2, p. 243.
71. Ibid., IV. v. 7–13, p. 347.
72. Ibid., III. ii. 95–7, p. 293.
73. Ibid., II. i. 75–100, pp. 234–5.
74. Ibid., III. i. 50, p. 277.
75. Ibid., I. ii. 137–56, pp. 188–9.
76. Ibid., I. ii. 5, p. 178.
77. Ibid., I. ii. 102, p. 185.
78. Ibid., III. i. 56–60, pp. 277–8.
79. Ibid., III. ii. 57–74, pp. 290–2.
80. Ibid., III. i. 64–82, pp. 278–9.
81. Ibid., III. i. 83–8, pp. 280–1.
82. Ibid., III. iii. 61–2, p. 315.
83. Ibid., III. iii. 69–71, p. 316.
84. Ibid., III. i. 54, p. 277.
85. Ibid., IV. v. 66, p. 346.
86. Ibid., II. ii. 259, p. 251.
87. Ibid., V. i. 178, p. 386.
88. Ibid., V. i. 116–17, p. 383.
89. Ibid., I. ii. 74–5, p. 183.
90. Ibid., V. ii. 229–35, p. 408.
91. Ibid., V. ii. 76, p. 398.
92. Ibid., V. i. 293, p. 393.
93. Ibid., V. ii. 363–6, p. 416.
94. Ibid., V. ii. 402–5, pp. 418–19.
95. *Hamlet*, I. iv. 13–38, pp. 208–11.
96. *Othello*, edited by M. R. Ridley (London, 1958) III. iii. 71–9, pp. 72–3.
97. *Hamlet*, IV. v. 99–102, pp. 353–4.
98. Prudentius, *Psychomachia*, 875–7.
99. See Sander L. Gilman, *Seeing The Insane* (New York, 1982) p. 5.
100. *An Humorous Dayes Mirth* in *The Plays of George Chapman: The Comedies*, edited by Allan Holaday (Urbana, 1970) I. i. 15, p. 67.
101. *Every Man out of his Humour*, in *Ben Jonson*, edited by C. H. Herford and Percy Simpson (Oxford, 1927), Vol. III, Prologue 88–109, pp. 431–21.
102. *Every Man in his Humour*, Herford and Simpson, Vol. III, II. iii. 40–72, pp. 329–30.
103. Ibid., II. iii. 72–4, p. 330.
104. Ibid., II. iv. 1–23, p. 331, III. v. 1–29, pp. 353–5, IV. xi. 1–9, p. 390.
105. In the Epilogue to *Every Man out of his Humour* 'which, in the presentation before Queene E. was thus varyed . . .' pp. 599–600.
106. Ibid., V. xi. 65, p. 597.
107. Ibid., Prologue 110–22, p. 432.
108. Chapman, *An Humorous Dayes Mirth*, I. i. 7, p. 67.

109. Ibid., I. i. 13–20, p. 67.
110. Ibid., II. i. 26–34, p. 83.
111. Ibid., I. ii. 79–80, p. 70.
112. Ibid., I. iv. 154–72, p. 76.
113. Heywood, *An Apology for Actors*, a3[r].
114. Chapman, *An Humorous Dayes Mirth*, I. i. 11–19, p. 68.
115. Ibid., II. ii. 1–11, p. 86.
116. Ibid., IV. iii. 82–3, p. 106.
117. Ibid., II. ii. 58–60, p. 87.
118. Ibid., II. ii. 68, p. 87.
119. Ibid., II. ii. 134, p. 89.
120. Ibid., II. ii. 116–21, p. 89.
121. *Twelfth Night, or What You Will*, edited by M. M. Mahood (Harmondsworth, 1968) V. l. 385, p. 131.
122. Ibid., I. 5. 258, p. 65.
123. Ibid., I. 5. 300, p. 66.
124. Ibid., II. 3. 134, p. 73.
125. Thomas Middleton, *A Chaste Maid in Cheapside*, edited by R. B. Parker (London, 1969) III. ii. pp. 55–67.
126. *A Refutation of the Apology for Actors*, by I. G. (London, 1615). Reprinted with the *Apology* (New York, 1973) pp. 42–3.

5

Character and the Passions

I COMMON SENSE AND THE UNIVERSAL MIND

The Elizabethan development of a rhetorical theatre as the arena of politics and historical representation has at its basis assumptions to which middle-class Protestantism opposes itself – an opposition to the idea of a visible, common, indivisibly social life, an opposition that expresses itself in the construction of interiorities and in the assertion of an authoritative basis for the self in individual relation to God and his revealed word. But, as we have seen, that theatre, in its articulate self-reflexivity, its complex mapping of the unsaid against the spoken, can at least point to the opposite of itself. It has no simple unitary value as the symbol of a certain kind of social 'order'. To examine the representation of the human as a political praxis (which is how Aristotle and the rhetoricians examine it) is to become aware of the complexity of Elizabethan theatrical practice, especially in an area that often unexamined notion of character has tended to obscure.

I intend to move on from this theatre to a later theoretical construct arrived at in opposition to it: Thomas Rymer's neo-Aristotelian critique of *The Tragedies of The Last Age*, in the light of its French sources and of Dryden's careful attempts both to conciliate and counter it. The neo-classical theatre of the later seventeenth century is of interest not only as a stage in the development of something with which we are more familiar – the post-romantic Shakespeare – but also as a phenomenon of the general business of 'Restoration', and hence as a reflection back on what must be for my argument the massive historical 'given' of the revolution itself. It is too easy to invoke puritan opposition to theatre as a kind of impassable rift in the history of English drama. But it is precisely because the ideological project of Restoration culture is so thoroughly revisionary, not only as regards the memory of the conflicts of the mid-century, but also in the effacement or 'improvement' of a pre-civil-war culture marked by the emergence of those conflicts, that the interregnum appears as a gap, as that which could not be represented within available theatres, but did irrevocably change theatre. The civil war effected a revolution in

174

theatrical representation, but this is most marked in the evolution of precisely those forms which *need not* register it. The presence in drama of a revolution and its origins is most visible as a gap, a difference perceivable, but not explicitly accounted for, the difference between the new drama and 'tragedies of the last age'.

Rymer retells the story (or 'fable', to use his term) of one of the three plays on which he concentrates, *Rollo, Duke of Normandy*. After a brief narrative account he suggests a revision in line with his interpretation of Aristotle's prescriptions. Among other changes, the character of the virtuous successor to the throne should be strengthened, and thus the play's resolution made more fitting — '*Aubrey* should in all his words and actions appear great, promising, and Kingly, to deserve that care which Heaven manifests so wonderfully in his Restoration'.[1] As his choice of terms here suggests, Rymer proposes his revision with an eye to the larger cultural project of the restoration of the Stuarts. This is not to say that he is recasting the play as propaganda. His project is much larger. The things he wishes to excise from theatrical representation are presented as the untutored fancies of an age that did not know the *Poetics*, and the *Poetics* are seen not as rules but as methodical distillations of a knowledge of unchanging human nature. Hence their universal applicability. The full title of his volume is *The Tragedies of the Last Age Consider'd and Examin'd by The Practice of the Ancients, and by the Common Sense of All Ages*, the point being that the one is simply a formulation of the other. Rymer's language is consequently brusque and colloquial, his appeal is to groups outside the realms of learning — '... certainly there is not requir'd much Learning, or that a man must be some *Aristotle*, and *Doctor* of *Subtleties*, to form a right judgement in this particular; common sense suffices; and rarely have I known the *Women-Judges* mistake in these points, when they have the patience to think, and (left to their own heads) they decide with their own sense'.[2] To claim the *Poetics* as common sense (to use them as the foundations for a commonsense aesthetic of theatrical representation) may seem paradoxical from a modern point of view, but however quirkily he develops it, Rymer was only following contemporary French scholars and critics. 'When I come to examine the Manner in which Aristotle delivers them,' claims a slightly later text, an anonymous English translation of Dacier's preface to Aristotle, here discussing the matter of 'rules', 'I find them so evident and conformable to Nature, that I cannot but be sensible they are true; for what does *Aristotle*? He gives not his Rules as *Legislators* do their Laws, without any other reason than their Wills only; he advances nothing but what is accompanied with Reason, drawn from the common Sentiment of Mankind, insomuch that the Men themselves become the Rule and Measure of what he prescribes'.[3] Rymer's critique of Shakespeare's *Othello*, in a sequel volume, has given him a slightly misleading notoriety, as an eccentrically iconoclastic literary critic. But his reopening of a debate about Aristotle's *Poetics* has the importance of establishing this sense of a universal common sense as the grounds of a representation of the human. His opposition of this to the 'last age' may be mocked for its critical detail (he invites such a response, he finds the dialectics of common sense in provocative badinage) but his theoretical orientation is adopted not only by contemporaries like Dryden, but, in its redefinition of the proper ends of theatrical mimesis, its anglicisation of Aristotle's *to katholos* as 'common sense', it leaves its mark on such later Shakespeareans as Johnson and Bradley.

The 'universal' (*katholos*) is introduced into the argument by Aristotle as the special field of poetry, as opposed to that of history. This makes poetry more philosophical than history, more general in application, in that sense more true.[4] Later writers emphasise poetry's distinction from philosophy too, as being more concrete in its means of persuasion, and so potentially more effective as an educational force. Poetry's alignment with the universal governs accounts of how poetry and drama work — hence the necessity of justifying the rules themselves as 'the common sense of all ages' — accounts of effect on the audience, of the proper subjects of representation, of the proper mode of that mimesis. It is in this light that we should see Rymer's focus on the kings of pre-civil-war tragedy (a concern he shares with his French sources, though their worries are concentrated on democratic Athens). Rymer points out that we are too apt to confuse 'use' with 'nature'. In other words, what may happen, even what usually happens, is not as significant as that reality to which our reason points us, the reality that we deduce and refine philosophically. The verisimilitude at which the poet aims is achieved by such a selection and by a presentation (by however formal a means — for Rymer, the classical Chorus, in making plain the relevance of the action to the audience, is an aid to verisimilitude[5]) that opens up the universal significance of the performance. 'Use' (in the sense of 'the usual') by comparison points to the banal, the arbitrary and meaningless. 'Nature' is often used as a term for such things, but this is a misapplication of it.

'And far from all decorum is it, that we find the King *drolling* and quibling with *Bessus* and his Buffoons, and worse, that they should presume to break their little jests upon him.

This too is *natural,* some will say. There are in nature many things which *Historians* are asham'd to mention, as below the dignity of an History: Shall we then suffer a *Tom Coriat* in *Poetry*? Shall we on the most important day of King's Reign, and at Court be content with such entertainment as is not above a Cobler's shop? Might not a Poet as well described to us how the King eats and drinks, or goes to *Stool*; for these actions are also *natural* . . . .'[6]

Even (perhaps especially) those particularities proper to history are disallowed in Rymer's prescriptive development of the idea of *katholos*. The classical writers, according to Rymer, 'found that *History* grosly taken was neither proper to *instruct*, not apt to *please*: and therefore they would not trust History for their examples, but refin'd upon the History and thence contriv'd something more *philosophical,* and more *accurate* than *History*'. A story like that of Rollo on the other hand 'may well be a History; for never man of common *sense* could set himself to invent anything so gross'.[7] 'Common sense', as we can see from this, is not the common sense of empiricism, (for Rymer that simply amounts to an appeal to 'use'), but a sense of what is common, of what a king *is* as king, apart from the physical accidents of his being, or the often unfortunate particulars of his individual acts. The tragedies of the last age, in writing without a proper idea of universals, remain grotesquely in thrall to history. 'Some have remark'd, that *Athens* being a *Democracy* the Poets, in favour of their Government, expos'd Kings, and made them unfortunate. But certainly, examine the Kings of their *Tragedies,* they appear all *Heroes,* and ours but *Dogs,* in comparison of them. So respectful they seem to Kings in their *Democracy,* and so unthinking and unpolitick are our *Poets* under a *Monarchy* . . .. They made the Kings *unfortunate,* we made them *wicked* : they made them to be *pittied,* we make them to be *curst* and *abhorr'd*.'[8]

Rymer's strictures on the proper representation of hierarchy is not limited to the matter of the monarchy – a woman for example should not be shown to kill a man unless he is her social inferior. Nor is the idea of hierarchy he posits essentially different from that from which earlier seventeenth-century dramatists work. The difference lies in his idea of its proper theatrical representation. The notion of the universal as poetry's field allows the neo-classicists to bypass the historical particulars of the way such hierarchies operate. More crucially it represents such a hierarchy not as political praxis, as the rhetorical theatre did, but as 'nature', thus understood as universally valid, as knowable in common sense. These are arguments to which many earlier figures may well have assented. Rymer's point is that the existing modes of theatrical mimesis do not adequately represent them. The neo-classical theatre however would make anything else unrepresentable, would disallow the dangerously open, even subversive, mode of that earlier theatre.

Rymer's theatre is a theoretical construct, though an influential one, and it stands apart from contemporary stage practice, to which it opposes itself not only in terms of a taste for dubious revivals, but implicitly in the unrespectable naturalism of comedy and the disorderly violence of the popular tragedies. It does nonetheless give powerful expression to the project of a new restored theatre, on the model of the French theatre's exemplary liaison of absolute power and neo-classical decorum. Like so many products of the Restoration, the result is equivocal and contradictory. But it marks a distance from earlier tradition, and forces a redefinition of the terms on which those plays might be revived. Whatever the notoriety of the *Othello* passages, Rymer might be seen as laying the foundation for Shakespeare's pre-eminence, in depressing the reputations of Fletcher and Jonson, and in giving Dryden the terms in which to present Shakespeare as the universal genius. Though Rymer uses 'the universal' to exempt tragedy from history in a way that finds Shakespeare and the other 'dramatists of the last age' equally defective, 'the universal' becomes central to later attempts to recoup Shakespeare for at least some neo-classical values. But by then it is developed in terms of an anti-Aristotelian evaluation of 'character' above 'action'. Samuel Johnson, in labelling Shakespeare 'the poet of nature' claims that his 'characters are not modified by the customs of particular places . . . by the peculiarities of studies or professions . . . or by the accidents of transient fashions or temporary opinions: they are the genuine progeny of common humanity, such as the world will always supply, and observation will always find'.[9] This judgement is taken up (it seems to have become so much common sense that it need not be acknowledged as Johnson's) by A. C. Bradley, opposing it to a morbidly modern interest in psychological particularity.[10] That Shakespeare is a 'universal genius' is still one of the first things we 'learn' about him. Its origins would seem to lie in Dryden's answers to Rymer. Dryden grounds this universality in the affective use of character (though he does not, as Johnson does, link the two into an account of 'human nature'). In doing so he opposes Rymer, but he takes over and confirms the anti-historical, apolitically 'universalising' tendency of Rymer's argument.

Dryden's main argument in the notes he made for an answer to

Rymer was with the most uncompromisingly argued aspect of Rymer's Aristotelianism, his assent to the privileging of *praxis* above *ethos*. Like Rapin, and other French writers whom he follows in this, *ethos* is carefully translated as habitual knowable behaviour – *mores* becomes *moeurs* becomes 'manners'. But another more up-to-date term is added – 'the passions'. 'The manners' as Dryden defines them in his 'Grounds of Criticism in Tragedy' 'are understood to be those inclinations, whether natural or acquired, which move and carry us to actions, good, bad, or indifferent, in a play; or which incline the persons to such or such actions.'[11] The term then is a rather pedantic translation of *ethos/mores*; a point which needs to be stressed in order to counter our more trivialised sense of the term, and consequent trivialisation of this aspect of Restoration writing. Character too is defined by Dryden in carefully classical terms. 'From the manners, the characters of persons are derived; for indeed the characters are no other than the inclinations, as they appear in the several persons of the poem; a character being thus defined, that which distinguishes one man from another'.[12] So Dryden puts character in relation to *ethos*/manner as the mode in which it becomes apparent and distinct. But by invoking the passions he adds into his equation a term more recently developed, by the French philosopher Descartes, in opposition to the Aristotelian tradition. 'Under this general head of manners, the passions are naturally included as belonging to the characters.'[13] The passions form the central plank of Dryden's reply to Rymer, as developed in the 'Grounds of Criticism' out of the *Heads of an Answer to Rymer*, written in the end-papers of his copy of *The Tragedies of the Last Age Considered*. They provide the means of reconciling Rymer's neo-classical prescription of universality with the intense deployment of character devices, in Shakespeare's and Jonson's plays particularly.

Traditional accounts of the passions, like Thomas Wright's *The Passions of the Mind* (1604), combine rhetorical study with post-classical medical theory to account for and classify the passions of *affectus* on which, as for Cicero and Quintillian, it was assumed that rhetoric had its effect.[14] Descartes, however, initially in response to the queries of an aristocratic patroness, produced a version of a then current genre of treatise which decisively makes a break with Aristotelian tradition. At the beginning of Article I of *Les Passions de L'Ame* (1649), Descartes declares that 'there is nothing in which it is so clear that the sciences we have from the ancients are defective, as in what they have written of the passions'.[15] He aims to remedy this by logical deduction from empirical evidence. Where a writer like Marin

Cureau de la Chambre presents in his *Les caracteres des passions* (1604–62) a massive taxonomy of the passions in terms of their readable signs, their characters, Descartes traces them to their origins, classifying six 'primitive' passions, from which the others are derived, and presenting them in order according to the sequence with which we tend to experience them in relation to some outside object – wonder, love, hatred, desire, joy and sorrow.[16]

The most radical and most influential aspect of Descartes's philosophy is his redefinition and description of the distinctness of soul and body, and of the relation between the two. This is the basis of his account of the passions. For Descartes, the passions are an effect of the relation of the soul and body. Passions are a kind of perceptions, or registerings, sometimes of the soul itself, as in its awareness of the operations of its own will, but more often caused by the body. Of these perceptions Descartes only classes as passions in the proper sense those that, though felt in, and in Descartes's terms 'sustained by', the body, refer back to the soul – unlike hunger, for example, which 'refers' to the body, or sensory perceptions (taste, smell and so on) which refer to external objects. The ingenious and intricate physiology with which Descartes supports this description is not strictly relevant here. But it is important to note the essential separateness of soul and body. The soul in itself is unified, single, individual. The body is a kind of machine, powered by heat and the internal motion of heat-generated 'animal spirits'. It is endlessly divisible, literally and in the method of Descartes's mechanistic descriptions. But the internal division of the soul (the conflicts that seem to take place in it in post-Aristotelian accounts) involve, for Descartes, a gross misrecognition of the nature of the soul. 'There is only one soul in us, and that soul possesses no diversity of parts within itself; it is sensitive and rational too, and all its appetites are volitions. The error that has been committed in setting it to play a variety of roles, usually opposed to each other, comes simply from the fact that its functions are not clearly distinguished from those of the body; one should attribute only to the body all that can be seen in us to oppose reason'.[17] Descartes's destruction of the rationale of the psychomachia idea – which he seems to be referring to not only here but in the next article, his account of the 'arming' of the will – is a necessary part of his redefinition of the subject. The Cartesian subject is a unified 'soul', essentially separate from its body/machine, by means of which it receives perceptions of an equally separate 'external' reality. There are not good and bad passions, the passions are indifferent in themselves, and they exist not as faculties of the soul, needing regulation from within it, but as aspects of the soul/body relation, requiring the soul's attention and discipline. The analogy Descartes uses is with training dogs.[18] The Cartesian subject is not the always potentially disordered state or kingdom of the post-Aristotelian model, but the private individual, educating and controlling the defective animal-machine that his bodily existence requires.

Rymer and his French sources adopt this more satisfyingly modern account of the subject in preference to that of the rhetorical tradition. Its use as the basis for re-interpreting *The Poetics* creates as much of a hybrid as did Scaliger's importation of the *mores/affectus* distinction into his discussion of Orestes's crime. The confusion it causes Rymer (the self-evident paucity of his subsequent account of the tragic effect) leaves Dryden the room to formulate a new theatrical theory of the passions, one more favourable to English drama.

The doctrine of the passions allows first Rapin and then Rymer to re-examine Aristotle's idea of pity and terror. For Rapin, of all the passions on which theatre can act, these are the most important, as governing the moral life.[19] An area of ambiguity opens up here, as to how pity and terror are evoked in the audience – by the fable or by the characters? By the fable, it would seem – it is as for Aristotle the operation of *mythos* that creates audience response, here by evoking pity and fear as to the outcome of the story.

For Rymer, as for Rapin, Aristotle's point in giving pre-eminence to *praxis* is simple in itself, however powerful its implications. If *mythos*, or 'fable' is the soul of tragedy then, according to Rymer, it ought to be a rational soul.[20] Both as the organising principle of the play and as the source of its impact on the audience, it ought to make sense (common sense). Hence his provocative re-telling of the stories of the plays. Rymer's rational fable is the source of a play's effect on its audience, and so it ought both to participate in a rational knowledge of universals, and it ought to be organised purposively to lead the audience's feelings to rational and ameliorative conclusion. Pre-civil-war tragedy patently fails to do this.

Where for Aristotle the climax of tragedy was in moments of recognition, in the plot's remaking of identities conceived of as social or familial rather than 'personal', for the neo-classicists it is in the healthy exercise of the passions, their retraining to proper ends through the exercise of a rational fable. The audience is acted on as individuals, who perceive universal forces at work in themselves; recognition is therefore a species of self-recognition, the recognition of 'human nature' in oneself. Tragedy provides the minatory recognition of a disastrous potential in human nature, and so both invokes pity and fear and corrects them. The persons in the play serve to impress this on us, to open the wider significance, the 'verisimilitude' of the action. Rapin's example, the Oedipus story, shows Oedipus experiencing such a purgation within the play, whose action turns on the presentation of the fable (which is him) to him.[21] It thus makes a powerful but ambiguous example – do we feel pity and terror because Oedipus is feeling them within the play, or do we feel something larger (more universal) on which his experience reflects? Probably the second. But Rapin's example is problematic in other ways. After describing the massive emotional effect such a play should have on his audience, he then forswears this particular example, whose anti-royalist implications may have pleased the Athenians (Rapin is probably the source for the similar point made by Rymer), but are as foreign to contemporary French society as the amusements of the insular and blood-thirsty English.[22] Rapin thus elegantly sidesteps (as Rymer does not) the prescription of theatrical practice, while opening up the possibility of a powerfully emotive theatre of moral persuasion. As in his account of the poet of genius, early in the *Reflections*, self-examination and self-recognition play an important part in both art and morality and it is this (rather than any simple notion of didacticism) that seems to provide the common ground between them.[23] Both he and Rymer end in a position where the audience is conceived of as individuals, with responsibility for implicitly defective passions, which the play, by asserting the universal human nature, acts on and reforms. But the figures in the play, whose passions and manners are depicted 'fitly' by writer and performers, are conceived of as components in the fable/*mythos*, not discussable as 'characters' abstractable from it (any more than they would have been for previous writers). The example of Oedipus points in a different direction – as a figure who *is* his story, his citation by Rapin would seem to indicate an interest in the possibility of a theatre of empathetic individualism, as a development of the neo-classical mode.

Dryden however takes an anti-Aristotelian line; a reply to Rymer should stress ' . . . that the fable is not the greatest masterpiece of a tragedy, tho' it be the foundation of it'.[24] The building metaphor is developed in the 'Grounds' to redefine the nature of the primacy of *mythos*, in a way that elegantly allows *ethos* a more effective role, while preserving the sense of a necessary interrelation.

After the plot, which is the foundation of the play, the next thing to which we ought to apply our judgement is the manners, for now the poet comes to work above ground: the ground-work indeed is that which is most necessary, as that upon which depends the firmness of the whole fabric; yet it strikes not the eye so much as the beauties or imperfections of the manners, the thoughts, and the expressions.[25]

In the context of the passions, this allows a more inclusive account of audience response than Rymer's and Rapin's. For them pity and terror are the keys to tragedy, the passions that they work on and through to produce an educative catharsis. But Dryden claims that 'all the passions in their turns are to be set in a ferment: as joy, anger, love, fear are to be used as the poet's commonplaces; and a general concernment for the principal actors is to be raised by making them appear such in their characters, their words and actions, as will interest the audience in their fortunes'.[26] Dryden concedes to neo-classical theory an interpretation of *katharsis* as an education of the passions, like Descartes's dog-training, and the notion of a proper universality. But the source of the universality is in the 'working' up as vividly as possible of the whole gamut of 'passions'. This aspect of 'manners', made 'apparent' and 'distinct' as 'characters' is the meeting-ground of audience and play, the accessible and habitable spaces of the tragic edifice, where 'fable' is its necessary, but only broadly deducible, 'foundation'.

This version of the tragic is obviously a great deal more accommodating to English tragedy than Rymer's. Dryden does not want universality to rule out national difference; a patriotic desire to establish English writing as *more* universal than Greek or French underlies Dryden's arguments, and indeed remained a cornerstone of Shakespeare's pre-eminence. Shakespeare emerges from Dryden's reassessment as the poet of the passions, thus understood; perhaps inferior to Jonson in making his characters fully apparent, wholly distinct, but possessed of 'an universal mind, which comprehended all characters and passions'.[27] Character, passion, manners, are distinct though interrelated things — character here is still character as visible, readable sign. But Dryden's subtle revision of Rymer's precepts involves his taking over basic ideas — the universal, the Cartesian account of the human subject — while perceiving that they develop an anti-Aristotelian notion of what we now inclusively call 'character' more successfully than they serve Rymer's own Aristotelianism.

Furthermore, he is able to build persuasively on a sense of where the richness of the Shakespearean texts lies – their fertile and problematic exploitation of character devices. This is instanced for Dryden, in an example brilliantly chosen to oppose the orderly and decorous presentations of the human privileged by neo-classical theory, by the disorderly and indecorously non-human Caliban, 'a person which was not in nature',[28] but a person nonetheless. At the end of the 'Grounds' Dryden promises to return to the issue of 'character'; 'I had intended to have proceeded to the last property of manners, which is that they must be constant, and the characters maintained the same from the beginning to the end; and from thence to have proceeded to the thoughts and expressions suitable to a tragedy: but I will first see how this will relish with the age'.[29] Working here from the familiar Aristotelian/Horatian prescriptions for character, Dryden has isolated, as an issue consequent on the idea of character he assembles and promotes, the problem of unity within an individuated 'character'. He returns to it to some degree in the remarks on Chaucer in the preface to *Fables Ancient and Modern* – another English genius, whose superiority lies in 'character', another reputation persuasively and lastingly defined.[30] But Dryden's own penchant for visual metaphors compounds his conservative definition of character as *visible* ('apparent') distinctiveness – this 'unity', as he describes, it remains a matter of repetition and blatancy in visible characteristics. The question of individual coherence and identity was to be developed in the next century, for which Dryden's work and Rymer's becomes in itself a kind of 'foundation'.

II UNITY OF CHARACTER

Spectator and role in the late seventeenth-century theatre are Cartesian subjects. Their subjecthood, unified and coherent, lies a little beyond the incoherent and often warring forces not only of the world, but of their own bodily selves, their 'persons'. So it is distant too from the passions which are its perceptions of all that is not it, of body, world and of other subjects. Descartes conveys this by two examples, the first rather startling, the second more conventional.

> For example: a husband weeps for a dead wife whom (as sometimes happens) he would be distressed to see brought back to life. His heart could be broken by sorrow (excited in him by the trappings of mourning and by the absence of someone to whose conversation he

had become accustomed) and perhaps some traces of love or pity, presenting themselves to his imagination, draw real tears from his eyes. Nonetheless he feels, at the same time, a secret joy, in his innermost soul. This emotion possesses such power that the sorrow and tears which accompany it can in no way diminish its force. And when we read strange adventures in a book, or when we see them represented on a stage, sometimes it excites sorrow in us, sometimes joy, or love, or hate, and all the passions together, according to the variety of objects which it offers to our imaginations; but together with this we have pleasure, to feel them excited in us, and that pleasure is an intellectual joy, which could as well be born of sorrow, as of all the other passions.[31]

This intellectual joy is the basic position of the spectator. For Descartes it is a token of the control the soul can possess over the passions, and his theatrical illustration could be used to justify the very existence of theatre, as the means by which the passions could be exercised and reformed. This is, as we have seen, what neo-classical critics took *katharsis* to be. Applied to the actor, Descartes's formulation anticipates Diderot's famous paradox, the paradox embodied in the great English actor David Garrick, of the passionate performance (the performance that presents and works on the passions) which comes from some point of essential detachment and control in the actor himself. Garrick is often credited with the invention of a new style of acting, a style that can be seen as a discovery of 'real' Shakespeare or simply an improvement in acting 'technique'. In my terms his achievement is a redefinition of character for the actor, a decisive move from the rhetorical model to a new 'substantive' mode. Garrick is the embodiment in theatrical terms of the newly dominant post-Cartesian subject; hence what his contemporaries saw as his cultural centrality.[32] His theatrical revolution focused the decisive outcome of a debate where philosophy and literary theory converge.

Baroque acting had as its object the rhetorical expression of common passions. For a seventeenth-century actor a role was a sequence of loci, a series of places in the progress of a plot where the decision to act, a choice of actions or the consequence of action were articulated. Leading actors on the Restoration stage would take a large number of roles in each season, but give only half-a-dozen to twenty performances of any one play. Roles would not necessarily be distinct from one another in terms other than those of plot, or of what is an essentially moral perception of general distinctions of feeling – of 'the passions'.

Garrick's fame depended in part on a vivid presence, an ability to agreeably astound. But, as has been generally recognised, his vogue was more than simply personal; he established a new style of acting, not only in his own work but in that of his protèges and in the companies he managed. In acting terms, Garrick changed his contemporaries' sense not just of the means of presenting character, but of what character was. For Garrick and his followers, acting was the presentation by all the means at the actor's disposal of a coherent and consistent individual, not of the actor or the writer or any real person. It was the creation of an imaginary but possible being. His farce *The Irish Widow* (1772) turns on the familiar comic device by which a woman assumes a disagreeably shrewish persona to punish an older man who wants to marry her, and so secure a younger whom she chooses for herself. But the widow of the title, a lady of exemplary moral sensibility, shows an unwillingness to participate in the pretence perhaps surprising in a play written by the greatest actor of his time. 'Could I bring my heart to act contrary to its feelings' she says to her lover, 'would not you hate me for being a hypocrite, though it is done for your sake?' His eventual answer does not meet her moral objections directly, but the model of acting it proposes shifts the grounds of her problem. 'You are an excellent mimic' he tells her 'Assume but the character of your Irish female neighbour in the country, with which you astonished us so agreeably at Scarborough ....'[33] This solves the Irish Widow's dilemma – she is not deceiving anyone, any more than any fiction can ordinarily be said to deceive. She is not saying things she does not feel, she is no longer herself, she has created, from observation and wit, a being who did not exist before and who has in a way replaced her. The difference between this idea of acting and the style it superseded is, in these terms, the difference between the creation of a distinct coherent persona which replaced the actor's own, and the presentation of a series of choices, decisions to act and reactions discrete in themselves but adding up to a recognisable moral profile – character in a neo-classical sense. Such a shift is more than a matter of technique. It redefines the objectives of acting. The new style of acting was characterised by both detractors and apologists as a kind of 'mimicry'.

Fielding sends Tom Jones and his companion, the village school-master Partridge, to see Garrick's *Hamlet*. Unimpressed by the ghost at its first appearance at 'the scene between the ghost and Hamlet . . . Partridge gave that credit to Mr. Garrick, which he had denied to Jones, and fell into so violent a trembling that his knees knocked against each other ... "O la! sir," said he, "I perceive now it is what you told me. I am not afraid of anything; for I know it is but a play: and yet if I was frightened, I am not the only person ... if that little man there upon the stage is not frightened, I never saw any man frightened in my life ...."' But Partridge's participation in Garrick's emotional mimesis, far from implying an admiration of the actor's skills, renders those skills imperceptible:

> at the end ... Jones asked him, 'which of the players he had liked best?' To this he answered, with some appearance of indignation at the question. 'The king without doubt'. 'Indeed, Mr. Partridge,' says Mrs. Miller, 'you are not of the same opinion with the town; for they are all agreed, that Hamlet is acted by the best player who was ever on the stage.' 'He the best player!' cries Partridge, with a contemptuous sneer, 'Why I could act as well as he myself. I am sure if I had seen a ghost, I should have looked in the very same manner, and done just as he did. And then, to be sure, in that scene ... between him and his mother, where you told me he acted so fine, why ... any man ... that had had such a mother, would have done exactly the same ... the king for my money .... Anybody may see he is an actor.'

Partridge 'from whom' as we are told, Jones ' ... expected the simple dictates of nature, unimproved indeed, but likewise unadulterated by art'[34] was no more at a loss than 'the town' itself. Adherents of the old-school actors – who liked it to be seen that they *were* actors – could attack those of the new school as 'low', as 'buffoonery' in Theophilus Cibber's terms, or 'mimicry' in Walpole's.[35] Garrick's answer to this was to publish anonymously '*An Essay on Acting, in which will be considered the Mimical Behaviour of a certain fashionable actor ...* ' (1744) in which he both accepted those terms and mockingly fulfilled them by impersonating his opponents in print. 'Garrick must be allowed all the merit that Mimicry can give him – which to be sure is very pleasant, over a bottle, tho' despicable on the stage. Why being a good mimic should entitle him to be a great actor cannot easily be comprehended.'[36]

Garrick's career is well-documented, in contemporary accounts and modern studies.[37] The style of character creation which is normally ascribed to him first made its impact in the Shylock of his friend Charles Macklin. Macklin concealed his conception of the role from the rest of the cast, which included James Quin, the most celebrated actor in what was then taken to be the leading role, Antonio. The performance suddenly revealed on the first night was a physically detailed, carefully costumed impersonation of an urban Jew. The shock effect of this against the performances of the rest of the cast ensured Macklin's sudden fame.[38] He remained to some extent a one-role actor, but it is tempting to see this moment as the subversion of *The Merchant*, an irrevocable deposition of Antonio, that creature of moral action and ambiguous choice, in favour of Shylock's resistant, obstinately coherent selfhood. 'This is the jew' Pope famously and inelegantly remarked 'which Shakespeare drew'.[39]

Garrick seized on this style of acting and promoted it in a series of famous impersonations of Shakespeare characters and a series of productions for the companies he managed. 'If the fellow is right' Quin remarked after seeing Garrick's Richard III, 'I and the rest of the players have all been wrong.'[40] Garrick eventually directed Quin as Falstaff, a choice of role for the great heroic actor that reflects ironically on the famous early engraving of his stout, beplumed Coriolanus.[41] A grander and more heroic conception of Falstaff colours critical accounts of the role in ways I will discuss later. But this reclassification of the great actor of the previous generation suggests the extent of Garrick's power, not just professionally but in terms of the aesthetic of acting which he promoted.

There are many accounts of Garrick observing actual behaviour and transposing it into his performance.[42] He acquired a realist vocabulary in order to externalise, to develop a fuller language of physical presentation. In Garrick's case this is the means to an end, the end of creating and presenting a coherent 'character'. Such a character would be essentially static: but nature would be perceptible at different intensity at different moments, and this would be the source of excitement. Garrick's performances had a particular appeal for painters and illustrators. High points in a Garrick or Garrick-style performance would be moments of intense revelation, of 'seeing'.

In tragedy the effect of this creation of complete being had initially a semi-magical effect, linked with ideas of terror. Garrick's performances gelled in moments of self-realisation which were also moments of extreme fear: Romeo at the tomb, Hamlet with the ghost, Macbeth after the murder, Richard III on the eve of battle. Impersonation is perhaps intrinsically disturbing, but one can locate the kind of terror involved here by reference to the problem of realism; or at the least the matter of the creation of 'real' presences. A ghost — except for Romeo they are all roles in 'ghost' plays — is something which is perceptible where logically it should not exist. It is inserted into a 'reality' constituted by rules which would ordinarily deny the possibility of its being there. To that extent it is like theatre, or more exactly, like theatre which claims to be real.

The neo-classical perception of theatre is put most cogently and memorably by Samuel Johnson.

> The truth is, that the spectators are always in their senses, and know, from the first act to the last, that the stage is only a stage, and that the players are only players. They come to hear a certain number of lines recited with just gesture and elegant modulation. The lines relate to some action, and an action must be in some place.[43]

This formulation, deliberately rather stark, tallies uneasily with the experience eighteenth-century theatre aimed to give its audiences. Theorists tried to argue against it, actors simply tried to make it untrue. The most positive responses to Garrick are like those of Partridge, which can stand in for all the non-fictional accounts with the concision of accurate caricature. They are responses in which the audience is out of its senses, in which, momentarily, it forgets. This is a problem which early forms of realist art set themselves: to what extent can the spectator take such art *for* real? Such realism is to be validated by the intensity with which the audience experiences it.

Johnson made scarcely any recorded comments on Garrick's work, and never discussed it in print. Johnson's Shakespeare is the Shakespeare praised because while 'in the writings of other poets a character is too often an individual, in . . . Shakespeare it is commonly a species'.[44] Johnson shares Garrick's sense that Shakespeare's source is observed human nature, but his attempt to account for the use Shakespeare puts this to painstakingly avoids the concept of individual character on the rhetoric of a perfect intuitive creation which, as we shall see, this came to imply. Johnson works within neo-classical terms but their conjunction with Shakespeare seems to be a move on Johnson's part towards a more inclusive aesthetic. The neo-classical language of dramatic criticism had been sharply left behind by developments in theatre practice. Literature and theatre had never been seen before as essentially distinct. It is perhaps romantic criticism that first imports a disdain for theatre and the theatrical into the self-confirming idea of a 'literary' sensibility. Such an opposition would never have occurred to anyone in the seventeenth or eighteenth centuries (except for puritan writers, who would not have had much time for most 'literature' either). Johnson, like everyone else, assumes that literature and theatre are aspects of the same thing. It would seem to be theatre, in this Garrick-inspired boom, which initiated that still apparent split between the stage and 'literature' which significantly alters the nature of dramatic criticism. Critics writing on drama rush for terms to describe a new aesthetic experience: then, having consolidated these terms, they are able to use them to place and distance theatre practice from their own 'real' knowledge of the texts, and so to characterise almost any theatrical representation as inadequate, by its very nature.

I have already suggested that Garrick's work was ahead of his critical contemporaries' attempts to rationalise it. This is the kind of relationship I wish to posit in the history of Shakespeare criticism. I am not suggesting that we instate Garrick or any other actor as a 'critic' of Shakespeare in the same way as we see Johnson, or Morgann or Coleridge. 'Interpretation' here means something different, as Johnson's remark on Garrick's Lady Macbeth, Mrs Pritchard, would warn us. Boswell records that:

> Mrs. Pritchard being mentioned he said 'Her playing was quite mechanical. It was wonderful how little mind she had. Sir, she had never read the tragedy of Macbeth all through. She no more thought of the play out of which her part was taken, than a shoemaker thinks of the skin, out of which the piece of leather, of which he is making a pair of shoes, is cut'.[45]

This returns us to Macklin, evolving a Shylock in isolation from the rest of the play. Garrick's importance lies not in how he read the plays but in what he did to them: he rendered them down to a series of discrete individual characters. The climax of this process was the procession of Shakespeare's characters in the Stratford jubilee of 1769.[46] A hundred or even fifty years earlier this would not have been possible, as it would not have been possible to distinguish one character from another, visually to distinguish them in *themselves*, apart from action. One aspect of the growing differentiation into 'characters' was the development of a visual iconography of Shakespeare illustration, to be consolidated by the opening of Boydell's Shakespeare gallery in 1789. This itself follows on from the impulses to read in terms of discrete character, character detachable from the action of the plays in which they appear. Arthur Murphy in 1753 styled Garrick '[Shakespeare's] best commentator. For it is certain, he has done our poet more justice by his manner of playing his principal characters than any editor has yet done by a publication'.[47] The issue of character was seen by Garrick's admirers to be the source of his pre-eminence over critics as well as actors. A few years later Joseph Warton described Shakespeare and Garrick as each other's only equivalents.

> We ... of Great Britain have reason to congratulate ourselves on two very singular phenomena; I mean Shakespeare's being able to pourtray characters so very different as FALSTAFF and MACBETH, and Garrick's being able to personate so inimitably a LEAR or an ABEL DRUGGER.[48]

Fielding's 'quotation' of Garrick's Hamlet suggests a broader critical context. In *Joseph Andrews* (1742) and *Tom Jones*, Fielding draws attention to his innovatory bringing together of those discrete external signs of type whose listing makes up 'character' as a literary mode in pre-eighteenth-century writing, with a sense of moral agency which those characteristics are now used to reveal. He claims that the result is a new kind of realistic fiction, or, to use his term, of 'history', and refers to both Garrick and Hogarth as exponents of a parallel approach to character.[49] Partridge's 'unadulterated' response is Garrick's vindication. The actor's physical presence is the means of developing further this common pursuit of an accessible moralised realism; it makes possible a wholly unified presentation of individual personality. Characters are perceived as what they are, not in what they do. This moral essence, once grasped, places every perceptible aspect.

The mid-eighteenth-century novel, as evinced in two otherwise dissimilar figures like Fielding and Samuel Richardson, is primarily the novel of 'character'. But both these writers use the term in the traditional sense. Character in their work is a set of knowable signs, or at least a set of known signs, continuous with the colloquial sense of the word as 'reputation'. So Clarissa Harlowe and her friend Anna Howe can worry at the real extent of their knowledge of Clarissa's suitor, the notorious Lovelace. They know his 'character', but what of his 'nature'?[50] The distinction is an important one for the development of the novel, in Clarissa's case as well as in Lovelace's. Both are 'characters' in the general social/moral/gossip-defined world to which their and others' letters give us access, but their natures provide the book with a vast and fascinating hinterland to which character can grant no clue. In *Tom Jones* too, character is a delusive clue to 'nature'. Fielding's method is more overtly theatrical that Richardson's, instating a rhetorical relation of writer to reader, playing quizzically with the classical tradition. The true recognition of the nature of his *dramatis personae*, as opposed to the 'characters' they bear in its world, is the task the book sets for the reader. Citations of Garrick and Hogarth invite us to recognise the possibility of a more coherent knowledge of human nature than the rhetorical tradition, wittily explored by Fielding, can seem to grant us. Rather than seeing 'character' in the modern sense as a 'novelistic' importation into other art-forms, one might recognise here Fielding's reliance on the theatrical and the visual to pose the question of character and nature – as one might recognise the traditional nature of the distinction both novelists make between the two.

III 'THE MIND AND ITS MOVEMENTS'

Contemporary analyses of Garrick's work employ a method and a terminology derived partly from the Aristotelian tradition and partly from Descartes. Samuel Foote, having taken Garrick's part against Quin in his *Treatise on the Passions, so far as they regard the Stage* (174?) continued his discussion of English acting in *The Roman and English Comedy consider'd and compar'd* (1747). The English stage, he claims, has added to the unities of Aristotle 'another, disregarded by the writers of other Countries, Unity of Character'. Shakespeare in particular, wrote 'without observing any one Unity, but that of character . . .'.[51] Foote's *Treatise on the Passions* places his argument in favour of the new style of acting in the context of a discussion of 'the passions', their objects, origin and mode of operation, which derives from Descartes. Garrick's practice, according to Foote, is closer to the true nature of human passion, as Cartesian enquiry has described it. Foote's framework of aesthetic thought remains Aristotelian, though his elegant formulation of 'the unity of character' implicitly challenges neo-classical theory. The problems raised by 'unity of character' are central to the native philosophical tradition; later commentators turn to Locke and Hume for their terms.

Philosophic discourse on the individual had been opened to Garrick's contemporaries largely by John Locke, in the *Essay Concerning Human Understanding* begun in 1671 and first published in

1689. Locke's exploration of the nature of knowledge involves an attempt to define the modes of human perception, and the nature of its objects. The question of individual identity is crucial to both. How does one define the individuality – the distinctness and coherence – of the object perceived? How does the perceiver experience the distinctness and coherence of his or her own self?[52] David Hume's *A Treatise of Human Nature* (1739) includes an elaborated version of Locke's position, and it is from the mid-century onwards that ideas of identity and unity replace discussion of distinct 'passions' in the criticism of acting and drama.

Character-criticism – such as began to exist around the mid-century – works initially within an externalised concept of individual identity. Analysis of psychological process as such is much less in evidence than the construction of imaginary biographies. The method is the accumulation of circumstantial detail, the literary model is the apologia. Colly Cibber's famous *Apology* (1740) may well lie behind the adoption of the form as an approach to theatrical character: Cibber's self-interrogation is a performance in itself, its modes of self-presentation are as cloyingly ingratiating as those of the characters he played. Maurice Morgann's *Essay on the Dramatic Character of Sir John Falstaff* (1777) sparked off a series of character sketches cast in this defensive mode. Polonius, Hamlet, Macbeth and even Iago were expounded and exonerated in a process that sometimes overlapped into identification and, in a way, performance on the writer's part.

Morgann's very enjoyable essay is the most interesting of these in combining the apologia form with a serious and ingenious exploration of ideas of perception. The apologia parodistically treats its fictional subject as real, but Morgann's aim goes far beyond parody: the form becomes a way of positing an object for an exercise in perception. The essay announces itself in an engagingly Shandeyan way

> The vindication of FALSTAFF's Courage is truly no otherwise the object than some old fantastic Oak, or grotesque Rock, may be the object of a morning's ride; yet being proposed as such, may serve to limit the distance, and shape the course; the real object is Exercise, and the Delight which a rich, beautiful, picturesque, and perhaps unknown country, may excite from every side.[53]

Morgann thus presents perception, the 'exercise' offered, as equal if not superior in interest to the object that allows and limits the

perception. As a statement of his choice of Falstaff this is of course
comically disingenuous. Falstaff is the *least* Aristotelian of roles, the
least defined by *praxis*. He exists apart from action, and has no sense
whatsoever of moral choice. The end-product of the essay is an
anti-Aristotelian proposition about the nature of character, a proposition worked out within the issue of perception, a proposition for which
Falstaff provides the ideal exemplar.

The terms of Morgann's argument are derived explicitly from
contemporary philosophy — specifically, from the distinction Hume
draws in *The Treatise* between 'ideas' and 'impressions'. The mind for
Locke is essentially passive, 'white paper, void of all characters'.[54] It
receives everything in the form of 'ideas'. But for Hume there are two
distinct forms in which the mind comprehends things: as 'ideas', but
also as 'impressions'.[55]

The exact nature of the distinction is never entirely clear. It seems
largely a matter of degree of intensity or 'liveliness' to use Hume's
term. Impressions are forceful and instantaneous, while ideas are
ratiocinated and less compelling. We act on impressions, not on ideas.
Impressions are the sole source of moral knowledge and moral action.
Ideas have no such power to move us. This distinction is deeply
problematic, as Hume himself is aware. But in Morgann's case at least,
the overlap between 'impression' and the traditional 'character'
metaphor allows its easy transposition into an account of identity.
Morgann uses it as the basis of a conception of character and replaces
the difficult area of 'ideas' with what he calls 'understanding'. Most
literature according to Morgann is morally suspect in that it appeals to
the rational consideration of character in action. It is therefore
defective on two counts: it is in thrall to the 'understanding', and so
debarred from moral knowledge, and it assumes that character and
action are significantly connected.

> this clear perception, in Novels and Plays, of the union of character
> and action not seen in nature, is the principal defect of such
> compositions, and what renders them but ill pictures of human life,
> and wretched guides of conduct.

His example of defective literature is drawn from Voltaire:

> in real life, I believe, *my Lord the Judges* would be apt to inform the
> *Gentlemen of the Jury* that my *Lord the Inquisitor* was *ill killed*; as
> *Candide* did not proceed on the urgency of the moment, but in the
> speculation only of future evil.[56]

Shakespeare, almost exceptionally, says Morgann, creates character as 'impression'. 'If there was one *man* in the world who could make a more perfect draught of real nature and steal such Impressions on his audience, without their special notice, as should keep their hold in spite of any error of their Understanding, and should thereupon venture to introduce an apparent incongruity of character and action, for ends which I shall presently endeavour to explain; such an imitation' (he rather tamely concludes) 'would be worth our nicest curiosity and attention'.[57] In other words, the claim Morgann makes for Shakespeare is that character exists apart from action or from anything else that can be apprehended rationally, by 'the Understanding'. It is a kind of moral knowledge communicated by the instantaneous and intense perception of one person by another. Shakespeare produced 'Impressions' of this kind. Hence his superiority to any other writer.

Morgann's use of a forensic language (judges, jury and so on) is heralded in his preface, where he styles himself 'rather . . . an Advocate than . . . an Inquirer'.[58] It is also written into the apologia form. In this, the most widespread early model for writing on Shakespeare's characters, the character is seen as somehow on trial. The critic has the freedom to interrogate different perceptions, and to call almost anything 'evidence'. He also has a professional interest in getting his client off. The problem of character had been linked explicitly with the matter of law since at least Locke's *Essay*. In the chapter entitled 'Of Identity and Diversity' Locke posits that personal identity is a matter of unity of consciousness. This must be imperfect, given such things as forgetting, sleep and drunkenness, and given that none but the consciousness itself can know itself as unified or conscious. Locke, typically, makes a double appeal out of this apparent deadlock, to the social and to the divine. The identity we ascribe to others is a kind of social convention made necessary by law ' . . . though punishment be annexed to personality, and personality to consciousness, and the drunkard perhaps be not conscious of what he did, yet human judicatures justly punish him; because the fact is proved against him, but want of consciousness cannot be proved for him. But in the Great Day, wherein the secrets of all hearts shall be laid open, it may be reasonable to think, no one shall be made to answer for what he knows nothing of; but shall receive his doom, his conscience accusing or excusing him'.[59] In other words we attain full knowledge of ourselves and so become unified selves only at that climactic moment. Human identity is thus a kind of deferred totality.

An eschatology of this kind is the ultimate resolution of all that is problematic in Locke's thought. The forensic dimension seems initially more suggestive; it remained an explicit part of the approach to character until the romantics. Locke's apocalytpic solution to the problem of ultimate knowledge was not so easily assimilated. The Humean idea of the 'impression' proposed a more accessible solution, accessible partly by virtue of its continuity with the still-current 'character' metaphor, of stamping and sealing. But in these 'impressions' we can, indeed *must*, perceive the 'reality', the unified moral being of another person. This is the knowledge that constitutes identity.

So character is a moral knowledge, the knowledge of what other people are as distinct, self-consistent beings. Character is not related to what people do, except in local, often insignificant, cases of cause and effect. It can only be accurately perceived in a kind of instantaneous intuition. Shakespeare somehow participated in this, and, equally mysteriously, could convey it in his plays. This is the position of Shakespeare criticism in the late eighteenth century.

Theatre has an exciting potential in an aesthetic of 'Impression'. As Morgann puts it, 'In Dramatic composition, the *Impression* is the *Fact*'.[60] Theatre provided Hume with a model for his conception of the workings of the mind:

> The mind is a kind of theatre, where several perceptions successively make their appearance; pass, re-pass, glide away, and mingle in an infinite variety of postures and situations . . ..[61]

The experience of theatre is, at its most intense, the experience of instantaneous, unrepeatable perceptions. These are the salient 'facts' of performance. So it is easy to see why theatre provided philosophers with an image of mind and why once the concept of the 'impression' had been formulated it was assimilated so promptly by theoreticians of theatre. Successive paintings by Fuseli of Garrick's Macbeth, for example, can be seen as attempts to get closer to the rendering of sheer 'impression'. Nor was it coincidental that the great Shakespeare characters as identified first by the stage and then by criticism are largely defined by their relationship to ideas of criminality. Richard III and Macbeth clearly belong in the dock. But the identities of Shylock, Falstaff and Hamlet are just as inextricably bound up with questions of legality and punishment. Garrick's presentation of these roles as unified quasi-autonomous 'characters' places them squarely within Locke's frame of reference. Sleep, drunkenness and forgetting, to refer back to Locke's version of the inevitable discontinuity of personal identity, are disordering forces in *Macbeth*, clues to the key play of mid-eighteenth-century sensibility.[62] The moment in *Richard III* which Hogarth chose to paint is the climactic soliloquy where Richard confronts his own character at the end of that parade of characters which can alone bring home to him the meaning of actions his exclusive selfhood prevents him from internalising. He is himself the last 'ghost'.[63] But the importation of the terminology of the philosophy of mind into an account of a series of fictional creations does nonetheless raise one overriding problem of identity: the identity of the author. For if Shakespeare can 'create' in this way, he is not as other writers, nor indeed as other men.

'There are but few Dramatic characters which will bear this kind of investigation' Morgann writes towards the end of his study, ' . . . but this is not the case with regard to the characters of *Shakespeare*; they are struck out *whole*, by some happy art which I cannot clearly comprehend, out of the general mass of things, from the block as it were of nature . . .'.[64] Characters become 'whole' – so they cannot show the marks of their genesis, which in turn becomes some other process than mere writing. It is presented as a kind of natural process: Shakespeare participated in the reality of human nature, and this participation becomes visible as a series of 'characters'. Morgann's 'as it were' tactfully clouds the whole passage, but as its function is obscurantist in any case, a 'clouding' of the processes which writing is normally seen to require, it helps rather than hinders his purpose of exempting Shakespeare from the normal contexts of criticism, of at once apotheosising him, and making him (or Him as Morgann would write it) invisible. Nonetheless the language Morgann uses cannot but imply some sense of the production of a text: 'out of' requires 'some happy art' however vague he must be about that art: 'out of' requires some 'block' of something. So Morgann has to project the character back into the 'real' (or 'nature' in his terms) from which Shakespeare 'by some happy art' retrieves it.

This version of Shakespeare is the foundation of romantic Shakespeare criticism. Coleridge manages to resolve Morgann's quasi-theological dilemma by positing the organic wholeness, the mysterious and perfect totality of Shakespeare's work. The idea of the author's agency which Morgann and his contemporaries veiled in deistic metaphor is irrelevant to Coleridge. Shakespeare's work does not seem to have 'come out of' anything. It is perfect, and its perfection is manifested in every character, for it is the perfection of a moral knowledge of human beings. Shakespeare himself, he remarks, is 'characterless, because characteristic. [He is the] poet lost in his portraits . . .'.[65]

Coleridge's own note to that remark is a jibe at Dr Johnson,

> The Frog-Critic. How nimbly it leaps, how excellently it swims – only the forelegs (it must be admitted) are too long and the hind ones too short.[66]

This seems irrelevant but I take it to be an irritated reminiscence of that account of character I quoted earlier – as the definition of 'species' rather than the creation of an 'individual'. Coleridge does not argue with Johnson's judgement, but he copes with it in a way entirely consonant with the logic of his own position. Once Shakespeare is defined as late-eighteenth-century criticism defines him, then what is the place of his critic? A post-eighteenth-century idea of character does not work on Coriolanus as fully as Coleridge might wish, but he does not complain:

> I have always thought this in itself so beautiful a speech the least explicable from the mood and full intention of the speaker of any in the whole works of Shakespeare. I cherish the hope that I am mistaken and, becoming wiser, shall discover some profound excellence in what I now appear to myself to detect an imperfection.[67]

'Imperfection' is of course some challenge to the personal coherence of a character, in this case someone as secondary, as instrumental, as Tullus Aufidius. But this humility goes together with and to some extent depends on the critic's sense of himself as the sole authentic interpreter. Coleridge is anxious to establish himself as the *first* to discover Shakespeare; the true Shakespeare, that is. Hence the ferocity with which he fends off charges of indebtedness to Schlegel with one hand, and pushes his English contemporaries aside with the other.

> Mr Hazlitt, whose hatred of me is in such an inverse ratio to my zealous kindness to him as to be defended by his warmest admirer, C. Lamb (who besides his characteristic obstinacy of adherence to old friends, as long at least as they are all down in the world, is linked as by a charm to Hazlitt's conversation), only under the epithet of 'frantic' – Mr Hazlitt himself replied to an assertion of my plagiarism from Schlegel in these words: 'That is a lie . . . ' etc. etc.[68]

Johnson could write about Shakespeare as one literary man among many writing about a literary man now dead. Coleridge is participating in a moral knowledge whose medium is something called Shakespeare, once a person but now de-materialised by sheer creativity.

When an idea of character, detached from action and summing up a complex moral knowledge, is pushed beyond the Hogarthian aesthetic of readability, or a Fuselian aesthetic of intense impression, it comes to contradict the ways of seeing and knowing that the stage offers. Lamb states irritatingly but honestly a position that underlies Romantic criticism when, in '*On the Tragedies of Shakespeare, considered with reference to their fitness for stage-representation*', he argues that Shakespeare's true place is in the mind of the sensitive reader, and attempts incidentally to destroy Garrick's reputation as a Shakespearian. This is an argument from theory – he never saw Garrick, as he admits. Looking at the stage, according to Lamb, tempts us to read action, not character. It shocks us with crude facts – that Othello is black for example. He echoes Coleridge here in preferring a tasteful coppery colour but where Coleridge argues this from his assumption of Shakespeare's sensibility (he would not do anything as gross as have a white woman love a black ex-slave, so he *must* have meant Othello to be a kind of beige aristocrat), Lamb merely refers us to his and our own; 'that beautiful compromise which we make in reading' tones Othello down a bit.[69] The basic problem is that:

> What we see upon the stage is body and bodily action; what we are conscious of in reading is almost exclusively the mind, and its movements . . . .[70]

Romantic criticism discovered that the sensitive apprehension of character is something the critic can do *better* than the actor; that it was an actor, as I have argued, who invented this kind of 'character' and established it as the grounds of the Shakespeare criticism the romantics practiced simply makes it more strongly imperative that acting be put outside the pale of critical consideration. Shakespeare's privileged interpreters, like their version of Shakespeare, must be seen to be without origins, to reveal a truth without a history, always there but hitherto somehow missed.

When Hogarth 'saw' Sarah Malcolm's crime written on her as her 'nature', he affirmed a notion of character in which the colloquial idea of 'reputation' or the more complex tradition of readable, constructed, perhaps mendacious, signs, has been replaced by a knowledge of essence – 'character' and 'nature' have become one. Malcolm's defence was that she had fallen among bad company, been misled. Eighteenth-century judges and juries increasingly had to puzzle at 'psychological' defences, of a kind which develop Lockean controversies as to the identity and responsibility of the individual into 'expert' evidence.[71] Fielding too, one might remember, was a magistrate. Placed in this context, the evolution of a new notion of 'character' becomes much more than a matter of dramatic theory. But that context in itself suggests the way that the stage is still in this period the arena of a debate of identity, a space in which the controversies of philosophy and government found vivid if temporary realisation. It may well be, though, that the notion of 'character' which Garrick did so much to establish worked in the end to displace the stage from this cultural centrality. If 'character' is real, rounded, out there/here, then only in exceptional circumstances will acting be anything other than disappointing.

Notes

1. Thomas Rymer, 'The Tragedies of the Last Age Consider'd and Examin'd by the Practice of the Ancients, and by the Common Sense of All Ages, in a letter to Fleetwood Shepherd, Esq.', in Curt A. Zimansky (ed.), *The Critical Works of Thomas Rymer* (Westport, Conn., 1956), p. 26.
2. Ibid., p. 18.
3. A. Dacier, *The Preface to Aristotle's Art of Poetry* (1705; repr. Los Angeles, 1959) A4r.
4. Aristotle, *Poetics*, 1451b.
5. See Rymer's account of the chorus of Greek Tragedy, and his own plan for a tragedy on the Spanish Armada in *A Short View of Tragedy. The Critical Works*, pp. 84–93.
6. Rymer, *Tragedies of the Last Age*, p. 44.
7. Ibid., pp. 23–4.
8. Ibid., pp. 28–9.
9. 'Preface to Shakespeare' (1765) in *The Yale Edition of the Works of Samuel Johnson*, Volume VII, *Johnson on Shakespeare*, edited by Arthur Sherbo, p. 62.
10. A. C. Bradley, *Shakespearean Tragedy* (first edn 1904, repr. London, 1976), p. 7.
11. John Dryden, 'The Grounds of Criticism in Tragedy' from the preface to *Troilus and Cressida*, in John Conaghan (ed.), *Dryden: A Selection* (London, 1978), p. 558.
12. Ibid., p. 559.
13. Ibid., p. 562.

14. See Joseph R. Roach, *The Players' Passion* (Newark, 1985), pp. 29–31. Roach provides a valuable account of the links between rhetorical theories of acting and early medicine.
15. Descartes, *Les Passions de l'Ame*, part 1, Article 1 (my translation).
16. Roach, *The Players' Passion*, p. 32. Descartes, part 2, Articles 51–148.
17. Descartes, Part 1, Article 47.
18. Ibid., Part 1, Article 50.
19. René Rapin, *Les Réflexions sur la Poetique de ce Temps et sur les Ouvrages des Poetes Anciens et Modernes*, ed. E. T. Dubois (Geneva, 1970), XVIII, pp. 98–100.
20. Rymer, *Tragedies of the Last Age*, p. 24.
21. Rapid, *Réflexions*, XIX, pp. 100–2.
22. Ibid., XX, p. 103.
23. Ibid., XIV, pp. 27–8.
24. Dryden, *Heads of an Answer to Rymer*, in Conaghan (ed.), *Dryden: A Selection* [p. 546].
25. Dryden, 'Grounds of Criticism', p. 557.
26. Dryden, *Heads of an Answer to Rymer*, p. 548.
27. Ibid., p. 567.
28. Ibid., p. 561.
29. Ibid., p. 568.
30. Dryden, 'Preface to *Fables Ancient and Modern*' in Conaghan, *Dryden: A Selection*, p. 618.
31. Descartes, *Les Passions de l'Ame*, Part 2, Article 147.
32. Pat Rogers raises the question of Garrick's cultural centrality, in 'David Garrick: the actor as culture here' in J. Redmond (ed.), *Drama and the Actor*, Themes in Drama Series, Vol. 6 (Cambridge, 1984), pp. 63–83.
33. *The Plays of David Garrick*, edited by Harry William Pedicord and Frederick Louis Bergmann (Southern Illinois, 1980) Vol. II. I. ii. 6–8, 47–50, pp. 162–3.
34. Henry Fielding, *The History of Tom Jones*, edited by Fredson Bowers (Oxford, 1974) Vol. II, Bk XVI, Ch. V, pp. 852–4, 856–7.
35. Cited in *David Garrick* by Carola Oman (London, 1958), p. 46.
36. Garrick, *An Essay on Acting in which will be consider'd the Mimical Behaviour of a Certain fashionable faulty Actor* (London, 1744), pp. 25–6.
37. See especially George Winchester Stone and George M. Kahrl, *David Garrick: a Critical Biography* (Southern Illinois, 1979).
38. See, for example, Georg Christoph Lichtenberg's account of Macklin's performance; A. M. Nagler, *A Source Book in Theatrical History* (New York, 1952).
39. Oman, *David Garrick*, p. 32.
40. An often quoted remark. See, for example, Helen K. Smith, *David Garrick* (London, 1979), p. 12.
41. For illustrations of both the Falstaff and the Coriolanus see *Shakespeare from Betterton to Irving*, George C. O. Odell (New York, 1966), Vol. I, p. 354.
42. See, for example, Garrick's preparation for Lear: Oman, *David Garrick*, p. 48.
43. Samuel Johnson, 'Preface to Shakespeare', p. 77.
44. Johnson, 'Preface', p. 62.

45. From Boswell's *The Life of Samuel Johnson* (1793) II. 222, quoted in Brian Vickers (ed.), *Shakespeare: The Critical Heritage*, Vol. 6, 1774–1801 (London, 1981), p. 571.
46. Oman, *David Garrick*, pp. 285–300.
47. Arthur Murphy, *The Critical Heritage*, Vol. 4 (London, 1976) p. 105.
48. Ibid., p. 263.
49. See, for example, Fielding, *Joseph Andrews*, edited by George Saintsbury (London, 1910, repr. 1965) Bk III, Chapter I, pp. 142–6; *Tom Jones*, Vol. I, Book VIII, Chapter I, pp. 405–7. See also his 'quotation' of Hogarth's *Morning* from *The Four Times of Day* (1738) in the description of Bridget Allworthy; *Tom Jones*, Book I, Chapter XI, p. 61.
50. Samuel Richardson, *Clarissa Harlowe* etc. See, for example, Vol. I, letters X–XIII, Vol. 2, letters LXVIII, LXXXIV, LXXXV.
51. Samuel Foote, *Treatise on the Passions*, pp. 22–3.
52. Locke, *An Essay Concerning Human Understanding*, edited by Alexander Campbell Fraser (Oxford, 1894) Book II, Chapter 1, pp. 121–43.
53. Maurice Morgann, *Shakespearian Criticism* (1777; Oxford, 1972), p. 144.
54. Locke, *Essay*, Book II, Chapter I, p. 121.
55. Hume, *A Treatise of Human Nature*, edited by L. A. Selby-Bigge (Oxford, 1888, repr. 1964), Book I, Part I, Chapter I, pp. 1–7.
56. Morgann, *Shakespearian Criticism*, p. 148.
57. Ibid., p. 148.
58. Ibid., p. 143.
59. Locke, *Essay*, Book II, Chapter XXVII, 'Of Identity and Diversity', pp. 448–70.
60. Morgann, *Shakespearian Criticism*, p. 146.
61. Hume, *Treatise*, p. 253.
62. Bartholomeuz gives a full account of reactions to Garrick in this role. *Macbeth and the Players* (Cambridge, 1969), pp. 38–81.
63. See Lawrence Gowring, *Hogarth* (London, 1972), p. 50. Garrick's playing of the scene in question is discussed in Julie Hankey's volume on the play in the *Plays in Performance* series (London, 1981), pp. 237–8.
64. Morgann, *Shakespearian Criticism*, p. 203.
65. Thomas Middleton Raysor (ed.), *Coleridge's Shakespearean Criticism* (London, 1930), Vol. I, p. 82.
66. Ibid., p. 82.
67. Ibid., p. 91.
68. Raysor, *Coleridge's Shakespearean Criticism*, p. 19.
69. *Works of Charles and Mary Lamb*, edited by E. V. Lucas (London, 1903), Vol. I, p. 108. For Coleridge, see Raysor, *Coleridge's Shakespearean Criticism*, p. 47.
70. Lamb, *Works*, Vol. I, p. 108.
71. See Joel Peter Eigen, 'Intentionality and insanity: what the eighteenth-century juror heard', in W. F. Bynum, Roy Porter, and Michael Shepherd (eds), *The Anatomy of Madness: Essays in the History of Psychiatry* (London, 1985), Vol. II, pp. 34–51.

Afterword:
The Modern 'Subject' and Pre-Modern Drama

I   BRECHT AND THE FORMALISTS

Brecht's introductory notes on his opera *The Rise and Fall of the City of Mahagonny*[1] include a table of comparisons between the 'epic' theatre, of which this is an example, and the theatre it seeks to replace:

DRAMATIC THEATRE	EPIC THEATRE
plot	narrative
implicates the spectator in a stage situation	turns the spectator into an observer but
wears down his capacity for action	arouses his capacity for action
provides him with sensations	forces him to make decisions
experience	picture of the world
the spectator is involved in something	he is made to face something
suggestion	argument
instinctive feelings are preserved	brought to the point of recognition
the spectator is in the thick of it, shares the experience	the spectator stands outside, studies
the human being is taken for granted	the human being is the object of the inquiry
he is unalterable	he is alterable and able to alter . . .
. . . man as a fixed point	man as a process
thought determines being	social being determines thought
feeling	reason

In his notes on *The Mother* Brecht identified epic theatre as 'anti-metaphysical, materialistic, non-aristotelian drama. This makes nothing like such a free use as does the aristotelian of the passive empathy of the spectator'.[2] His definition of his own theatre practice in opposition to the 'Aristotelian' is most fully developed in *A Short Organum for the Theatre*, an ambitious summary of the tendency of his earlier work. Its title echoes that of Francis Bacon's *Novum Organum* where Bacon opposes the Aristotelian tradition in learning with a new empirical approach to knowledge. Bacon privileges experiment and observation above tradition and elaborated theory. Brecht cites this moment of intellectual history as the emergence of a scientific materialist knowledge of the world. His drama is similarly scientific, it engages the spectator in enquiry and criticism rather than in a confirmatory 'mirroring'. As such it is the product of an intellectual revolution of which, in this context, Bacon becomes a forerunner — Marx's scientific, materialist analysis.

This set of analogies is worked out also in the play from which the *Organum* to some extent derives, *The Life of Galileo*. Galileo's proof that the earth circles the sun decentres man from the ancient model of the cosmos. Popular balladeers and the Vatican hierarchy can recognise the implications of this, but Galileo himself cannot proceed from it, and so his revolutionary empiricism remains inert (as Marx's, the play implies, does not). A decentering of man from the model of the world constructed in humanist theatre had been Brecht's aim as theatre revolutionary, and it is in this context that he begins to characterise his work as anti-Aristotelian. Like other of his contemporaries, he opposes a 'holistic' theatre, of which Wagner's *'gesamkunstwerk'* was the most developed example — theatre as a unity of all available languages, tending to a unitary experience, undergone by the audience passively and uncritically, empathetically received. Brecht extends this to an account of empathetic art as bourgeois, stultifying, counter-revolutionary. This historical analysis of theatre is in turn the programme for a new theatre, a theatre for which the 'empathy' on which Brecht takes all post-Aristotelian theatre to be based is exhausted and discredited. And this is because the idea of the human which the Aristotelian theatre affirmed in its construction of the audience-as-subject is no longer valid.

In this final chapter I want to give some contexts for Brecht's decription of his work as 'anti-Aristotelian', and so to use it as a starting point for a reconsideration of the issue with which the rest of the book has been concerned — the representation of the human on the pre-modern stage. This is not in order to provide a summarised conspectus of 'modern approaches' to character – though such a thing would doubtless be useful, and such summaries will play some part in the argument of the chapter. Modern controversies – character/anti-character – have been focused very much on the novel, particularly on the realist novel. Work that takes into account the particular nature of theatre *as* theatre is comparatively rare. In theatre the human is material, present in the performers. The participation of the recipient subject is equally 'present'. Performance requires a reconsideration of the nature and position of 'the human', it raises issues different from those of that quintessentially modern situation, the private consumption of narratives, the individual engagement with the traces of dematerialised human presence. Different approaches to early-twentieth-century theatre converge on the question of a humanist/holistic theatre, on their own relation to a romantic/realist legacy. Theatre practitioners and theorists work, independently but in response to the same ideas, towards theatre(s) whose revolutionary role is defined by their exploration of new representational possibilities, by their reconsideration of a post-Aristotelian notion of the centrality of 'the human' to theatre. This body of work remains the source of exploratory theatre. It is doubly relevant here, in tending to exploit the possibilities offered by pre-modern and oriental theatre.

Brecht is too often cited in English accounts of theatres as the possessor of a 'theory', a theory which can be pointed to as a monolithic marker of a successful Marxist aesthetic practice, or, apolitically, as the description of a set of techniques. The issue at the centre of his attempt to define his theatre – its representation of the human – is worked out in a series of stage pieces, most notably *Mahagonny*, *Man equals Man*, and *The Mother*, in notes for audiences and actors, rehearsal practice as recorded by Brecht, and in the published text. The *Organum* and the dialogues tend towards retrospect and consolidation. Written in exile, they form a bridge between the experiments of Brecht's earlier career in Weimar Germany, and his return to build a theatre in a Marxist society. Seen as process, Brecht's work is so deeply implicated in historical change as to allow of no abstractable 'timeless' theoretical precept. The *Organum* takes 'theoretical' form by parody and analogy, and so by that very form sets up a dialogue with other writings and other historical moments – Brecht's writing 'deconstructs' the very idea of an individual in the possession of a timelessly valid wisdom. Like the plays, the so-called 'theory' fragments the individual subject to give us instead a process of work, marked by, and so representing back to us, the history it traverses, and like the plays this is formally an exploitation of the decentring effects of a dialogic, a multi-voiced 'theatrical' language.

Brecht's anti-Aristotelianism is more thoroughgoing than a matter of isolable techniques. His plays climax at *anti*-recognition scenes, the opposite of the confirming recognition of human identities that Aristotle posits as the climax of tragedy. The family structure, the taken-for-granted (or the 'natural', if you like) of motherhood, provides Brecht with his sharpest focus. The Mother does not greet her son in his return from prison, she is busy printing leaflets for the revolution.[3] Mother Courage cannot acknowledge her son, as commerce is more pressing – she cannot then acknowledge his corpse.[4] Galy Gay denies his wife – he has become a soldier. She decides the soldier is not her husband.[5] Instead of individual family-defined human identities, these scenes direct us to the larger process that overrides and redefines them – revolution, business, militarism. In *Galileo* too, the heroic possessor of knowledge breaks down, fails us, but then what in the play's ironic title is the 'life' of 'Galileo' after all? Knowledge matters, and it is the progress of this that is at the centre of the play – the human, in Galileo himself, is decentred, by a process Brecht sees as analogous with the discovery for which we remember Galileo's 'life'. But this decentering creates a problematic human subject – Brecht arrives not at a definable theory (which can be seen as either accurate or not) but to an open dialogue of the human, as theatre, that intensifying focus of recognition and reaction, of character and social praxis, represents it to the culture of the West.

Brecht's often cited '*V-affekt*', the alienating effects by which audience empathy is disrupted and the epic theatre made articulate, is a formulation arrived at comparatively late in his work.[6] It may owe its status in Western accounts of Brecht to its convenient declension of theoretical project into invented 'technique' (a more acceptable mode of innovation) and to its openness to commonsense rebuttal. The *V-affekt* is a bringing together of two things encountered in a visit to Moscow – the performance of a Chinese actor, and (though this is not overtly acknowledged) the notion formulated by Shklovsky as 'making strange' (*ostranyenye*).[7] Art should employ the means to make us see the world anew. Only then, Brecht implies, can we act on it, only then can we have a critical and purposive art. Habits of confirmatory empathetic spectatorship block our way to this. The distanced, formalised, but urgent and expressive modes of other theatrical cultures (and, perhaps as importantly, a recognition of the difference of these cultures and a consequent reappraisal of our own), can suggest ways forward for the new theatre. Brecht's development of a Marxist theatre practice involves a careful negotiation between formal experiment and the acknowledgement of an official Soviet aesthetic that proceeded from a Marxist consolidation and reinterpretation of Romantic positions to an increasingly stringently enforced version of 'realism'. But his tactful adoption of some aspects of formalist aesthetics is more than simple eclecticism. The formalists parallel his own interest in a non-humanist art, in the invention or discovery of alternative representations of the human.

The great innovator in this field is the Russian analyst of folklore, Vladimir Propp. Propp's idea of folklore studies came to be seen as 'formalist' in treating folklore not as representations, or records, of customs of labour or of national identity, but as an aggregate of conventions of narrative and of representational devices, which could be described as developed structures in their own right, transferable from one milieu to another. Propp's vastly influential *Morphology of the Folk-Tale* breaks Russian folktale down into a limited number of basic 'types' to reveal the constituent parts of its structure. This involves a shift from 'character' (however sketchily individuated in these forms) to 'function' – the role played in the story structure.[8] To quote Erlich's summary – 'Depending on the period or ethnic milieu the role of the grim foe can be played by a monster, a serpent, a wicked giant, or a Tatar chief; the function of the obstacle in the hero's path can be performed by a witch, an evil sorcerer, a storm, or a beast of prey'.[9]

For a Formalist position on character one could put this with Shklovsky's account of *Don Quixote*. Shklovsky draws on the formalist notion of 'motivation of the device' (*motivirovka priema*). The 'device' – the narrative structure, the figure of speech – tends to be 'motivated' for the readership by some appeal on the writer's part to 'life'. But the 'motivation' is always secondary to the 'device', to the pleasures and significance of form. So, the depiction of Hamlet's 'madness' could be seen as the 'motivation' of his 'wild and whirling words'. The formalist critic would reverse the priorities of the psychological critic for whom Hamlet's language is a set of clues to his mental state.[10]

For Propp, of course, psychology is irrelevant given the nature of his material. This perhaps has made his hypothesis much more acceptable than Shklovsky's, who provocatively chooses in Quixote a well-known, well-loved, 'rounded' character. What critics had traditionally thought of as Quixote's *reality as character* – a coherent identity determined by social and psychological likelihood – is for Shklovsky the 'motivating device' of Cervantes's linguistic play. (It goes without saying that works which 'motivate' in this way are less liked in a formalist aesthetic than those with a minimal contexting, a maximised 'foregrounding' of linguistic and narrative structure – Sterne's *Tristram Shandy*, for example.)

Shklovsky's study seems to have incidental value in drawing attention to discontinuities in an apparently homogenous character. But to point this out is of course to neutralise the thrust of his polemic. The Russian Formalists share with their Futurist allies a determination to de-psychologise art – to remove from it the centred, individuated, self-coherent human subject. Already in their work the shift from psychological theories of language had been extended to an attack on psychologised accounts of authors. An anti-character stance in literary study is the logical concommitant.

Early 'formalist', or, given its basis in Saussurian semiotics, 'structuralist' accounts of theatre practice are£ mainly the work of the 'Prague school'. Figures associated with the Moscow Linguistic Circle transferred operations to Prague in response to an increasingly unsympathetic political climate at home and helped to develop a substantial body of interrelated studies of aesthetics and linguistics, of which only a portion is currently available in the West. The work of the 'Prague School' is marked by an attempt to isolate, through semiotic analysis, the characteristic operations of individual art forms, and thus to move towards a structuralist account of art as such. The project was signalled by Jan Mukarovsky's 'programmatic statement' to the Prague Congress of Philosophy, *Art as a Semiotic Fact* (1934).[11] Every mode of artistic representation is relevant to this study which thus tends to pursue an eclectic policy of attention to widely different cultural phenomena towards the conversely universal goal of a formalist account of *all* art.

Theatrical representation is especially relevant here as a combination of different arts. Like the Russian Formalists, the Prague school combined a practical commitment to avant-garde theatre with an exploratory study of folk drama and folk art generally. This apparently unlikely combination of interests served both aesthetic and tactical ends. Folk theatre and pre-Renaissance theatre had for some decades provided Russian directors with the basis of an experimental approach to stage technique. Yevreinov's Starinny Theatr (1907/8 and 1911/12), Meyerhold, and Diaghilev's Paris-based Ballets Russes, like Honzl and Burian in Prague, exploited the strangeness of these forms, not only for their novelty value, but for the access they provide to a new range of structural and representational possibilities, that can be seen to parallel those sought by the futurist and surrealist avant-garde. A theatre that precedes bougeois humanism and one that seeks to supersede it combine in the formulation of a theatre aesthetic to which the native folk theatre, with its strictly limited and conventional modes of representing the human, could easily be assimilated. Tactically, folklore was simply a much safer subject than modernism. When Bogatyrev, taking a typically anti-holistic view of theatrical performance, points to the stylistically discontinuous nature of folk art, to its abrupt shifts of medium and stylistic register, he cites Futurism and Cubism, collage and montage, as contemporary parallels.[12] But the priorities of comparison are implicitly reversible. Folk art is itself cited here in opposition to the tendency of bourgeois realist or romantic theatre to a homogeneity, to the stylistic uniformity and smoothness which it presents as a property of 'correct' artistic theatre. An avant-garde aesthetic enrolls folk art in a tactical alliance against the inherited traditions of art theatre.

One might compare the Czech operation of a folk art/'high' art opposition with Brecht's development of a new theatre aesthetic *through* Marxism. For the Eastern European avant-garde, folk theatre has the function of a 'making strange' of theatrical representation itself. Karel Brusak's *Signs in Chinese Theatre* (1939) parallels the role played by similar explorations in the development of both Brechtian and Artaudian theatre.[13] That is, attention to the initially mystifying theatre of other cultures (that is those which like the folk and the mediaeval are outside the assumptions of Western bourgeois humanism) allows one to see afresh the process by which theatre communicates and so to become aware of the possibilities of a 'modernist' theatre. This does nôt, of course, involve any interest in oriental theatre as such. Its difference is invoked tactically, as an intervention into Western theatre. The idea of the 'folk' functions similarly — it is a theoretically hazy category, conceived of ahistorically, even as 'timeless' — it can be drawn on selectively, like the generalised European orientalism in which Japanese, Chinese and Javanese performance come out as seeming much the same. Folk art and 'high' art can be contrasted locally, but their difference cannot be theoretically accounted for. Brecht's Marxism, in contrast, does account for this theatre's relation to 'bourgeois' theatre, a term which may seem simplistic, but which establishes a dynamic basis for his work as an historically necessary aesthetic project. When Bogatyrev invokes Shakespeare's and Molière's plays as a liaison of individual genius and proto-typical dramatic materials, corresponding to art and folk aspects, it becomes apparent that, at the level of establishing a relationship between his two terms, Bogatyrev's theory remains inert.[14] As a distinction, 'high' versus 'folk' functions best through concrete examples of artistic practice — as contrasts in which analogies to contemporary avant-garde art are to be understood.

Bogatyrev's two translated essays on folk theatre — *Semiotics in the Folk Theater* (1938) and *Forms and Functions of Folk Theater* (1940) — set out the basis of a semiotic theory of theatrical representation. Bogatyrev defines the way we perceive material objects on the stage and in life as follows:

> What exactly is a theatrical costume or a set that represents a house on stage? When used in a play both the theatrical costume and the house-set are often signs that point to one of the signs characterizing the costume or the house of a certain personage in the play. In fact, each is a sign of a sign and not the sign of a material thing.[15]

So when an object, or as Bogatyrev goes on to add, a gesture, is transposed to the stage, the way we read it changes. A piece of clothing is a material object and, in any particular dress-code, it is a sign — of age, class, sex, nationality and so on. On stage its sign value as part of such a code refers to another sign — character, action or idea presented in the performance. It thus loses its specific value as a material object — it may be a silk dress, but it may as well be rayon, or paper, or represented by the actor's mime, so long as it succeeds in being the sign of a sign of a rich woman. This points to two related properties of the theatrical sign which distinguish it from other kinds of signs. The theatrical sign is highly *selective* in its reference. The signs encoded in a 'real' silk dress (dress as material object) are many, and, in their aggregate, individual to each example. But in a theatrical performance utilising such a dress the material would not matter if it was to signify 'chic' but the style would; the style would not matter if it was to signify 'money', but the material would have to appear to be lavishly used.

The second property of the theatrical sign is *transformation*. The change in sign value which objects undergo in their transposition from everyday life onto the stage can be extended to shifts of reference within the performance itself. A piece of cloth which an actor playing a rich woman wears as silk may become in the same performance the table cloth of a middle-class family, the bundle of a beggar and so on. Both limitation and transformability are properties of the theatrical sign, properties it derives from a heightening of sign value, a 'semioticisation' which objects, gestures and, implicitly, people undergo in performance.

Bogatyrev's account of the process tends, as in his initial formulation of it, to identify the source of that extra sign, of that heightened semiotic function, with character. Certainly, these kinds of example are easier to grasp. A book is a material object *and* a set of signs. When an actor playing Hamlet carries it on stage, it is a sign of a sign (the Hamlet character). It is thus transformed (it could be an English-Portuguese dictionary, but in that context it comes to be the sign of a Renaissance philosophical treatise) and this sign value is focused and limited (it is not a sign of emergent empiricism, or of the decay of scholasticism, it is a sign that he is unhappy). But what of a drama that is not character-centred (in the way that an application of this formula shows *Hamlet* to be, in that an investigation of any object or gesture in it takes one back to character, in some sense)? Religious drama, like the Japanese Noh, or the Christian drama of the West, represents a sacred concept as that which 'semioticises' things and people on stage, as the signified to which the various signifiers tend. In the Japanese play which Arthur Waley translated as *Early Snow*, the ladies on stage and their dead singing bird are signs of the sign of the transmigration of the soul through the stages ordained by Buddha.[16] Similarly in the mediaeval *Croxton Play of the Sacrament* the sign of 'transubstantiation', of the consecrated bread's identity as Christ, is that which organises the signs involved in 'wicked Jew'.[17]

Bogatyrev does not explore such examples here, though his primitive/folk interests would certainly seem to raise the problem. It is symptomatic that a centrality of the human presence – of performance thus tending to become readable as character - is not itself questioned; indeed, through the accumulation of examples it is actually reinforced. Two essays by Jiri Veltrusky – *Man and Object in the Theater* (1940) and the complementary *Dramatic Text as a Component of Theater* (1941) – take up this point, building on Bogatyrev's account of signification in order to interrogate the role of human presence in theatrical performance.

Veltrusky points to a double 'subject' of dramatic action – one subject who 'originates the intent' of the action and one who performs 'who may be identical with the basic subject but may also be his mere tool and thus only a partial subject'.[18] This second performing subject need not be human, as is often assumed (though presumably the first, the originator, must). Anything that is a 'component in the action', whether human animal or object, can be constructed by the audience as a 'performing subject'. It must then be the case that men and objects are interchangeable in function and indeed this can be seen to be so, though to a different degree in different kinds of theatre.[19]

In *Man and Object* the fact that the performer cannot fully 'edit' the properties of his/her presence lead him to the following proposition:

> not all the components of the actors are purposive; some of them are simply given by physiological necessity (thus, for instance, various automatic reflexes). The spectator of course understands even these non-purposive components of the actor's performance as signs. This is what makes the figure of the actor more complex and richer, we are tempted to say more concrete as compared to the other sign carriers. It has in addition to its sign character also the character of reality. And the latter is precisely that force which forces all the meanings to be centred on the actor.[20]

The doubleness, or 'duplexity' of the person on stage, the fact that some aspects of him/her signify and others do not, is a recurrent concern of theories of performance. But that the spectator 'understands even these non-purposive components of the actor's performance as signs' is more questionable. Why should not a human being signify in the same way that the objects in Bogatyrev's examples do, through an intensified transformable sign-value, edited not by their purpose (necessarily) but by the demands of that action of which they are 'components'? In a particular role it may signify that an actress is small or has red hair, or moves stiffly, in another the audience may not notice, in another it becomes a distraction because it seems to contradict the signs that action demands of her. Veltrusky wishes to exempt human presence from the implications of his analysis and so to resist the 'decentring' to which it seems to tend, first through its being more complex (different in degree) but then through a difference in kind—it possesses 'the character of reality' (the reality which Bogatyrev assumes material objects somehow forfeit by appearance on the stage) and by virtue of this 'forces all the meanings to be focused on the actor'.

In *Dramatic Text*, the presence of an actor invokes a semiotics 'diametrically opposed' to that of the language of the written text, in that the basic tenet of a semiotics of language, that 'meaning is so tenuously tied to sensory material' (of sound or whatever), is overthrown in acting where 'the material bearer of the meaning—the actor's body in the most general sense—absolutely predominates over the immaterial meaning. In theatre, the sign created by the actor tends, because of its overwhelming reality, to monopolise the attention of the audience at the expense of the immaterial meanings conveyed by the linguistic sign'.[21] Again, 'reality' is invoked to exempt the actor's presence from the process of signification which the written text determines. All the other 'languages' which make up theatre can be 'eliminated' by the text or 're-enter' by means of the actor (or presumably vice versa); they are dependent on the dialectic between text and acting, between the two opposed sign systems by which they operate, the dialectic of which dramatic performance consists.

Underlying Veltrusky's formulation one can see the traditional post-Aristotelian distinction between *ethos* and *praxis*. *Ethos*—'being' or 'presence'—would be the most appropriate term for that communication of the human which the actor brings with him on stage, which operates separately from, even in opposition to, the other languages which make up the performance text. Veltrusky's account of action (*praxis*) at the beginning of *Man and Object* is explicitly Aristotelian in the teleological nature of its definitions. Honzl, in *Dynamics of the Sign*, achieves a more ingenious liaison of semiotics and Aristotelian theory in his attempt to define the essence of the theatrical as 'action' which '. . . taken as the essence of dramatic art, unifies word, actor, costume, scenery and music in the sense that we could then recognise them as different conductors of a single current that either passes from one to another or flows through several at one time'.[22] The 'current' in this analogy is dramatic action, understood by Honzl both as Bogatyrev's transformable sign *and* as the Aristotelian *praxis*; the *praxis* of performance is that semioticisation of people and things. If we interpret action/*praxis* in this way 'the theatricality of dramatic character and that of place and that of plot will not appear to us as things permanently separated from one another'[23]—as they do for the later Aristotelians and for Veltrusky. In this definition of the theatrical, the mysterious 'thereness' of the actor's presence, Veltrusky's equivalent of *ethos*, ceases, precisely, to signify.

The Prague work, like aspects of Brecht's, might lead one to think again about pre-modern theatre, about exempting it from the character-based theatre of which a certain idea of Shakespeare is still the axis. The controversies surrounding a post-humanist theatre extend of course far beyond the reassessment of the pre-humanist theatre which it, often simply tactically, invokes. A currently fashionable parallel is the work of Bakhtin, whose *Rabelais and his World* offers the simultaneous possibilities of a post-Marxist construction of the subject as collective rather than individual, of an anti-Cartesian poetics of the body (in his terms, anti-Renaissance, or at least opposed to the special status of the Renaissance in post-Hegelian histories of art) and of a reassessment of the status in Marxist theory of pre-modern writing. The special status Bakhtin gives 'the folk', his identification of mediaeval art with collective popular voice(s) imperils his work from a purely historicist point of view, but it gives it its raison d'etre as a late and initially unsuccessful intervention into an increasingly authoritarian official aesthetics. The book's opposition of authority and the revolutionary popular energies of carnival as expressed in pre-humanist art is a kind of typology of Soviet aesthetics, as well as a fertile and suggestive attempt, parallel to Brecht's, of redefining the subject from within Marxism.

Brecht himself takes on some of the orthodoxies of a Soviet position in his later statements from East Germany. Praise of Stanislavsky,[24] and a careful reassessment of Aristotle in the notes to his version of Sophocles's *Antigone*,[25] realign his thought with an aesthetic of socialist 'humanism'. But the Aristotle of the earlier work was a symbolic figure, necessary to the structure of typologies that aligned Brecht, Bacon, Marx and Galileo. The Aristotle of the 'Antigone model', like the later discussions of Shakespeare, offers the possibility of fiercely negotiated compromise, between what were by now official dicta, and the interests of Brecht's earlier theatre practice. If the 'human' remains a problem in the Prague work as a limit on a formalist aesthetic project, in Brecht's work it is a problem of necessity, the necessity of participation in a still urgent debate, as to the place of the human subject in Marxist thought.

II   SUBSTANTIVE 'CHARACTER' IN SOVIET AESTHETICS AND IN ENGLISH STUDIES

Though the early Formalists took their anti-character, anti-psychology, stance to be appropriately modern, even revolutionary, Soviet anti-formalist polemics took an opposed position, to be realised decisively in political terms. Trotsky's *Literature and Revolution* (1924) sets out a theory of progress from bourgeois culture through the transition periods of revolutionary and proletarian art to a truly socialist culture. Futurism and Formalism are paid special attention, the first as a movement with a potential contribution to make to socialist art, the second as 'the only theory which has opposed Marxism in Soviet Russia'.[26] Links between the two movements are not discussed, the inference being that Trotsky's aesthetic offers the Futurists the opportunity to disown Formalism and to become a 'necessary link' in the 'evolution' of a socialist art. But both movements share the same objectionable tendency—to deny the centrality to art of the representation of the human subject.

'The whole conception' of the Formalists is for Trotsky 'simply based upon the fact that they ignore the psychological unity of the social man, who creates and who consumes what has been created'.[27] Individual psychologies are formed by material and social conditions (they are individual in that the aggregate and proportion of these factors is likely to be unique to each case) and the experience, knowledge and desire personal to each require artistic expression. This expression may in turn require new techniques (directly analogous for Trotsky with technical developments in, say, engineering) but these are an answer to the needs of a new psychology ('this new man') which new social conditions have created. Artistic innovation must wait on social change—thus the Futurists, like other examples of avant-gardeism 'anticipate history'.[28]

Trotsky invokes the classic idea of the 'mirror to mankind'[29]—realistic representations of individuals are crucial to the function of art as he sees it. It cannot otherwise fulfil its secondary, often long delayed but still valuable role in political and social change, that of helping to form 'this new man'. The character study is the main mode of Trotsky's polemic. Against the 'new man' are set a whole series of caricatures of old and newish men and women, including more or less every practising writer of note, whose dubious class backgrounds produce ludicrous art through warped psychologies: the only hope for whom is to scientifically recreate himself in line with the process of the revolution.[30]

References to literature made by Marx and Engels (though relatively sparse) tend to reaffirm the centrality of 'character', understood in its nineteenth-century sense. These remarks were developed by Lukács, as a justification for a specifically Marxist aesthetic of realism.[31] 'Realism, to my mind,' Engels writes in a letter of 1888 to 'Margaret Harkness', (a pseudonym of John Law) who had sent him a novel (s)he had written, called *City Girl*, 'implies, besides truth of detail, the truthful reproduction of typical characters under typical circumstances'.[32] That Engels means something more by 'typical' than simply 'representative' is shown when he goes on to criticise Harkness's portrayal of working-class figures; their passivity does not convey the historical role of the workers as Engels perceives it. So characters are to be 'typical' of moments and forces in history, as revealed by materialist analysis. They are to be constructed and read as focuses of conflict and transition, and are for this reason, when 'realistically' depicted, the highest aim of art.

In opposition to Brecht, Lukács also developed a contrast made apparently independently by Marx and Engels in their response to Ferdinand Lasalle's play *Franz von Sickengen*—a contrast between Schiller and Shakespeare. Shakespeare is, in this context, the play-wright of character, Schiller that of ideas. 'You would then have been automatically compelled to write more in *Shakespeare's* manner', Marx writes to Lasalle, 'whereas I regard as your gravest shortcoming the fact that *à la Schiller* you transform individuals into mere mouthpieces of the spirit of the time'.[33] And Engels defines his 'view of drama, which consists in not forgetting the realistic for the idealistic, Shakespeare for Schiller . . .'.[34] The Shakespearean characters in which Marx and Engels find the typicality of realism are the 'Falstaffian' figures in the history plays—similar figures would have 'automatically compelled' Lasalle to provide a more 'realistic' account of historical struggle. To link 'character', 'realism' and 'Shakespeare' is scarcely a revolutionary move in itself, but in conjunction with the idea of the typical it lays the foundation for a character-centred and in that sense 'humanist' Soviet aesthetic. It is this which Trotsky opposes to Futurism and Formalism. Gorky leads a move towards the creation of great 'typical' figures. Brecht, in adapting Gorky's *The Mother*, seems to want to create a liaison between this and his 'epic' theatre. The great emotive moment of the novel—'the mother' Vlasova, picks up the workers's flag when the demonstrator holding it is shot down, so choosing solidarity with the workers—is presented by Brecht in an 'alienating' narration, not enacted but presented as an appeal to our understanding, not our capacity to empathise.[35] But the thrust of early Soviet art is towards a new understanding of the great figures of the past and the creation of new revolutionary types—the only surviving film of Lunacharsky shows him addressing a rally from the stage of the Bolshoi theatre calling for the creation of characters 'like Hamlet and Don Quixote'.[36] The realistic depiction of character—character as read in terms of materialist analysis—is the dominant mode of representing the human, and that representation is the aim of art.

When Engels reminds Lasalle of 'the significance of Shakespeare in the development of drama',[37] it is as the inventor of realistic character. The source for this strand in Soviet aesthetics is of course Hegel – doubly important here, as the formulator of an account of tragedy as conflict embodied in great individuals, and as the consolidation of that romantic view of Shakespearean drama as a kind of epochal breakthrough which allows one to consign all that comes before it to museum status.

'In the tragedies of Shakespeare' Trotsky wrote, 'the fates of the ancients and the passions of the mediaeval christians are crowded out by individual human passions such as love, jealousy, revengeful greediness and spiritual dissension. But in every one of Shakespeare's dramas the individual passion is carried to such a high degree of tension that it outgrows the individual, becomes super personal, and is thus transformed into fate of a certain kind. The jealousy of Othello, the ambition of Macbeth, the greed of Shylock, the love of Romeo and Juliet, the arrogance of Coriolanus, the spiritual wavering of Hamlet, are all of this kind. Tragedy in Shakespeare is individualistic . . ..'[38]

Trotsky's argument here allows, perhaps unexpectedly, a transition to the equally fierce but less decisive controversies of English studies. To link Trotsky to A. C. Bradley is in this context more than simply paradoxical. Both have an ideological investment in a certain idea of literary and dramatic character and both derive their formulation of that idea from the same source, Hegel.

For Hegel, tragedy is the expression of the 'Ideal' through conflict. In a certain 'world condition', 'ethical principles' find form in those situations which allow of a tragic action, and this produces tragic character as described in the following equation:

> *First*, we have the universal forces which constitute the essential content and object, for the sake of which the action takes place.
> *Secondly*, we have the *realisation* of these forces in the *individuals* who act.
> *Thirdly*, the two aspects above mentioned have to unite themselves in that which, in default of any better generic term, we will here call character.'[39]

Those 'universal forces' require individualised figures in which they appear as 'an affecting *pathos*', the 'meditative link'[40] to audience or reader. Such figures in a slightly later stage of the argument are seen to 'acquire the concentrated unity and concreteness of a *whole* and a *single whole*. This totality is man apprehended in his fulfilled spiritual content and the subjectivity therein comprised, in one word the entire self-contained human individuality which we designate as character'.[41] Hegel finds these conditions fulfilled in the Greeks, in Shakespeare, in Goethe and in some Schiller. He is emphatically opposed to the romantic ironies of character (the discontinuous, the paradoxical, the bizarre) as exemplified for him by Kleist. This generates false readings of Shakespeare that he is anxious to refute. 'If . . . Shakespeare is distinctive in any one quality it is in the firm and decisive delineation of his characters . . . they [the Kleist school] would assimilate even Shakespeare's characters to a world of ghosts, and appear to think that this futility and indecision of ups and downs can by itself contribute to our interest.'[42]

Trotsky describes Hegel as of use when 'turned inside out'—his historical dialectic is important to Marxist theory, but only when reversed, when the material is its base, not the 'Ideal'.[43] In this sense the historical conditions which Hegel sees as necessary to produce tragedy are the object of interest which tragedy illuminates, not simply part of a causal chain which results in a 'pathos' that is the communication of the Ideal. This is evident in the continuation of the passage I quoted earlier:

> Tragedy in Shakespeare is individualistic and in this sense has not the general significance of *Oedipus Rex* which expresses the consciousness of a whole people. Nonetheless compared with Aeschylus [sic] Shakespeare represents a great step forwards and not backwards. Shakespeare's art is more human. At any rate, we shall no longer accept a tragedy in which God gives the orders and man submits.[44]

Trotsky takes Hegel's readings of the plays more or less unquestioned—he puts them to a new use. More generally he takes over Hegel's character-centred critique, partly historicises it, but maintains a balance which allows both Greek tragedy and Shakespeare some progressive validity.

Trotsky's Hamlet is Goethe's, via Hegel. Bradley's Hamlet is conceived in opposition to Hegel, as are some of the details of his tragic theory. The tragic conflict or collision which Hegel locates in the external world is for Bradley *internal* to Shakespeare's characters. This builds to some extent on Hegel's idea that the human takes precedence over the divine in tragedy, a centring of the human subject, thus understood, that both Bradley and Trotsky locate historically in Shakespeare's period. Trotsky's 'great step forward' is echoed in Bradley's judgement that religious ideas 'do not materially influence his representation of life, nor are they used to throw light on the mystery of its tragedy. The Elizabethan drama was almost wholly secular . . .'.[45] Where Bradley and Trotsky disagree (and where Trotsky seems more Hegelian) is in their reaction to that 'pathos', that intense affective expression of 'universal power', to which the tragic character tends. Hegel's passionate admiration for Juliet 'transpierced with and carried away by one single emotion' is carefully, if a little evasively, worked out by Trotsky as 'the individual passion . . . carried to such a high degree of tension that it outgrows the individual, becomes super-personal; and is transformed into fate of a certain kind'.[46] But for Bradley this 'fatal tendency to identify the whole being with one interest, object, passion or habit of mind . . . is for Shakespeare the fundamental tragic trait',[47] in the sense that it is this which leads the protagonist(s) towards disaster. True, it reveals that which is 'noble' in them, but his choice of term here takes him away, perhaps unconsciously, from Hegel's 'Ideal'. However careful Bradley is to gainsay the idea of a 'moral order' operating in the tragedies, 'noble' invokes a level of accessible moral judgement and one which maps too easily onto a 'gentlemanly' ethos of duty and behaviour out of which Bradley addresses the students at his Edwardian redbrick university. (Again, he is careful and shrewd in dealing with the 'high' social status of the tragic heroes, but 'noble' slips into unwanted ambiguities in this context.)

As anyone teaching English knows, this unconscious moralism is the trap Bradley sets incautious imitators. Here I want to tackle a common assumption about Bradley—that his interest in character is 'novelistic'. Hegel makes available to Bradley a new version of the relation of character to action. For Bradley the 'centre of the tragedy, therefore, may be said with equal truth to lie in action issuing from character or in character issuing from action.'[48] Bradley's formulation thus creates a dynamic link between the two components of dramatic form which Aristotle had so puzzlingly separated. Its palindromic shape places 'the centre of tragedy' between action and character, in the meaning they give each other.

Shakespearean Tragedy is in fact scrupulously attuned to the demands of acting and the stage. Eschewing historical or linguistic scholarship, he addresses the book to those who read a play more or less as if they were actors who had to study all the parts. They do not need, of course, to imagine whereabouts the persons are to stand, or what gestures they ought to use; but they want to realize fully and exactly the inner movements which produced these deeds and no other, these words and no other, at each particular moment. This, carried through a drama, is the right way to read the dramatist Shakespeare.[49]

The great tragic figures on which Bradley concentrates are constructed from a few 'essential traits' – contingent or externalised detailing of the kind that builds realist (in that sense novelistic) character is denied or minimised. 'Little peculiarities' have no place in tragedy, but neither has attention to 'differences of period, race, nationality and locality'; these have 'little bearing on the inward character'. Here, as I mentioned in my last chapter, Bradley invokes the 'universalism' of Johnson. Nor is psychology *in itself* of any interest. To say that 'Shakespeare's main interest lay in *mere* character, or was a psychological interest, would be to make a great mistake, for he was dramatic to the tips of his fingers'.[50] So the methods and interests of the realist and novelistic modes of Bradley's own time are rejected in favour of a version of character that seems to him to be wholly dramatic. 'The tragic world is the world of action, and action is the translation of thought into reality'.[51] Bradley is surely right in seeing this as inherently dramatic, as a paradigm, almost, of theatrical realisation.

The process of his reading of the plays, then, is his construction of the meaning of action through character, and vice-versa, to produce the 'line-through', the necessity of action and utterance that a knowledge of the 'inner movements' of the *dramatis personae* should give. Bradley falls victim on a superficial reading to the connotations of his own rhetoric, his tendency to cast his readings in the perfect past tense of narrated fictions, to do without the kind of critical distancing devices by which, as Seymour Chatman suggests, we talk not of Iago, but of 'Iago'.[52] Bradley can say (in an example chosen at random) that 'Iago did not clearly understand what was moving his desire'.[53] But even in his carefully detailed 'narrative' account of Iago, every point is the result of a close reading of the action (including past action narrated in the play, particularly important in *Othello*). The real limitation of Bradley's method lies in his attempt to reaffirm a holistic unity of character and action. His reading of *Hamlet* breaks down in his account of the scenes with Ophelia. In the face of the apparent discontinuity of Hamlet's behaviour here, he recognises that:

the actor who plays the part of Hamlet must make up his mind as to the interpretation of every word and deed of the character. Even if at some point he feels no certainty as to which of the two interpretations is right, he must still choose one or the other. The mere critic is not obliged to do this. Where he remains in doubt he may say so, and if the matter is of importance, he ought to say so. This is the position in which I find myself in regard to Hamlet's love for Ophelia.[54]

Shakespearean Tragedy remains a rich and complex study of its subject largely because Bradley is shrewdly aware of the limits as well as of the advantages of his method. Bradley is also *rhetorically* self-aware; that tendency to frame his reading as narratives ('Iago thought X and so did Y'), the most cogent way, after all, of conveying the links between character and action, may mislead his detractors into seeing his work as novelistic, but never diverts his own writing into fantasised extensions of Shakespeare's texts. L. C. Knight's parodistic title 'How many children had Lady Macbeth?' is a ridiculous question only in its statistical precision. Most actresses playing the role would still be likely to ask—had she children? What happened to them? Did she expect to have any more? (What kind of marriage was it? How long had they been married? . . . and so on). Whether the actor for whom the role was written would do the same is a different matter. Bradley's continued currency is at least partly due to his awareness of a still predominant tradition of acting, and thus to the way most audiences (and readers) encounter the plays.

The model of acting that Bradley requires seems startlingly avant-garde in terms of his own context—the 'line-through' a role that he seeks to establish, and takes almost as a theatrical norm, is formulated and developed for the modern stage by Stanislavsky. Bradley cannot have known Stanislavsky's work, or vice-versa, but the two share a common source in English romantic acting. Salvini's Othello was the model Stanislavsky analysed to come to understand his own shortcomings as an actor.[55] The performance had been much admired in England, and had helped to form the great tradition of nineteenth-century Shakespearean acting. In other particulars, of course, Bradley would not concur in a Stanislavskian approach, but the two are close enough to help explain the commonsense currency of Bradley with actors and audiences of a largely Stanislavskian English theatre. The current vogue for books by and about Shakespearian actors, normally centering on the Royal Shakespeare Company, fills a gap for the average playgoer that academic criticism has deliberately vacated—the gap where 'character' used to be. Bradleyans to a man or woman, the classical actor as celebrity sets the tone for all but the most stringently academic 'discussions' of Shakespeare—which is fine as a focusing of attention on the stage, but limiting in its unanalytic repetition of received wisdom, its preservation of the traditional 'Shakespeare' as a valued cultural object.

Considerations of character in Shakespeare still tend to return to Knights's critique of Bradley as a *locus classicus*. I did so myself at the beginning of Chapter 3, to make the point that the divide between language and character, across which they oppose each other, is a false distinction in terms of the idea of character with which the historical Shakespeare was working, and that Knights's intervention merely serves to confirm literary criticism in it. Knights's title parodies the notes that Bradley provided as an appendix to his work—'Where was Hamlet at the time of his father's death?' or 'Did Emilia suspect Iago?'.[56] Knights refers at the start of his essay to 'signs of a reorientation of Shakespeare criticism', a move away from character towards 'thematic', 'symbolic' or 'poetic' readings.[57] His own piece involves, first, an introductory polemic, then an account of the eighteenth-century background of character-based criticism, and then a study of *Macbeth* which Knights offers as a modest proposal for the future of Shakespeare studies.

Compared to Bradley, Knights seems anti-theatrical. The self-imposed task of describing a play without invoking 'character' produces a rash of inverted syntax and passive constructions. 'Theme' gradually takes on a musical connotation; an anti-character stance makes it impossible for him to see 'themes' as tending to cluster around or be associated with 'characters', as Kowzan, one of the few theatre theoreticians to explore 'theme' finds in his *Littérature et Spectacle*.[58] Knights is of course no formalist—the play is a statement of values, organised around binary oppositions (natural/unnatural, chaos/order) and presented dramatically, in so far as it *is* dramatic, as a kind of Wagnerian symphonic drama. 'A Shakespearean play is a dramatic poem. It uses action, gesture, formal grouping and symbols, and it relies on the general conventions governing Elizabethan plays.'[59]

Knights's deliberate devitalisation of the theatricality of the plays goes together with a deprecation of their popularity. Again character is the crux. Character reading reduces the plays to the level of 'best-sellers'—on which his authority is Q. D. Leavis.[60] Knights sets out to rescue the plays for readers on a higher level of culture.

Nonetheless, the *Scrutiny* approach has had a vast influence on Shakespeare production, through the university-trained directors who emerged in the fifties and sixties. Peter Hall and Trevor Nunn, for example, still invoke F. R. Leavis's teaching at Cambridge as the major source of their approach to texts. Though the integrated theme-based Shakespeare productions of the sixties and seventies now seem out of fashion, the Leavisite influence is still claimed for Nunn's populism, and Hall's literalist criteria of 'fidelity to the text'.[61]

Knights later qualified his anti-character stance. It is clear that his readings of Shakespeare, like those of the Leavisite *Scrutiny* group, with which he was at this point associated, require the centrality of character to their morally educative project. Leavisite readings often depend on our seeing a figure, or indeed a writer, as defective in themselves—in Knights's reading of Hamlet for example, the urge to empathise reveals in the reader an 'immaturity' to match Hamlet's own, and this is Shakespeare's moral purpose in the play.[62] To cite Knights as anti-character is thus a red herring. Nonetheless a Leavisite investment in character is ideologically different from the more celebratory brand of character recognition practised in English studies and seen at its best in John Bayley. A. D. Nuttal, for example, can end a recent essay by urging:

> let us not be scared by L. C. Knights. We met when we first read Shakespeare a wonderful company of heroes and ladies, fools and wisemen, poet-kings, old, mad despots with flowers in their hair, melancholy humorists, men of action, distracted maids and acid commentators. They will stay with us through life. We shall find ourselves wondering about them even (be it said) when we have forgotten the plots in which they appear. There is much more to the plays of Shakespeare than the characters which appear in them. But then there are certainly characters in the plays of Shakespeare.[63]

E. M. Forster's distinction between 'round' and 'flat' characters consolidates this tendency to talk about Shakespeare's characters as people we 'meet', who 'stay with us'.[64] To be flat is to be like a page (and so not 'come alive off the page'). It is to remind the reader of textuality. To be 'round' is to be beyond textuality, to be the object of that anti-textual mode of critique by which Dryden—its earliest proponent?—saluted Chaucer's work with 'here is God's plenty'.[65]

In *The Characters of Love* John Bayley boldly counters the notion that character is essentially novelistic, and imported into the criticism of drama improperly. *Othello*, with Chaucer's *Troilus and Criseyde* and Henry James's *The Golden Bowl*, is the object of a detailed character-based analysis, and also an illustration of Bayley's overall claims as to the centrality of character to great writing. Bradley, for Bayley, is not novelistic enough in one way, and too novelistic in another.

> Bradley devotes most of his study of the play to Iago, and to asking questions like: what did he hope to gain from his crime? Such a question shows the wrong sort of fictional analogy, for it makes a demand on plot which the novel by convention upholds, but which the poetic drama need not. Bradley also asks the proper question: without Iago would the lovers have achieved happiness?—proper because it sets us to consider the nature of that love and how Shakespeare portrays it, and these considerations are deeply relevant to the world of the play.[66]

The distinction Bayley makes here is clearer in the context of the overall statement of his book. Before turning to this (and before leaving Bradley) one might consider Seymour Chatman's argument in *Narrative and Discourse*. Unlike Bayley, Bradley or for that matter, Trotsky, Chatman's interest in reinstating character into his broadly structuralist-phenomenological account of narrative is not primarily ideological—it depends on a commonsensical attention to 'how we read'. Chatman's discontent with functionalist accounts of *dramatis personae* or *personnages* centres not on drama but on early modern fiction, and he proposes the idea of 'open' character, whose opposition to 'closed' character depends on the amount of extension or variation that the 'traits' that make up either kind are open to. Character is classed by Chatman, in his two-part classification of the components of narrative as an 'existent' as opposed to an 'event'.[67] This obviously maps on to the Aristotelian character/action distinction, in a way that would more obviously beg the question if drama was at issue. Similarly, 'open' and 'closed' character parallels, as Chatman acknowledges, E. M. Forster's 'flat' and 'round' characters. 'Open character' can be set against Bayley's more mysterious, even inexplicable, 'open consciousness', possessed by great fictional characters.

'Character', one might say, is what other people have, 'consciousness' is ourselves, and—as Shakespeare's Troilus discovers—the lover is uniquely capable of feeling the difference between the loved person as an extension of his own consciousness and as a separate 'character' . . ... The great author can make us see his characters both as we see ourselves and as we see other people. Chaucer's Criseyde, for example, is both an unfaithful mistress and an open consciousness in the complexity of which—as we experience it—this description loses its power of definition.[68]

As one can see from this example, Bayley attempts to convince us of this by (a) appeal to a common fund of experience (and implicitly of culture) and (b) to rhetorically assertive value judgement. Both coincide in an essentially ethical perception of the nature of love and of literature, and of the relationship between the two.

What I understand by an author's love for his characters is a delight in their independent existence as *other people*, an attitude towards them which is analogous to our feelings towards those we love in life; and an intense interest in their personalities combined with a sort of detached solicitude, a respect for their freedom.[69]

Bayley's fascinating, and at times rather beautiful, book consciously sets out to reinstate character at the centre of English literary culture, as an expression of liberal humanist values. His enemies are not the structuralists, writing as he is in England in the late fifties, but the *Scrutiny* group, whom he shrewdly accuses of transferring, via their criterion of 'significant life', a lot of the freight of interest which character carries into the study of works of fiction as wholes, as authored statements. For Bayley the author is 'neutral' and his characters possess 'significant life'.[70] Or rather the *great* author; he is just as prone as the 'scrutineers' to defend his ideas with exclusive value judgements as to the texts to which they properly apply. Bayley's book stands as the most daring statement from within English studies of an ideological investment in the idea of character as such, in the centrality of the human subject as individuated, knowable, coherent but somehow open, somehow 'free'. Though it may not have been vastly influential within English studies it represents a sophisticated and personal development of the assumptions of a humanistic literary culture and as such may stand as an index of what are still the attitudes of an English cultural 'élite'. In English studies Bayley had identified the wrong enemy—his book was overtaken by the revival of structuralism in the sixties.

III   CHARACTER AND SUBJECT: SOME
POST-STRUCTURALIST APPROACHES

In Keir Elam's *Semiotics of Theatre and Drama* (1980), a usefully concise guide to the field, there is no entry in the index for 'character'. Wherever possible Elam uses *dramatis persona* as an alternative, references occuring sporadically, and usually very briefly. (Compare 'discourse' or 'deixis'.[71]) Elam's avoidance of the word is of course wholly justified. The project of semiotics—the application of the methods and terminology of Saussurian linguistics into other modes of signification—is implicitly anti-humanist. Like the Russian Formalists, the 'Structuralists' who revived this project in the sixties and later prefer an approach to fiction in which *dramatis personae* are seen not as 'characters', as human subjects of interest in themselves, but in terms of the 'functions' that they fulfil in a narrative structure (or indeed in any other kind of structure that can be analysed in terms of 'the grammar' of its components). The French theoretician, A. J. Greimas, develops this into a distinction between the *dramatis personae* as *acteur*, as individuated character in the traditional sense, and as *actant*, as a function in a narrative structure, classifiable according to a strictly limited taxonomy, as one of six categories understood as a grid of possibilities; subject, object, sender, receiver, helper, obstacle.[72] 'Thus' in Roland Barthes's summary, 'one actant may combine several characters just as a single character may combine several actants; an actant may be figured by an inanimate entity.'[73] The resultant 'grammar' of story-telling gives one the basis for a structural analysis of narrative, and in doing so effectively displaces from our reading all those   assumptions   about   the   representation   of   the human—assumptions   as   to   its   autonomy,   wholeness   and primacy—which 'character' has come to imply.

Greimas, of course, only represents a part of a still ramifying project. But this example should indicate how closely the idea of a Structuralist 'approach to character' approaches to paradox. Much of the recent hostility towards 'Structuralism' coming from within English studies can be read as an anxiety consequent on that displacement of 'the human' from the study of literary texts. A structural analysis operates on a level which forbids notions of 'essential' or 'substantive' character as the object of knowledge to be approached 'through' texts. This would seem to align it more closely to the rhetorical tradition, as outlined in previous chapters. But a post-formalist account of the reading and construction of 'signs' differs radically from the rhetorical tradition in its assumptions as to the nature of the text (written or otherwise) which those signs make up. The rhetorical notion of the text as a transaction between human subjects, of character as the identifying impress of these and other subjects, is unavailable to a modern tradition which seeks to problematise and displace the subject as the source of the text, as its referent or its *telos*. To reinvoke my initial dichotomy between substantive and transactional modes of character, the opposition between semiotics-oriented writers and the post-eighteenth-century 'substantive' mode is clear, and clearly articulated by Barthes among others. But Barthes's occasional citation of Aristotle and the rhetoricians should not confuse the point that the purposive human-centred rhetorical account of what writing is differs radically from modernist accounts of the text as a site for meanings generated, not by the human presences somehow 'stamped' upon it, but by the discourse, the particular language of which it consists, operating in a kind of free play of signifying practices.[74]

Literary semiotics may thus seem to signal 'the end' of character, and thus traverse the limit of this book. This is certainly how some of its proponents would see it. As in *S/Z*, Barthesian narratology comes to devolve on quizzically tracking traces of the human through the texts of its readings. The human 'figures' in the discourse(s) that make up the texts, but flexibly, without closure into 'individual' 'characters', in a mode of 'open' play.

> From a critical point of view, therefore, it is as wrong to suppress the character as it is to take him off the page in order to turn him into a psychological character (endowed with possible motives): *the character and the discourse are each other's accomplices*: the discourse creates in the character its own accomplice: a form of theurgical detachment by which, mythically, God has given himself a subject, man a helpmate, etc., whose relative independence, once they have been created, allows for *playing*. Such is discourse: if it creates characters, it is not to make them play among themselves before us but to play with them, to obtain from them a complicity which assures the uninterrupted exchange of the codes: the characters are types of discourse and, conversely, the discourse is a character like the others.[75]

A contemporary analysis of character, and a reassessment of pre-modern drama and 'Shakespeare' in its light, can be seen to have stemmed from the liaison of structural linguistics, Freudian psychology, and Marxism in the work of Lacan and Althusser.

Freudian psychology makes limited use of the term 'character', an exception being Wilhelm Reich's formulation of 'character-armour', to describe repeated defensive actions.[76] But in the main Freudian accounts of the psychic 'economy' displace 'character' as a way of knowing the human, in favour of more complex account of individuation and subjecthood. By drawing on structural linguistics in order to account for the formation of the individual subject, Lacan extends Freud's work towards a further decentring of the subject, which Althusser pushes towards an account of 'ideology'. To become a subject, an 'I', is to be part of a pre-existing 'structure' of language, a structure made present to us in our relation to our parents, in the Oedipal drama of which that consists. For Althusser that structure is inescapably ideological; we can, in other words, have no simple faith in an 'I', an 'ego', from and as which we encounter an outside 'reality'.

> Not in vain did Freud sometimes compare the critical reception of his discovery with the upheavals of the Copernican Revolution. Since Copernicus, we have known that the earth is not the 'centre' of the universe. Since Marx, we have known that the human subject, the economic, political or even philosophical ego is not the 'centre' of history—and even, in opposition to the Philosophers of Enlightenment and to Hegel, that history has no 'centre' but possesses a structure which has no necessary 'centre' except in ideological misrecognition. In turn, Freud has discovered for us that the real subject, the individual in his unique essence, has not the form of an ego, centred on the 'ego', on 'consciousness' or on 'existence' . . . that the human subject is decentred, constituted by a structure which has no 'centre' either, except in the imaginary misrecognition of the 'ego', i.e. in the ideological formations in which it 'recognizes' itself.[77]

So the familiar historical analogy returns, in a typological sequence of revolutionary decentrings.

The Copernican analogy returns us to the problem of the kind of history that an Althusserian approach requires. Jonathan Dollimore in particular seems to see the radicalism of English renaissance tragedy as lying in a 'decentering' analogous to that of Marxian materialism—but where do we find the other side of this equation, a pre-renaissance 'centering'? Here the Copernican analogy misleads. Dollimore switches attention to 'humanist' critics—it is *their* centering of the human to which he and (somehow) the texts he cites are opposed.[78] History as analogy becomes history as Möbius strip. 'Character', as a discourse, requires an examination both of current academic and theatrical practice, and an attempt to recover a historical past. One should both make possible and justify the other.

Notes

1. Berthold Brecht, *The Rise and Fall of the City of Mahagonny*, introductory notes, translated by John Willett in *Brecht on Theatre* (London, 1964), p. 37.
2. Ibid., p. 57.
3. Brecht, *The Mother*, scene 9.
4. Brecht, *Mother Courage and her Children*, scene 3.
5. Brecht, *Man equals Man*, scene 8.
6. Brecht/Willett, *Mahagonny*, pp. 91–9.
7. For a summary see Victor Erlich, *Russian Formalism: History—Doctrine* (The Hague, 1965), pp. 176–8.
8. Vladimir Propp, *Morphology of the Folktale*, trans. Laurence Scott (Texas, 1968).
9. Erlich, *Russian Formalism*, pp. 249–50.
10. Ibid., pp. 196–7.
11. Translated in Ladislav Matejka and Irwin R. Titinuk (eds), *Semiotics of Art: Prague School Contributions* (Cambridge, Mass., 1976), pp. 3–9.
12. Peter Bogatyrev, *Semiotics in Folk Theater*, in *Semiotics of Art*, p. 40.
13. Karel Brusak, 'Signs in the Chinese Theater' in *Semiotics of Art*, pp. 59–73.
14. 'Forms and Functions of Folk Theater' in *Semiotics of Art*, p. 55.
15. Bogatyrev, *Semiotics in Folk Theater*, p. 33.
16. *Hatsuyuki* ['Early Snow'] in *The Noh Plays of Japan* by Arthur Waley (London, 1921), pp. 244–6.
17. *The Play of the Sacrament*, edited by Whitley Stokes (Berlin, 1862).
18. Jiri Veltrusky, *Man and Object in the Theater* in *A Prague School Reader on Esthetics, literary structure and style*, edited and translated by Paul L. Garvin (Georgetown, 1964), p. 83.
19. Least so in the realist theatre perhaps; objects or animals become signs of a character sign through association with present or absent human beings (General Gabler's pistols, for example) or through an identification often described as 'symbolic' (Nina and the Seagull, Hedvig and the Wild Duck). Objects which have significance in themselves—Chekhov's Cherry Orchard—are almost always kept off stage; perhaps the only way of keeping their meaning still potent beyond narrowly associative or symbolic reading is to keep them free of the character based hierarchy of devices on which the realist stage depends. The symbolic seems to be required to keep truce between the interpretative demands made by people and things; its persistent invocation in a realist theatre suggests that the relation between

the two is less settled than it may at first appear. Folk and avant-garde theatre predictably combine to occupy the other end of the spectrum.

20. Veltrusky, *Man and Object*, p. 85.
21. Veltrusky, *Dramatic Text as a Component of Theater* in *Semiotics of Art*, p. 115.
22. Honzl, *Dynamics of the Sign in the Theater* in *Semiotics of Art*, p. 91.
23. Ibid., p. 91.
24. *Brecht on Theatre*, pp. 236–7.
25. Ibid., p. 209–15.
26. Trotsky, *Literature and Revolution* (New York, 1957), p. 162.
27. Trotsky, *Literature and Revolution*, p. 171.
28. Trotsky, *Literature and Revolution*, p. 134.
29. Wittily, 'one cannot get along without a mirror, even in shaving oneself', Trotsky, *Literature and Revolution*, p. 137.
30. See, for example, Trotsky, *Literature and Revolution*, Introduction, pp. 14–15.
31. See George Bisztray, *Marxist Models of Literary Realism* (New York, 1978), pp. 24–8.
32. *Marx and Engels on Literature and Art* (Moscow, 1976), p. 90.
33. Ibid., p. 107.
34. Ibid., p. 105.
35. Gorky, *Collected Works* (Moscow, 1907), Vol. III, 29, p. 173.
36. Shown on a BBC documentary on the Bolshoi ballet company, summer 1987.
37. *Marx and Engels on Literature and Art*, p. 104.
38. Trotsky, *Literature and Revolution*, p. 242.
39. *Hegel on Tragedy*, edited by Anne and Henry Paolucci (New York, 1962), p. 131.
40. Ibid., p. 157.
41. Ibid., p. 152.
42. Ibid., p. 162.
43. Trotsky, *Literature and Revolution*, p. 182.
44. Ibid., p. 242.
45. A. C. Bradley, *Shakespearean Tragedy* (first edn 1904, repr. London, 1976), p. 17.
46. Trotsky, *Literature and Revolution*, p. 242; *Hegel on Tragedy*, p. 157.
47. Bradley, *Shakespearean Tragedy*, p. 13.
48. Ibid., p. 7.
49. Ibid., p. xiii
50. Ibid., p. 172, p. 7.
51. Ibid., p. 19.
52. Seymour Chatman, *Story and Discourse* (Ithaca, 1978), p. 138.
53. Bradley, *Shakespearean Tragedy*, p. 187.
54. Ibid., pp. 122–3.
55. See David Magarshack's introduction to *Stanislavsky on the Art of the Stage* (London, 1967), p. 12.
56. Bradley, *Shakespearean Tragedy*, Note B, pp. 341–3, Note P, p. 375.
57. L. C. Knights, 'How Many Children had Lady Macbeth?' (1933) in *Explorations* (London, 1946), p. 1.
58. In Kowzan, *Littérature et Spectacle* (Paris/Warsaw, 1975), pp. 79–159.
59. Knights, 'How Many Children had Lady Macbeth?', p. 4.
60. Ibid., p. 14.

61. See *Peter Hall's Diaries*, edited by John Goodwin (London, 1983), p. 347. '*Tuesday 18th April* News today that F. R. Leavis is dead. A terrible shock . . .. All the textual seriousness at the basis of Trevor's work and of mine comes from Leavis, and there is a vast band of us. Comical to think that Leavis hated the theatre and never went to it. He has had more influence on the contemporary theatre than any other critic'.
62. See Knights, 'Prince Hamlet' (1940) in *Explorations*.
63. A. D. Nuttall, 'The argument about Shakespeare's characters' in D. J. Palmer (ed.), *Shakespeare's wide and universal stage* (Manchester, 1984), p. 30.
64. E. M. Forster, *Aspects of the Novel* (London, 1949), pp. 65–75.
65. Dryden, *Fables Ancient and Modern*, edited by Conaghan, p. 618.
66. John Bayley, *The Character of Love* (London, 1960), p. 140.
67. Chatman, *Story and Discourse*, pp. 107–38.
68. Bayley, *The Character of Love*, pp. 33–4.
69. Ibid., pp. 7–8.
70. Ibid., pp. 37–9.
71. Keir Elam, *The Semiotics of Theatre and Drama* (London, 1980).
72. 'Greimas's own account can be found in *Semantiques structurale* (Paris 1966), Chapter 10.' Note to *Image-Music-Text*, edited and translated by Stephen Heath (London, 1977), p. 84.
73. Barthes, 'The Struggle with the Angel', in *Image-Music-Text*, p. 137.
74. See, for example, 'Structural Analysis of Narratives' in Heath, *Image-Music-Text*, p. 105.
75. Roland Barthes, *S/Z*, translated by Richard Miller (New York, 1974), p. 178.
76. Simon Callow's *Being an Actor* provides an interesting if anecdotal combination of Reichian analysis with Stanislavskian practice as an account of his own development as an actor. See also J. Laplanche and J. B. Pontalis, *The Language of Psycho-analysis* (London, 1983), pp. 67–8.
77. L. Althusser, 'Freud and Lacan' in *Essays on Ideology* (London, 1984), p. 170.
78. Jonathan Dollimore, *Radical Tragedy, passim* (Brighton, 1984).

Index

84
122, Conceit

vice from Vygt. (53)

130
131 138- Concit
139 - Q - 2 Subj
154 - 5 Hamlet's interiority

226